The Bri

Beyond Lucky

A Story of Extraordinary Redemption
by
Brian "Glaze" Gibbs with Joseph Verola

Amazing *Glaze* how sweet the sound
That saved a wretch like me
I Was lost, but now am found
Was blind but now I see
'Twas g*laze* that taught my
Heart to fear!

Dedication

This book is dedicated to my mother Dorothy Gibbs,
I love you and there is not a day that goes by
without you in my thoughts;
and my little brother Juneau "Sty" Wilson

Seventh Edition: January 2020
Website: http://beyondlucky.biz
ISBN: 9781519792242

Table of Contents

Preface

The Brian "Glaze" Gibbs Story

Brian's story is the blueprint for every black or white drug lord who grew up in the five boroughs of New York City.

By the age of 22, he was head of his own crew which he proudly initialed M&M. He worked with his mentor Lorenzo "Fat Cat" Nichols. Fat Cat was once the most dominant power in heroin and cocaine trafficking in the five boroughs of New York City.

Brian reveals infernal stories, never exposed, that can no longer be told by those who didn't survive the streets and the prisons. Deposing individuals that often perished as a result of their own criminal actions, lack of loyalty to their crew, or died violently by the command of, or directly by Brian. Others were dispatched to kill, a consequence for interfering with him in prison, with his territory, with his crew on the streets or by the order given by Fat Cat. In his world no one was spared, including so-called friends.

Glaze tells the real facts behind the killing of a rookie cop and how the NYPD accused him of having committed one murder a week from June 1987 until November 10, 1988.

"One more thing, when you start to read my story, some of you will hate me from the "Get Go", for others it will take a while, and some will relate and won't judge. However, it isn't important that you like, or believe I've been redeemed or reformed. But hopefully, my story will save someone you want to influence. Recommend this book for anyone that might be falling in love with the street. I guarantee; they'll fall out of love with the street."

In Brian's Words

Drug Dealers Anonymous

Welcome to Drug Dealers Anonymous (DDA). My name is Brian "Glaze" Gibbs. I'm the only member right now. All the drug lords, associates, and dealers that I have known are either dead, or serving life sentences. You don't have to be a drug dealer to be a member of DDA, you just have had to survive living in the inner city tenements, and projects or just want to help a friend or family member from falling victim to drugs, dealing drugs, domestic violence, rape, stabbings, shootings and death. For those of you who haven't experienced the joys of being a drug dealer, well... that's why I'm telling my story of drugs, sex, rape and murder. If you want to or think you want to make $40,000 a day? Take a journey with me; I'll tell you how I did it and if you think you're fly you better think twice. Eventually, by telling this story, my new identity will be known and hopefully without risking my life to those looking for revenge.

It is my intention to take my violent past, day to day experiences and present them to the *teens and* adults in the inner-city tenements, and low-income housing projects across the United States. Then based on my reputation and experiences, I hope and believe people will learn from my story. As for adults with the power that will read my story, I ask that they think about this. What impact can we substantiate, if we are packed; hundreds of thousands of young people into areas of a few square miles? How are they provided a proper education and jobs to support them; never mind their parents? There is only so much room for a few to succeed in such an environment an escape to a world that is only an illusion, a hologram they see or have seen on TV or in the movies and not on the inner-city streets.

Don't dismiss the consequences. I will tell you what led me to making $40,000 per day as drug lord. The steps may not be in order. Step one: start getting rid of your conscience. This will also apply if you want to be a stockbroker.

Chapter One - The Initial Formative Years

What Was the Stork thinking?

My journey started in Bedford Stuyvesant. It was on Sunday, around 4 AM, October 20, 1963 when my mother, Dorothy L. Gibbs went into labor. She called 911 pleading for an ambulance to rush to her home on Herkimer Street, Brooklyn NY. If you knew our neighborhood, it was needless to say that a NYPD squad car would arrive first. When the two officers arrived, my mother's water broke. The officers made a judgment call and decided not to wait for the ambulance and headed immediately for the hospital. Along the way, one of the officers assisted my mother and brought me into the world, in the back seat of that police car. My biological father, Samuel Clark, was not present then or during my "Wonder Bread Years." Thinking about it, maybe my start into this world, in the rear seat of a NYPD green, black and white, was a sign of The Ghost of Christmas Future. Well, from 1979-1997, I would spend over eighteen years in crime, fighting both the State and Federal judicial system, and fourteen years as the guest in their prisons. You gotta be able to laugh at yourself occasionally or put a bullet into your own head.

Like many other children my youth had its ups and downs. For the first ten years of my life, *as* many mothers, Dorothy also filled the role of father to my brother, sister and me. My mother almost never denied us anything, always granting our wishes in due time. I would describe my mother as a wonderful and supportive person, who truly fulfilled her responsibility in her dual role.

Welcome to Cypress Hills

During the spring of 1975 our family moved from a brownstone on Halsey Street in Bedford Stuyvesant to Cypress Hills, ENY section of Brooklyn. Bedford Stuyvesant was a residential area; the average street would have approximately twenty-five to thirty brownstones on each side with each brownstone having three to four floors and two apartments. <u>During this time Cypress Hills was known as the murder capital of New York</u>, with the most homicides – not bragging. There should have been a sign as you entered the area, instead of the usual, "Welcome to Cypress Hills," it should have read, "Welcome to Cypress Hills, Enter at Your Own Risk!"

The area we lived in was protected by the 75th Police Precinct. It was responsible for thirty building's spread out from Sutter Avenue to Euclid Avenue to Linden Boulevard to Fountain and Fountain to Sutter Avenue. Each building had seven floors with seven apartments on each floor, totaling forty-nine apartments in one building; totaling fifteen hundred and fifty-eight apartments, all filled with different nationalities in such a small confined space. The first building we lived in was 455 Fountain Avenue, Apt 6G. *A lesson, in the drug business like all businesses, it is a numbers game. Like a good salesman you need to know your territory and your prospects.*

Cypress Hill Houses - Police Protection

Our family later moved into the in Cypress Hills Projects at 1266 Sutter Avenue, apartment 4b. After my mother moved, it eventually became my headquarters. There were five rooms: kitchen, living room, bathroom and two bedrooms; one of which I shared with my sister and brother. When the FEDS raided us on August 11, 1988 the rumor was that they found several dead bodies. Again, I was their key suspect. Go figure.

Cypress Hill Houses are part of The New York City Housing Authority (NYCHA) which continues to provide public housing for low- and moderate-income residents throughout the five boroughs of New York City. NYCHA also administers a citywide Section 8, Leased Housing Program in rental apartments and homes. However, new applications for Section 8 have not been accepted since December 10, 2009, due to lack of space.

NYCHA has approximately 13,000 employees serving about 176,221 families and approximately 403,736 residents. Based on the 2010 census, NYCHA's Public Housing represents 8.2% of the city's rental apartments and is home to 4.9% of the city's population. NYCHA residents and Section 8 voucher holders combined occupy 12.4% of the city's rental apartments.

I'm would like you to ask yourself, if the area you live in requires the following; to protect its inhabitants of the Cypress Hills Houses, the Patrol Bureau, the largest of the bureaus, created and deployed Project Stabilization Units, Narcotics Units, Anti-Crime Units, Bicycle Units, and Emergency Rescue Units. The Detective Bureau deployed a Homicide/Major Case Squad, Robbery Squad, Burglary Squad, Warrant Squad, Elevator Vandalism Squad, and each PSA had a Precinct Detective Unit assigned. The Internal Affairs Bureau had a Special Investigation Unit, and the Civilian Complaint Review Unit. Support Services Bureau had the Motor Pool, responsible for the acquisition, and maintenance of all Department vehicles now numbering over 200; and the Personnel Services Bureau fielded the Police Academy Unit, the Firearms Training Unit and the Driver Training Unit, making the Department the largest and most professional Housing Police Department in the world? Obviously, jobs and money were scarce and putting that many people in such tight areas, was extremely costly in man power, not to mention the cost to house the people. If the above doesn't give you an idea of the hell that my neighbors and I lived in, again please ask yourself this question. Does the area you live in require the above protection?

It was finally realized that it was better to give those living in the projects a point of reference for better living and to place them among the more financially responsible, therefore Section 8 Housing. Unfortunately, not in time for me to change the direction my life was taking.

I'm No Angel - Really?

"I know I'm no angel and at one time I thought I was too smart to allow myself to get caught up into a web of chaos and destruction, yet I became known as the MOST RUTHLESS CRIMINAL/MURDERER ON THE EAST COAST BOARDER - not my quote. How did that happen? I was brought up going to church with a Christian background, sang in the choir, and served as an usher. So, the question I pose, how in the hell did I become a monster, and a killer with no conscience, until now? Unfortunately for those I killed it was too late - sorry.

Maybe I did it all because I felt I had something to prove. I knew right from wrong. I would love to know what you think about the good, the bad and the ugly?

At one point in my life I went to church every Sunday and attended Sunday school classes. The family also attended evening services that were usually between 4pm and 6pm. Keep in mind this went on weekly for five to six years. My sister Tia, brother James and cousins, close friends and myself all from that church grew up as a close knitted family. Most of us hated the fact that we had perfect attendance in church. Yet I knew a few of us were destined to be outcasts. We were very rebellious at the time, always doing things that we shouldn't have been doing, such as cracking jokes and making fun of other church members during service. Often, we fight with each other. Apparently, my mother's wisdom realized that forcing the issue would make no difference; she urged, but eventually no longer demanded we go to services.

Was I a common senseless thug? Maybe there is such a thing as a bad seed. I can't change the past, but I can control my thoughts and surely control my future actions. To change, like an alcoholic, you must first admit your shortcomings to yourself. Many times, I would get into fights with the kids from the neighborhood who teased us for being church goers. The church was dead smack in the heart of the Bedford Stuyvesant section of Brooklyn. The area slogan was and still is, *Do or Die Bed-Sty*. The church continues to be until this day, some 30 years later. Those of us that are still alive stay in contact.

As I reflect back upon it, I was definitely no angel and I wasn't always a hell raiser either. My frame of thought even as a regular member of the church, knowing right from wrong, I still was committing crimes whenever the chance was presented. Despite my mother and stepfather, aunties, friends and church teachings I still allowed myself to become "Glaze."

What I notice back in my earlier life of crime, most of the criminals could not read or write. If you can't read or write, how were you going to fill out a job application? You couldn't even deliver the right package to the right address? But they were rocket scientist when it came to counting money. My objective is to use my good, bad and ugly experiences to teach critical thinking relating to the use and dealing of drugs. There are no winners. Just a fast ride, which will end in destruction for all those involved and those loved ones surrounding you, those you think you can protect, but find that you only bring pain and possible death to foes, friends and family.

So again, the question that I pose is, how in the hell did I became a monster, a killer with no conscience? When, where and how did I become so violent and blood thirsty? Was it in my DNA? Maybe my father who was a hot head, with one hell of a temper and didn't take shit from a soul? It's not like my father was in my life, like a normal family. I knew who he was, but I really didn't know him. Science may say it's in my genes - one excuse anyway. When I was disciplined by my family members, they used extension cords and broom handles when I stepped out of line for being disrespectful or getting into trouble at school. I would get my ass whipped. Literally, I would get the shit beaten out of me. Well-deserved I believe - discipline was needed. What doesn't break you makes you stronger, or meaner, I guess. Although, in 1994 my biological father murdered someone in self-defense; someone shot him, and he shot back. He testified on his own behalf in front of a Brooklyn Grand Jury seeking to indict him on a murder charge. As he was telling his version of the shooting, blood from his wound started seething through his shirt and every member of the grand jury refused to indict him. He did receive probation for possessing an illegal weapon.

Chapter Two - Personal Responsibilities

1972-74 - The Wonder Bread Years

During my "Wonder Bread Years," I was a typical kid growing up, and an average student. I attended Public School #5 in Brooklyn, with math being my favorite subject. I did get into a couple of fights in school, didn't kill anybody yet. Normally the guys that picked a fight with me would be bigger in height and weight, but it didn`t matter because I would attack first, jump on them swinging until my hands were too tired to swing anymore. Even at an earlier age I was taught right from wrong: including yes sir, no sir, yes ma'am, no ma'am, even though I still allowed myself to become the lost sheep that went astray. Even as a youth I hated that word **no**, and never seemed to get out of those terrible twos. I hated the fact that if I was even denied an extra piece of chicken, a pair of sneakers, or clothing. *Patience was a quality I hadn't perfected, which led me at a very early age to do things that aren't recommended and come with severe consequences.*

At the age of eight years old, going on nine, I can recall my siblings and me confronting our dear mother as we traveled on Sundays to my mother's sister for Sunday dinners in Fort Green, another section of Brooklyn. We would ask her why when went to family gatherings to visit her sisters, our aunts, her nieces, nephews and our first cousins, why were we always giving them gifts for birthdays, Christmas and graduations, while none of them ever gave us anything? We were three pissed off little kids that didn't quite understand. My mother would pause and look us eye to eye, one at a time and utter those famous words, "It's better to give, then to receive." We were still three pissed off little kids.

At approximately age eleven, the man I called Spann became my mother's common-law husband. As may be expected, it was difficult for me to accept another man as my father, not that my biological father set the bar very high. A great deal of time had passed, but with some enlightening from my mother, reality soon set in. I now realize that Spann had been more of a true father to me, my brother and my sister than our biological father was or ever attempted to be. I truly loved Spann as my father. I am so much more appreciative to him for being part of my life than he will ever know.

My First Job - Thanks for the Tips

In some respects, I wasn't any different than other kids starting out. I wanted and needed instant gratification and became a product of my environment. At eleven years old, I would hang out with my first cousin on the weekends. Nickel was a few months older than me but every Saturday morning, from 1974 to 1975, Nickel would get up and we would head to one of the largest meat markets and grocery warehouse in the Fort Greene section of Brooklyn. There he taught me the bagging and delivery game; for just helping the customer pack their meat, groceries and help carry their bags they would normally tip us fifty cents to two dollars.

For my next job I went independent and started delivering newspapers. Unlike in the suburbs I didn't flip papers from my bike; I walked my route, delivering the paper to those living in apartment buildings. I would get up early on Sunday mornings to purchase bundles of the Sunday news at .35 to .50 cents each and hit the Projects, going into the buildings and knocking door to door. It's amazing how the neighbors had no problems paying a dollar or more for the paper. I would easily collect no less than $30.00, of clean, honest dough every Sunday before going to Church.

I also had a half-brother named Country from my father's side. Again, my father wasn't really in my life. He was a cab driver and ran numbers on the side, but I didn't get too many tips from him. He is still alive, eventually moved out of New York and we now have a much better relationship. My father felt that if he was more involved in my life growing up my life might have been different. I disagree - maybe? Instead of drugs, I'd be running numbers. He did try to watch out Mark "Country" Garnes; he had his mother's last name. At one time my father told my mother that Country was hanging out with me and I was encouraging him to go around killing people. I denied it of course. Yes! It was true – again, sorry.

It was my mother and her common law husband Spann who kept a roof over our heads and food on the table. At that time I was still having trouble accepting another man playing the role of my biological father; you just don't feel they have the right to discipline you. With that as I said, Spann was the best father that my sister, brother and I could have had. I truly appreciated everything he did for our family knowing he didn't have to.

He even forgave me for taking his nickel-plated Smith & Wesson 22 revolver to school. That sucker was sweet. I carried the gun in my brief case with my books. In between classes when everyone was in the process of going to class I'd stopped at one of the many dice games in the stair cases and placed my brief case down to roll the dice when all of a sudden, the Dean and school security chased me and the other would be gamblers off to our classes. Arriving to class, I realized I left my brief case behind, I panicked, knowingly once they found the gun in my brief case my ass was going to jail. I started thinking and asked my teacher for a bathroom pass. As I left the classroom and headed to the Dean's Office, all of a sudden, a fight broke out. As the staff went to break it up and regain order, I spotted my briefcase. I quickly snatch it up and got the hell out of school with a big sigh of relief. Once again, I beat the odds. *Not thinking that eventually luck would dessert me. The odds are odds, because they are not always on your side and for some more than others.*

The Brooklyn Gold Rush

It wasn't long before an older guy from the projects and I came up with the idea of selling fake jewelry when gold jewelry was in style. I still think it is. Everybody wanted it but couldn't afford it. Even back then, how do you give the people what they want at a very reasonable price? The answer was what we called slumming. We would go to lower Manhattan jewelry stores and purchase ten chains from a blue velvet tray and then buy ten 14 karat gold clips at $2 dollars apiece. Once we arrived back to Cypress Hills, we would use a fingernail file to remove the round clips that read 1/20 12kt gold filled on the chains then replaced them with a genuine 14kt gold clip. Our whole investment was $100-$120 dollars. Once that task was completed, we would catch women coming home from work on pay day, Friday. We sold those chains for $35 dollars apiece making 23 to 25 dollars on each, totaling $230 to $250 per tray, not bad for two kids from the projects. Then we would head right back to Manhattan to repeat the process. Our little scam only lasted a couple of months until the gold chains started to tarnish - it was time for a new hustle.

To Get the Girls - You Gotta Be Fly

When I was thirteen, if you wanted to get the girls, you had to be "Fly," meaning, shakin', money makin' and stylin'. I needed money and I wasn't going to get a summer job. And as for me delivering papers - I was done. Watching other kids with summer jobs getting paid, buying clothes; British Walker Playboy Shoes, trench coats, etc. We waited for those who had summer jobs and robbed them. I am sorry now but not then, we took their money, their clothes, or anything of value. If we saw a white person, we knew they usually had money. I was robbing people my age, as young as thirteen to seventeen, and older. Sometimes we'd get away with two to three thousand dollars and sometimes only five bucks. Again, sorry.

Once Yours, Now Mine

Our victims were always those who we assumed had money. Gentlemen dressed in nice suits, ties, riding the trains, or those who drove new or expensive cars were always targeted - especially if he was white. No one could call us prejudice. *However, we never robbed women, maybe because they would start screaming right away.* Our approach was usually the same; me being the youngest and with that baby face look would approach an intended victim, and say "Mister don't make a move, my partner next to you has a gun, and it's cocked and aimed at you. If you wish to make it home to your wife and kids tonight, give up your wallet and all of your jewelry." Ninety percent of the time those gentlemen would give it up without any resistance. *My friends and I would split up to $2,000 amongst three to four of us, but sometimes we'd make out with zero. I know, poor us.*

Any gold that we ripped off the victims was always taken to the Manhattan Diamond Exchange, 47 and 50th street between 5 and 6 Avenue. They would buy all our stolen gold and diamond jewelry, no questions asked. Any type of gold; for a graduation rings we would receive three hundred dollars an up. For diamond rings, bracelets and watches we would receive up to three thousand dollars. Back then we were kids without any real responsibility, so our money was mostly spent at Delancey Street clothing stores for Quarterfields, Sheepskins, Trench coats, British Walker Playboy shoes, Pumas, Adidas, and gabardine slacks, etc. Our motive, we wanted to dress up and be "Fly" for the girls; shaken', money makin' and stylin!

Welcome to Get Your Ass Kicked 101

Robbing and burglarizing had presented risks and we knew that, but some came with violent consequences. Some were obvious; others were much unexpected results that would one day bring tears to my eyes. My friend

Cisco and I assumed people who lived in Linden Plaza, (a more affluent section in Brooklyn) were better off than us living in the Cypress Hills Houses, and were just trying to survive like myself, but at a different level. *In time you learn everything in life is relative.*

Cisco and I had a couple of friends from school who happen to live in Linden Plaza. What these friends would do, is befriend kids their age that lived in the Plaza in order to get themselves invited into their apartments. *Once inside, they would scope out the apartments and make a mental note of any items worth stealing -- didn't want to steal a bunch of cheap knick-knacks.* Based on their information, I decided which apartments to hit, or not to hit. We would steal the basics: money, jewelry, anything electronic that we could conceal and sell for a profit - that was the name of the game. *Sorry, but I have to laugh, a profit. What did we invest, time and wear and tear on our sneakers?* The most we ever nabbed out of these burglary gigs was $5,095 cash which we divided four ways. We were really into it, being so young and receiving $1273.75 each was indeed a large sum of money for thirteen to sixteen-year olds. Linden Plaza consisted of five, twenty story high rise buildings. The plaza was built in 1971 over the MTA's train storage depot. That meant that the first floor of apartments didn't start until the seventh floor. So, in reality the apartment buildings were twenty-seven floors high. The scary fun part was, in most instances, we gained access to people's apartments by climbing from terrace to terrace. We could start out on the twentieth floor of our friend's terrace and climb three over and then up three to enter an apartment. We were young and reckless, fearless; maybe stupid is more appropriate. Could you imagine slipping and falling? We didn't! Instant death, twenty-seven stories high, with your body hitting the railroad tracks.

Like pirates, we always spilt any and all bounty: cash or the money from stolen items we sold. We were invincible for six months, the police were clueless, and nothing was going to stop us -- until we hit the wrong apartment. It belonged to this lady and among the items we stole was her late mother's diamond wedding ring, along with a camcorder, cameras and stereo equipment. The woman sent word on the street, that she didn't care about the cameras and stereo equipment, all she wanted back was the ring. She gave us exactly one week, *seven days* to return her beloved mother's ring. If your being true to the street code, you never give anything back.

This woman was obviously well loved. She also had a nephew who was recently paroled from one of New York's finest prisons. This lady received word that Cisco was one of the persons who had burglarized her apartment. How she heard was unknown. Anyway, *on day eight*, Cisco, my friend and partner in crime was walking from the store when he was snatched up on the corner of Sutter and Eldert Lane, in broad daylight into the back of a cargo van. He was blind folded, taken to an unknown location where they stripped him butt naked. His abductors used a hot curling iron and burned him all over his body. They tortured him for information on how we accessed her apartment and for our names. He never gave up a word. They beat him with belts and with what he said felt like a baseball bat. Cisco was found in the wee hours on a sidewalk, near Yankee stadium, butt naked, and left for dead. A street sanitation worker found him and called for an ambulance which took him to a Bronx hosptial. He was initially identified as a John Doe. His family had placed a missing person's report and after a few days they were able to locate and identify him. He remained in critical condition for over a month before he was released from the hospital. When Cisco came home from the hospital, I went to his mother's apartment to visit him. It brought tears to my eyes. He could have died all because we burglarized the wrong person's apartment. *Despite that, you think I would have seen the light and changed my ways. You'd think.* It only made me bitter, more devious, and gave me the desire to want more; I began getting involved in other ways to make money -- Linden Plaza was done.

Introduction to Drugs

The first time I got high from using drugs was in the seventh grade. My classmates called me into the bathroom of l.S. 218, where I was shown a "joint" – a marijuana cigarette – and asked if I wanted to get high. That was the first time I smoked marijuana during my Junior High School days. Next, I tried alcohol; beer and hard liquor, whereas, I liked the marijuana high because it made me mellow, so in a short time I became a regular smoker. Although, I never used cocaine, I once placed a small amount on my tongue, the result was a numbing feeling known as a "freeze." As for heroin, I never even experimented, although I did later sell it.

Therefore, ages thirteen thru sixteen I was robbing, burglarizing and *slumming* jewelry. Those crimes were committed to buy new, expensive clothes so we could be "fresh." To be "fresh" was to be exceptionally clean and sharply dressed. We were all on some fashion fair. Everyone wanted to be fresh to continue impressing the girls. However, my next moves of selling drugs would up the ante.

Back to The Future - The Mayor & Dead Bodies

Attending Thomas Jefferson High was bad news when I attended. In time it only got worse. The school officials believed they were making progress until February 27, 1992, although students were still finding it hard to focus on getting good grades.

An Excerpt - Los Angeles Times

NEW YORK — A principal's dream to show off a high school (Thomas Jefferson High), nationally recognized for making educational progress in one of this city's toughest neighborhoods, was shattered Wednesday when a 15-year-old student, firing at point-blank range, killed two other students before being captured.

The killings at the Brooklyn school were called one of the worst incidents of school violence here in decades. Until today's mass shootings. They took place less than an hour before Mayor David N. Dinkins was scheduled to tour the school. Dinkins kept the date. Stepping over the bodies, he was shocked and saddened; he spoke in Thomas Jefferson High School's auditorium, issuing an urgent plea for gun control and self-control. "It is not a good day," the mayor told classmates of the slain students. "If this tragedy had not occurred, I would have been here saying how important it is for you to stay in school, to study hard to learn how to read and write and count and think. . . . *The problem was you've got to survive to get an education.* "We've got to do everything we can to eliminate the violence, not just in the schools, not just around the schools but in the city. In large measure, the problem is guns. . . . If you don't have a gun, you will not use the gun," he said.

Horrified classmates told detectives that the teenager, whose name was withheld because of his age, pulled a .38-caliber revolver from beneath his jacket and opened fire, striking Ian Moore, 17, in the chest and Tyrone Sinkler, 16, in the head. Both died minutes after being rushed to Brookdale Hospital.

Later that day, a 16-year-old classmate, distraught over the killings, attempted suicide. Police said the student shot himself with a .32-caliber revolver and was in critical condition at Brookdale. A police spokesman said the teenager was "very despondent over the deaths of his classmates."

Sinkler's father told reporters that his son had transferred to Jefferson in the fall because he feared violence at his previous high school. Detectives said the shooting was the result of a grudge, dating back to December, but they declined to elaborate.

Jefferson is in the East New York section of Brooklyn in a police precinct that recorded 109 homicides in 1990. Latest statistics show that 104 people were slain during the first 11 months of 1991--more than in many large cities. In the last five years, 35 Jefferson students have been killed, mainly in street violence. Faced with these stark statistics Beck set up therefore a special grieving room for students was allotted.

"We do not celebrate the positive aspects of people, of caring and loving and just being. As a society, we don't even seem to be interested in developing the music and the art--the sensitive parts of the human being," she said. "As budget cuts and fiscal crises affect the city, our school system, those are some of the first things that go, that aesthetic that undefined part of the human development.

That was the end of the article, but not the violence. Yet we get politicians who feel that spending money on art, music and sports is an entitlement. We're still building this country. It cost money and we must all chip in, because everybody wins in the long run. Everybody pays for the prisons. Better to invest in creativity, than creating more prisons.

Domino Nicknamed Me Glaze

I got the nickname Glaze in the summer of 1978 when I was fourteen by my buddy, Domino. The name was prompted by my brother James, nicknamed "Kool-Aid," so Domino and I went with "Glaze" - and not a fucking glazed donut!

I had another unwanted nickname, Sugar Bear. It was given to me by some female classmates at J.H.S 218, during the seventh grade. The reason for the name was because of my chubby cheeks, like the bear from the cereal commercial. It's strange when the girls like Wanda, Helen and Melba called me Sugar Bear, it was no problem but when my male classmates called me Sugar Bear, I wanted to fight. *That was a clear case of a double standard.*

Delivering flyers and Stealing Cash

Occasionally, we tried to earn an honest buck. My man, Domino, (his real name was Curtis Gibbs), we weren't blood related, but the bond that we created establish us as family. We hung out together, from going to school to parties. We even had a side job together; going around from borough to borough placing flyers on cars and sliding brochures under apartment doors. We did it for a plastic slipcover company and it was a legit hustle until a few older guys, who were from the Bronx, were telling the owners of the slip cover company that we were to slow in doing our job. So, after a few weeks, these chumps (excuse me - employers) were talking about firing us. That was when the great schemer that I am, watched and saw one of the partners return and place a large sum of cash in a desk drawer before walking to another office in the back. That was my cue; I went into motion as Domino served as the lookout, I grabbed the large stash of cash, and ran out of there. I placed the cash in a brown paper bag that I obtained when I left the shop and purchased a soda; then placed it under a rock in the co-op courtyard nearby. That was June of 1978, I was fifthteen years old. When I arrived back, no one noticed that I was gone, which was great for me. Once they all came from the back office, they decide to pay us and cut ties. Once they realized the money was gone the NYPD was contacted and that was my second contact with NYPD.

The first was when I was born in the back seat of police car, but that's a very vague memory now. Once we got paid, Domino and I walked about six or seven blocks to the F train, instead of going directly for the hidden money,

23

just in case we were being followed. I then doubled back to the courtyard and retrieved the money from underneath the rock. I was somewhat surprised the money was still there, after all, it was Brooklyn. We split the $600 and boarded the F train to Delancey Street, where I bought my first pair of British Walker shoes for $54. In 1978 that was a considerable amount for fourteen and fifteen-year-olds.

My crime spree with Domino was different. He wasn't the typical guy from the neighborhood, he was around and down. It was as if he was playing chess, ten moves ahead of everyone else. Domino was also a ladies' man, getting more pussy than anyone of us. Back then he had females ten and fifteen years older than himself.

Moochie and The Nut Hut

Moochie was the first person that placed me in the drug game. I meet Moochie when I was about fourteen or fifteen and Moochie probably was about thirty. Moochie had all of the expensive items, cars and clothes. He was the first man I saw who wore a mink coat; he had some of the most beautiful women that I have ever seen. Back than he had a game room called, **The Nut Hut**, it was right across the street from Cypress Hill Houses, on Sutter Avenue side, right next to Dan Supreme's supermarket. In the game room most kids played the pinball machines and pac-man, while the older guys would be shooting pool. Moochie had several guys working for him. One who stood out was Sheldon, he had a dark complexion, about 6'2", muscular build and his head was covered with braids. Sheldon was Moochie's number one problem solver; if anyone needed a beat down, to collect money from or be killed he was it. However, Moochie could and would also take care of the problems at hand.

The Nut Hut was always busy, people moving in and out either playing pool or arcade games. Although, the majority of clientele would bypass the games and head straight to the back to the bullet proof glass petition to purchase what they wanted: a bag of dope, aka heroin, or a bag of coke or pot. Others would gamble in Moochie's private casino downstairs. He held some of the largest dice and poker games back in those times, right there in the famous Nut Hut. When my friend Domino and I had the opportunity to hang out downstairs behind the bullet proof partition, we saw so much money stacked up, it was amazing. I had never seen so many stacks and stacks of green currency in my life. Back then when tough guys came through an acted up, Moochie would place a .38 revolver in their mouth and played Russian roulette. Trust me those so-called tough guys never gave him a problem again. One night something must have gone awfully wrong, Moochie kicked everyone out of the game room early and several hours later, about 3:00 AM, Domino and I were watching the Nut Hut from his apartment window and we saw Moochie and one of his guys place what look like a body wrap up in a rug in a the back of a van. And for some reason that made us feel secure, we both knew Moochie liked us and knew that if we ever had a problem Moochie would take care of it.

As time passed, my crew and I continued hanging out at The Nut Hut as we participated in our own crimes, doing whatever it took to make fast dollars. I can recall one day being downstairs with Moochie in his private office, he had stacks of drugs each one looked like white shaped sized bricks wrapped up in saran wrap. He was telling us, "If you ever want to become filthy rich, this product right here is the way." Then he took out his pocketknife and dug a little hole in the top of the package removed his blade with a little white powder and guided the blade to his nostril. He sniffed it up, jumped back and said, *"This is some strong shit right here. This dope is so strong it'll make you want to slap the shit out of your closest relatives."* As a youth, I *thought why would I want to do that if that shit was that good?* Nevertheless, at that age I was totally against selling any type of drugs. My reasoning was that I witnessed so many people who would actually be nodding out in the streets, on the steps of apartment buildings, inside the halls, on the staircases, that were literally lost from sniffing and shooting heroin. I didn't want any part of that. The Nut Hut later got hot! Too much traffic and the cops were watching Moochie, so he shut it down before he got arrested. We were sad when our #1 hangout was shut down, but we soon found a new hang out.

King Tut was No Bodies Mummy

As luck would happen, the notorious stick-up kid Walter "King Tut" Johnson and his family resided in the same building as my family. It was rumored for years that the Federal Government believed that he was involved in the murder of the rapper Tupac Shakur. As in the rapper's lyrics titled *Many Men by 50cent,* there is a verse that says, "The Feds did not know who Shot Pac, I got a kite from the joint that Tut got knock." Walter "King Tut" was also a suspect in the shooting of Tupac Shakur in 1994 outside of a NYC recording company, besides his murder in 1996 in Los Angeles. The attempt murder was also later part of the lyrics in rapper's Tupac's "Against All Odds" on The Killuminati: The Seven Day Theory, by Tupac himself.

Tut and I became friends after we got into a fight in school. Funny how many friendships start off that way; a bully befriends a guy who has the balls to fight back hard. In 1980, then sixteen, Walter "King Tut" Johnson and I started robbing any and everyone. He eventually became a major figure in the infamous Black Mafia Family street gang, operating out of New York City. He also had a business relationship with Sean John Combs, later to be known by his stage names Puff Daddy, Diddy, and P. Diddy, a record producer, actor, and business mogul.

He was bad, known for sticking up gangsta rappers. Tut who grew up in the same neighborhood with Michael

Tyson got away with a lot of shit, including the Brooklyn, N.Y. Barber Shop shooting of three NYPD cops. As luck would give out, he is now in Pennsylvania, Lewisburg Penitentiary for life without a *shot* for parole. *And some kids reading this, may wonder why their parents are so concerned about who they are hanging out with.*

Chapter Three - Boot Camp

First Trip to Rikers Island with King Tut

Of all the crime Tut and I did together it wasn't until spring of 1981 that we were arrested. One day while in a restaurant near our high school named Redirection, an Alternative High School for guys and girls, which meant it, was a last resort to complete your education because you either dropped out or were a truant. I as transferred there from Thomas Jefferson H.S. for being a truant. Most students there would do anything to make that fast dollar; from robbing, stealing, jostling, shop lifting, or selling drugs. You name it and someone at Redirection was the best at doing it - practice, practice – good or bad.

One morning before we went to school, Tut, Domino and I were having breakfast at Trudy's. Trudy's was a small restaurant located on Van Siclen Avenue and Fulton Street, under the "L" (elevated trains). They served breakfast and lunch, and we didn't pay much attention to what the health codes ratings were. Our main concern was we wanted to eat at affordable places. You could always tell if your fellow classmates had run into some fast cash, based upon what they were all eating. If they only had a toasted bagel with butter and jelly to go, they were broke. But if the whole crew was sitting there with steak, eggs, toast and washing it down with a large pitcher of orange juice, you knew they came off with a nice piece of paper (money from hustling, whatever).

On this particular morning we were broke and working on how we were going to get our next pay day. Bingo! In came Penny from Nostrand Avenue. She walked up to Domino and me, holding a 14 karat white gold diamond studded watch in her hand and ask if we thought it was real. Domino and I both examined the watch and knew instantly it was real. Suddenly, Tut came along, grabbed the watch and ran right out of Trudy's. Penny ran after Tut, but it was to no avail. Tut refused to give it back and off we went to the "Jewelry Heaven" a.k.a. the Diamond Exchange. Tut sold the diamond studded watch for $1500 dollars, which we split. Initially Tut didn`t want to give Domino anything.

I had to convince him to hook Domino up. Back then we called Domino a Jew, meaning if he made a move to make some fast cash, he was not giving up any cash to anyone. Nevertheless, we took our share and went shopping. I purchased a pair of green suede British Walker shoes, Damian knit shirts and a pair of sharkskin slacks. Tut and Domino purchased - I don't remember. Do you really care? We split up and I went home, showered, dressed into my new threads, and left to hook up with a few guys at the projects. Man, unfortunately, there's always a price to pay. As I headed toward Euclid & Sutter Ave, I stopped frozen. Approaching me was an undercover police car with Tut sitting in the back seat which made me real nervous as it passed. Tut and I had been on a rampage robbing everything and everyone we desired. Suddenly, the car came to a screeching halt. Then the wheels spinning in reverse, the car came to a stop with two undercover detectives jumping from the car, pulling their guns, and shouting, there's money green! I was wearing a pair of green sharkskin slacks, green Damien shirt, green diamond dress socks, green suede and leather British Walkers, and a green leather European craft coat. *No, I wasn't a pimp.* I began jumping up and down in the middle of the street proclaiming my innocence. That lasted about three minutes or so, until one of them placed a gun to my head, while the other cuffed me, and placed me in the back seat with King Tut. We were chauffeured to the 75th Precinct, which would become our 2nd home. From there we went to central booking, then court, and to Suite C-74 Rikers Island.

I recall while Tut and I were on Rikers Island's C74, it was so crowded that we were moved from bullpen to bullpen. As we went into the mess hall, to sit down to eat, all of the hardened criminals were talking about what they are going to do if we walked into their area and how they were going to rob us of our British Walker shoes. All of a sudden King Tut and I stood up back to back in the mess hall, dumped our trays and said, *fuck it,* "If you punk ass guys want our shit, let's go now." We were jumped by the correction officers and taken to the, "why me bullpen" in the receiving room. The "why me bullpen" stood for the "*fuck up, anyone who steps out of line."* At C-74, the "why me bullpen" it is a very small cell.

After Tut and I snatched the diamond studded watch from Penny, I don't recall if Penny got the watch from a family member, found it, or stole it. However, I knew she had us by the balls and we did whatever had to be done for Penny to drop the charges. Eventually, once we worked things out with Penny we were released, with no charges filed.

Unfortunately, still no lesson learned. *You don't get it, neither do I.* Our behavior became more out of control. We began robbing people on the Queen's Green Line bus services; for money, jewelry or anything of value. We must have been watching one too many westerns stagecoach holdups. One day, Tut came to me all excited about a plan he had about robbing the Kingdom Hall Jehovah Witness Church. Man, I laughed, told him he was going to hell, for sure. I was against it, and second of all, his mother and his whole family attended the church - a major No-No. We kept robbing with no remorse. One night I caught this older guy name Boomer across the street from the Cypress Hills Houses. He was wearing several gold chains with medallions on each of them. He had to be twenty-five to thirty years old. I could feel my heart pounding as I pull out my 25 automatic and put the drop on him. He said, "You must not know who the fuck I am?" He was right; I didn't know as I took the safety off and put the gun to his head, "I will blow your fucking head off if you don't comply!" with that said I ripped off all of his jewelry.

Destination Rikers Island

It's been said, *"It's sometimes more important to enjoy the journey, than the destination."* I agree.

The Rikers Island complex consists of ten jails and holds local offenders who are awaiting trial or bail. Other residents included those who could afford bail, not given bail, those serving sentences of one year or less, and or those temporarily placed their pending transfer to another facility. Rikers Island is therefore a jail and not a prison, which typically holds offenders serving longer-term sentences. *That is information; hopefully, you will never have to make use of.*

Between the years of 1979-1997 I spent over 14 years fighting both the State and Federal judicial systems, as well as spending over fourteen years in and out of jail. Years that I experienced the feelings of trust and betrayal, love and hate, sex, frustration, kindness and ruthlessness, births and deaths, peace, fear, heaven and hell. Many of the experiences I'm sharing, I'm not too proud of, but fortunately I'm trying to balance the scale, yet I'm not sure if that's possible, but I'm trying. *Actually, to balance them, I would probably have to shoot myself.* Fortunately, not part of any 12 Step programs.

Merry Christmas

The journeys that lead me to my first significant experience in Rikers Island began on December 26, the day after Christmas 1979 and twenty-five days after my sixteenth birthday. I was feeling blessed the day after Christmas; unfortunately, I lost the holiday spirit. Again, Sorry.

On that cold and dark night, I was like a junkie, addicted to some form of chemical substance like no other drug or alcohol. That substance came in a paper form, a greenish color, the O mighty dollar. Anyway, as my accomplice Crazy and I arrived at Pratt Institute via mass transportation. I like the one in a million fare beaters, would walk through the gate or jump the turnstiles to ride the train. Pratt Institute is a private, non-profit institution of higher learning located in the Clinton Hills neighborhood of Brooklyn. As Crazy and I got off the train at Pratt Institute we started looking for our target. Our target market 85% of the time was anyone who was white and dressed for success, which equaled money. *Well, maybe I helped cause some of the prejudice against my people.* My associate Crazy had gained my respect after he retrieved my coat which had been robbed by another hood at the time, named Sangria. Sangria has since gone straight and now host a radio show and has published a magazine dealing with crime and the Mafia. Crazy at the time was like a big brother, older and more knowledgeable. Crazy wasn't cut from the same cloth, not psychologically nor physically built like me. Years later, after the robbery at Pratt Institute, when we eventually both went away to do State bids (time in prison) for our felony convictions, I became ruthless and built a reputation that I was not the one to go against. The irony was that Crazy was known as a good guy, totally the opposite of the image he once portrayed when we were younger. However, years later in 1986, Crazy and I have a major falling out after he robbed a drug spot, that he knew I was responsible for sales and protection. Out of the thousands of drug spots throughout the five boroughs, why would he rob one under my domain? I treated him like family and had provided him financial assistance numerous times to help him get on his feet. His actions were unjustified and caused his girlfriend to be murdered and it was going to cost him his life--a time for living; a time for dying. Anyway, back to the Xmas heist.

Let me preface what I'm telling you with a question someone asked me, "How do you go out the day after Christmas and rob somebody? Even criminals take a day off for the holidays, don't they? It's Christmas, a time for giving!" I'll try to answer; I have to think about it. Anyway, we waited in the dark like animals waiting to attack the first healthiest prey. I don't quite understand what led me down that road. Why couldn't I be like most normal, typical sixteen-year old, pick up a newspaper and search the help wanted section? Find a job that would have allowed me to earn a legit income and purchase, in time, whatever I desired? *These are all good questions.*

It was the day after Christmas, and I had no good reason for placing myself in such a desperate life-threatening situation. My Christmas was great. I received way more gifts than the average kid, thanks to my parents. But I was desperate, selfish, and greedy, with no good explanation for wanting more. So that night, as the most perfect victim came along, looking like a sure payday I went into attack mode. I pulled out my weapon and placed the drop on this innocent white couple. BOOM, two NYPD Anti-Crime detectives came out of nowhere and arrested Crazy and me. The two of us were taken, by the squad car, from the 88th Precinct to Brooklyn Central Booking, where we were fingerprinted and photographed. We were then taken to a holding cell with other individuals before taken to court and released on our own recognizance. One week later I was arrested again for robbery, in midtown Manhattan. Fuck!

After all the criminal activities and crimes that I committed over the years I was finally officially arrested for the first time. When we were arrested, I took the weight for the whole stick-up, saying that I didn't know Crazy and he wasn't with me. I could have been shot and killed, all because I wanted a fast buck. It wasn't worth it, but I had a short memory. My parents finally bailed me out. Note: Brooklyn Criminal Court, my first arrest, Brooklyn, N.Y., Pratt institute, 12/26/1979, on robbery and carrying an illegal weapon. It was also my first felony conviction, and I was sentenced to five years' probation, as a youthful offender.

Well, I thought about the question. How do you go out and rob someone the day after Christmas? Even criminals take a holiday, don't they? What was I thinking when I went out the day after Christmas to jack up somebody? Whether burglarizing or robbing victims of their personal belongings: cash, jewelry, boom boxes, and clothing at the point of gun with very little remorse, I knew deep down in my heart it wasn't right. How could you not? It wasn't like I was stealing bread to feed the family. As a kid being robbed of my belongings on the street a couple of times and while a guest at Rikers Island, I hated the feeling of being the victim, feeling weak and having no power at the time to do anything about it. Yet, I chose with my crew to inflict that same type of displeasure on so many people. My main excuse or reason, which ever, I don't have a good one. Even burglarizing a vast amount of folk's residences, breaking into their homes while they were at work and their kids were at school was a total violation of those individual's lives. Imagine coming home after a long day at work or school, you open your door and your place has been burglarized of your money, jewelry, electronic equipment, memories and everything that is worth any value. Total violation, that offense if I was the victim, I would have left wanting revenge.

Even with a Christian upbringing and going to church my actions and behavior demonstrated that I wasn't serving our Lord and Savior Jesus Christ. I was serving Satan himself. I know things were getting out of hand when at the age of fourteen I started shooting at anyone who opposed me. I doubt this explanation and the events leading to this point gives you a logical picture of why, or what justifies my actions. Let's just leave it to bad judgment for now. As a young black man living in that urban environment, we weren't thinking outside the box, about the type of lifestyle we were living. We knew our days on the street were numbered, that we would wind up in the prison systems or dead at an early age. But back then we were too busy trying to stay alive and out of jail. We were learning to gamble but didn't know it. In the future it would be the stock market.

I was once asked, knowing the consequences of my actions, "Didn't you think about the future?" To be honest, I and the majority of my peers never talked about the future. *I never spent any time thinking about the future; it was life day by day, or as the saying goes, "Live in the present." They should add a phrase, "but don't let the past sneak up on you."* When I got involved in crime, and like many young people, we all thought we were invincible. "It's not going to happen to me." Wrong!

When You're Hot - When You're Not

As previously written, exactly one week from the Pratt Institute bust, I was arrested on January 1, 1980.

The crime went down in Manhattan on an Upper East Side subway station with me and Big Head Joe, from Cypress, known for *Geeing Off,* in other words making thousands of dollars. We were both arrested for felony armed robbery by New York transit undercover detectives, which provided me my second stay to Rikers Island.

The way it went down, it was early morning, during rush hour on a weekday, and it was freezing cold. Every New Yorker was bundled up with coats, hats, gloves and scarves. I stopped the first intended victim by grabbing him and saying these exact words, "Mister do not make a move, my buddy" who would be right there to the side of me, "just came home from jail, he is crazy, and he doesn't care about going back to jail." At that time Big Head Joe pulled out his gun, at which time I told this well-dressed white man to give up his wallet and watch. This man slapped Joe's hand holding the gun, and said, "Don't you think it is kind of too cold to be playing games this early in the morning" and walked away. Joe and I busted out laughing; it was too funny; this guy had a lot of balls. Like I said ninety percent of the time the mark would give in; this guy was part of the other ten percent. We composed ourselves and caught our next victim, another well-dressed white businessman. I stopped him and gave him my pitch and Joe pulled out his weapon. The gentleman was scared and handed over his wallet and valuables. As we were exiting, we were chased and apprehended by two New York transit cops.

After being arrested in Manhattan and bail was set, I can recall, there was a group of us handcuffed and placed on the bus, heading to the lovely resort known as Rikers Island. I remember going over the long bridge, and all you could see was water until we arrived at the security check point of the largest county jail in the United States. *Passing water had a whole new meaning.* HDM is a part of Rikers Island designated for adult men - not very pretty. We were escorted to one of the many different jail sections. C-74 was the home of the adolescent age group 16 - 20. Keep in mind you had guys in C-74 as old as 30 lying about their age, because they didn't want to be in HDM or C-95 or any of the facilities that housed adult males 21 and up.

The older inmates who were lying about their age were straight up playing Humphrey Bogart with the younger inmates, taking their clothes, sneakers and coats. Let's analyze sixteen to eighteen-year old. Youngsters don't start fully developing until about nineteen, making the average new inmate approximately five foot six to five foot ten, and one hundred and forty pounds to one hundred and sixty pounds. Skinny is an easy target for the Jail House Gladiators. When you got punched in the face by one of the many Jail House Gladiators it felt like you've just been hit in the face with a cast iron frying pan; like a scene from Tom and Jerry and hearing and feeling that throbbing *bong yong yong* sound.

Unlike my first trip, I was jumped, beaten up and robbed. Now I am the victim, being exploited how my partners in crime exploited others. However, they were innocent victims, robbed and attacked for no reason. That was when I learned the meaning of the old cliché, "What goes around, comes around." Didn't let it stop me; just made me understand, if someone steals from me and I steal from someone else - *The Merry Go Round.* Ninety percent of those processed at Rikers Island were robbed by fellow inmates of shoes, clothing, jewelry and sometimes even an individual's manhood was taken by force. I would become one of the fortunate ten percent. *Rikers Island was like the Roman Olympics - only the strong survived, as well as what doesn't kill you makes you stronger.*

I was involved in several fights, because other inmates were always trying to steal my clothes. On one particular day an individual by the name of Mel wanted to fight me for my knit shirt. Being ignorant to the jailhouse way of life I removed my shirt and handed it to a guy from the neighborhood to hold while Mel and I fought. A few punches were exchanged, when Mel suddenly picked me up and body slammed me to the floor. Guards soon arrived to break up the fight and I was transferred to another building. The guy from the neighborhood gave my shirt to Mel. The stay at Rikers Island lasted about a month. During that time, I began to participate in the "rock trademark" -- robbing people or being robbed. I started to rob fellow inmates of their clothing, shoes, jewelry and anything else which might have been considered as having at least some value on the rock.

I recall going to the mess hall with my housing unit. The mess hall was huge, loud and the food was awful, and I couldn't eat it. I spent most of my days in my cold cell crying like a little bitch wanting to go home. After a week of pure hell, I was finally bailed out, but did I learn my lesson, this time? Not really, I was still a stupid young knuckle head who didn't learn shit. I felt if I could survive C-74, I could survive anything. Like, if you can make it in New York City, you can make it anywhere. I was tough, I was bad, and I was a God dam fool. Back then I really lacked the basics -- common sense.

After a month or so on Rikers Island, my bail was reduced to $2,500, and my mother and Spann posted bail for my release -- that was the second time. Like before, I returned home with a tough guy attitude; feeling I must be tough, having twice survived the stay at Rikers Island.

While on bail, from October to November of 1980, I kept my nose clean, staying away from possible sources of trouble. I was scheduled to appear in court, with my mother, the week before Thanksgiving.

More Memories - Fighting at Rikers Island

As scheduled, I appeared at Kew Gardens Queens Supreme Court, with my mother and my court-appointed attorney who asked my mother to hire him as a privately retained counsel. The judge called her forward and asked if she could afford to hire the attorney. My mother said she couldn't and then the judge ordered me to be returned to Rikers Island and raised my bail to $5,000; all because the court-appointed lawyer felt if I could afford bail, I could afford to pay him.

I recall being greeted in the bullpen by the "Queens welcoming committee." Made up with Melvin, the person I fought earlier to keep my knit shirt, a guy named "Beanie," and several others who had robbed me of a pair of black British Walkers and a leather coat, which in return I was given a pair of Adidas sneakers and a goose down coat. The choice was to either give it up willingly or get my brains stomped out and still have to give it up. I personally wasn't a freak for pain, *although I eventually served up a lot of it.*

While back on the rock, I started once more to rob others of their personal property. My little crew consisted of two others: Chris Bullock, known as "Skill, and Michael Alexander, known as "Big Head Mike" and yes he had a big head. There were other "little crews" besides ours. Our motto was; "Do onto others, before it's done onto you."

Joining the Other Ten Percent

Visits to the Rock weren't pleasant. One night at Rikers, returning from a scheduled movie, I was attacked by this Puerto Rican and black guy who had their own crew. One of my attackers had a Rikers Island Special, a heavy metal rod, which had been sharpened into a dagger. When I was hit, I blanked out for about fifteen seconds, and then I tried to get away from the attackers. I was punched, and then pushed towards the guy in possession of the metal dagger, who was continuously jabbing the shank at me. Using only my bare hands and arms, I did all I could to protect myself. The assault lasted about two minutes before several correctional officers arrived and broke up the fight.

The result was a puncture in my left-arm, with several less severe cuts on my stomach. Medical staff and officers alike said I was blessed, because they thought I would have needed to be taken to the hospital in serious condition which usually is the result of being assaulted with a shank (Rikers Island Special). Fortunately, all that was required was a trip to the institution's clinic for a tetanus shot and some bandages. God was watching over and protecting me, *I was beyond lucky.* Although, I'm not sure why, *I know God* had better people to watch over. When I returned to my housing unit, officers allowed me to watch my crew, Skill and Mike, beat down and stomp this other guy who was involved in the fight earlier that evening.

Learning to Fight Back at Rikers

As I went back and forth to Rikers Island during 1980 the trend didn't change, I was jumped, beaten up, and my belongings taken by force. The first few times was rough. But by 1981 it was a different story.

The next time I arrived on Rikers Island was July 31, 1981 arrest. I went in raising hell, refusing to accept any forms of disrespect from anyone. The first problem was with another inmate who stepped on my Puma sneakers. I lost it, punched him in the face and slammed his head into the wall before the COs (correction officers) came and broke it up. From that point on I was treated with respect on Rikers Island or at any State or Federal prison *for the most part...*

Note: Manhattan Supreme Court, arrested on 01/02/1980 for robbery and weapons charge. This was my second felony conviction, and I was sentenced to 5 years' probation to run concurrent with my Pratt Institute, probation. I was sentenced mid-1980.

Dooms Day 1981 to 1984

Instead of learning not to commit crimes, I was focusing on how to not get caught. *By September 8, 1980 I perfected neither.*

While awaiting trial for sticking up the Q-7 bus I continued my criminal ways. On July 31, 1981 it was dooms day. We were robbing other kids that were willing to work for summer youth checks. We were on a rampage, being stupid and trying to catch as many victims as possible for their pay checks.

Well, that brought about my fourth arrest on July 31, 1981 for robbery and assault. This would also be my fourth felony conviction. I plead guilty. I was sentenced on

December 18, 1981 to 2-4 years for the robbery "beef" on September 8, 1980. And while in prison, at only age eighteen on January 1982, I was sentence to 2yrs, 6 months – 5yrs for the July 31, 1981 robbery and assault.

Both sentences ran concurrently. Therefore, I spent three years and six months in prison; until November 27, 1984 just before my 21st birthday. *Most men can't remember the day they were married or their woman's birthday, but they do remember the day they went to prison and the day they got out.*

Rikers Island to Elmira Correctional Facility

My three and a half prison sentences started with me temporarily back at my second home, Rikers Island. As soon as I walked through the door, I started raising hell. If another inmate said or did something I didn't like, the result would be several punches to the face, or a sucker punch if the other person happened to be bigger than me. I wasn't about to take anything from anyone -- and that was final.

I started building my jailhouse reputation in July of 1981. On January 13, 1982, I was transferred from C-74 Rikers Island to Elmira State Prison - upstate New York. The ride to Elmira ranged from seven to ten hours. I can recall about thirty other inmates and myself being shackled down on the bus as we headed into a snow blizzard. Upon arriving all I could see was Elmira's long, tall and grayish wall with its big steel doors. I was inmate number 82B82, which designated me as the eighty-second inmate to enter Elmira in the year of 1982. I was prepared for what was coming; my brother, Kool-Aid, had gone through Elmira only a few months earlier and informed me about what to expect.

As they slowly opened the large steel doors and the bus entered, we were escorted off the bus into the facility which was cold and wet. After leaving the bus, everybody was unshackled, and strip searched. Next was the disposal of our clothes and being sprayed for bugs. After the spraying we were processed, showered, given green uniforms, underwear and a blanket, and then shown to our cells. Man, I can still remember how hot it was that night.

In the morning we all left our cells heading to the cafeteria. After eating, we headed back to the dorms: a two-sided tier, three floors high and approximately eight feet high. The cells were divided into two sections; therefore, at any given time there could be a total of four hundred and ninety-two inmates, two hundred and forty-six on each side. As I walked thru, all I heard were all four hundred and ninety-two inmates yelling at the top of their lungs, "New jack! New jack! New jack!" Keep in mind these are all murderers, armed robbers, burglars, rapists and arsonists. That was an extremely scary feeling, if you were not a seasoned prisoner. Some of the virgin inmates were so scared they pissed on themselves on that long walk to the cafeteria.

From my stint and hell rising on Rikers Island, as I walked through the jail heard fellow inmates that knew me, calling my name, "Amazing Glaze." Similar words would repeat themselves, from time to time, reminding me of the song. "*Amazing grace! How sweet the sound, that saved a wretch like me! I once was lost but now am found, was blind but now I see.*" I wish that was my case. I was still blind.

My mother, Spann, and my sister would drive from New York to Elmira to visit me and to make sure that everything was alright or at least as well as could be expected under such circumstances. By that time Kool-Aid left the Elmira population and went to Camp Monterey, located in Beaver Dam, New York. Since Camp Monterey and Elmira were relatively close, the family would always visit Kool-Aid first and then on to Elmira to see me. My brother and I were fortunate in that regard, most inmates never receive visits, or at least rarely when entering Elmira reception because it was near Canada.

Welcome to Coxsackie Correctional Facility

I lasted in Elmira for a month and a half, before being re-classified as a Maximum B inmate, and being transferred to Coxsackie Correctional Facility, which had a security classification of Maximum B. Coxsackie was also known as "Gladiator School." Sack, as it was called, housed mostly adolescents and young adults with long sentences. The Sack reminded me of reformatory school and the mess hall could be compared to a fast food restaurant.

When incarcerated it's pretty much standard practice for an individual to establish himself by gaining respect from other inmates, as well as staff. Fortunately, and unfortunately, I already knew inmates who were respected at the Sack. However, being the strong willed 18-year-old, I wasn't seeking respect vicariously.

My first misbehavior report came from my interference with another inmate, Tony Rome. While he was conversing with a third inmate; he was actually threatening the other inmate. Rome told the unnamed individual, that he was "going to fuck him in the ass." I overheard and said otherwise, telling Tony Rome to leave the young man alone. I was now facing my first problem in upstate New York. A heated argument ensued between Tony Rome and me, ending with Rome wanting to stab me. Another inmate, Mike "Coca Cocker," advised Rome that such a move wouldn't be very wise. However, Rome did end up sucker punching me while in the mess hall, which caused us both to be locked down in our cells. Lockdown is commonly referred to as "keep lock" in upstate New York.

During the keep lock period Rome was allowed out of his cell, the reason is not recalled, and I proceeded to "throw piss all over him." Tony Rome immediately returned the gesture and I ended up having to clean everything in my cell, including my clothes and other personal property.

After the keep lock period had ended, Rome made an attempt to lure me into a fight. On our way back from breakfast one morning, Rome came to me and said that he didn't want any problems. Rome also said that when certain correctional officers came on duty, they would allow him and me to fight each other in the dayroom, undisturbed and one-on-one. Rome then displayed a homemade knife. I knew if I tried to fight that morning, I would have been stabbed.

Several weeks had passed before an opportunity for revenge presented itself. It was during a movie in the auditorium that I left my seat, ducked, and moved ahead three aisles to where Tony Rome was sitting. Once there, I started pounding Rome in the face. Rome ended up with a black eye and busted lip. Again, we were both placed on keep lock status, but that incident did end the feud between Tony Rome and mtself.

During the first part of my stay at the Sack I was housed in Unit D-2, where my activity assignments was in the institution's upholstery shop in the mornings, then precollege in the afternoons. I lasted only a short time, until I was transferred to Unit F-2, where I was assigned to mess hall duty. I worked in the mess hall for about a month before I received a misbehavior report, for getting into a "misunderstanding" with a staff member. My "misunderstanding" landed me in "the box" -- that is, in solitary confinement -- for thirty-days. Life in the box meant erratic exercise periods alone in a miniature yard, and two-and-a-half minute showers per week. The temperature was in the 80s and 90s, and the cells were bug infested including a myriad of flying insects. Thirty-days in the box was rough, but I had no-other choice than to deal with it as best as I could. After being released from the box my correctional counselor decided it was best to transfer me to Fishkill. On July 21, 1982, I was on my way out of Coxsackie, passing by my half-brother, Mark Garnes, (AKA) "Country" who was just arriving from Elmira. *Crime was becoming a family business.*

Welcome to Fishkill

I lasted six months in Coxsackie before I was reclassified and sent to Fishkill Correctional Facility. I stayed there from the summer of 1982 until the fall of 1983. Then I was kicked out.

Fishkill was classified as a medium A. facility and I would describe it as being "wide open." In other words, there were no controlled movements; inmates were allowed to move about freely. Fishkill was so wide open during that time that inmates were being murdered almost with impunity -- especially in the area known as the infamous "Fishkill Tunnel."

August of 1983, a friend of mine, Tank, had a "misunderstanding" with another inmate; a Panamanian guy whose name happened to be Panama. The exact nature of Tank's and Panama's "misunderstanding" is not recalled, but a fist fight between the two ensued and Tank proceeded to whip Panama's ass. This nearly brought forth a race riot in the unit that night, but Panama and his "crew" realized they simply were not strong enough. It was therefore decided that the Hispanics and the Blacks would meet in yard 21A after Saturday's brunch, to "discuss the matter." The meeting took place, but soon after it started it turned for the worst and nothing was accomplished. There was simply too much animosity between the Hispanics and the Blacks.

Most everyone had brought weapons to 21A that Saturday morning. I had a large screwdriver, a six-inch metal spike, a hammer, a piece of solid steel and a rock. For protection I placed several books around my body for armor, and wore a large, green coat. P.S. The weather was in the 90s.

Others on the scene were: Tank; Marcellous 'Tiny" Lawrence; Derek "K-Wop" Cade; and Big Baker. The main players in the opposition were: Panama; Flaco; and Vic. Many others were there for the so-called "meeting" which brought the total to over two hundred. Shortly after the fight started, the yard was raided by officers. The original plan to stab as much of the opposition as possible was ruined. Weapons were being thrown away and everyone was rushing through the doors. Tank, Tiny, and one other individual were charged with inciting a riot and locked down. Several people from both sides were charged with possession of a weapon and locked down.

The next day, while walking back to my unit, shortly before the afternoon count and the officer's shift change, I was returning from the library reading a sex novel. The corridor was open and so I continued to walk and read with tremendous concentration. I walked past a staircase, paused believing I thought I heard a noise and suddenly struck with an urge to turn around. As I turned, I lost my footing and slipped, awkwardly hitting the wall, and narrowly avoided being stabbed. My assailants were Vic and Big Panama, and both had homemade prison knives. The two continually stabbed at me as I weaved, wobbled, and hit the wall. Regaining my balance, I ran as fast as I could back to my housing area -- my heart beating like there was no tomorrow.

Later that same evening Panama, Flaco, and Vic saw me in the hallway, but I moved along quickly before any of them had the chance to do anything to me. I had no weapon with which to defend myself as they were confiscated the day before. I therefore went to the 21 Small Yard, where one of my *homies* gave me a butter knife from the mess hall. I sharpened the butter knife while I was in the shower.

After showering I stayed up all night, plotting against my enemies. The next morning, with my trusty, sharpened butter knife, I entered the mess hall looking for Panama, Vic, or Flaco. The first to be encountered would be the recipient of the butter knife. Panama was the unfortunate one.

Panama was just returning to the mess hall with the food cart from the box and went into the dish room. KWop and I spotted Panama, we got out of our seats, emptied our trays, and walked towards him. K-Wop asked Panama, "Why the fuck was you trying to make a move on my man?" The captain and some of the institution's lieutenants were just outside the door, so Panama's false sense of security took over and he started that gangster tough guy shit. I attacked him, stabbing him with the butter knife. I stabbed Panama several times before correction officers arrived. I was handcuffed and escorted to the box.

Panama testified against me at a disciplinary hearing, claiming that I had stabbed him without reason. Panama's arm was in a sling and his shirt was lifted in order to display the multiple stab wounds. I was found guilty and sentenced to 150-days in the box and the loss of six month's goodtime. Tank and Tiny each received only 30days in the box. In addition to the institution's disciplinary proceedings, I was also formally arrested by the Dutchess County Sheriff's Department and charged with assault and possession of a deadly weapon. I went to court several times, but since Big Panama didn't force the issue the charges were dropped, and I was allowed to "cop-out" to 30-days for the prompting of prison contraband.

Touring Prisons and Going Green

On September 16, 1983, Tank, Tiny and I were transferred to Green Haven Correctional Facility, classified as a Maximum A facility. The environment within Green Haven was completely different from that of Fishkill. Most

Green Haven inmates had life sentences. How many times can you get kicked out of prison? *God, I needed his help. You gotta laugh.* Movement was restricted, and the security was very tight. When I arrived at Green Haven, I was taken directly to the box to finish the 150-days I received at Fishkill. After appealing the Fishkill sentence to Albany, the 150-days was reduced to 90-days and the loss of goodtime was also reduced to 90-days, instead of the original five months.

While in the box at Green Haven I met Tank through an Ernest Bethel who went by the name "Big Kareem." Another buddy of mine, Jerry Watson, was also in the box at Green Haven as the results of an incident at Fishkill. You are *the friends you keep.*

The incident for which Watson was serving time in the box involved assaulting an officer at Fishkill. Apparently, officer, Ramond who was known to be "a real prick," had been harassing Watson. Watson was handcuffed and upon the arrival of a second officer, and in the presence of one Sergeant Davis who seems to have had a racist reputation -- Ramond allegedly stabbed Watson in the back, which was followed by laughing and racial slurs. This was apparently the reason for Watson's alleged assault on Ramond.

I met many people while at Green Haven, including a close friend, Frank Staker, whose nickname was "'Born Freedom." Staker originally was believed to have died from a blow to the head, with a steel flashlight, by a female correctional officer at Rikers Island during early 1988. It was later learned that he survived the ordeal. Others I recall having met while at Green Haven were Ivan Johnson, Ronald Inman, Albert Jenkin, and Robert "Maddog" Cole. *Dick Tracy didn't have any exclusive on comic book names.*

I was soon transferred from A-Block to H-Block where I would remain until my release from Green Haven. I was returned to the Dutchess County Sheriff's Department in order to serve the 30-days I received as the result of the attack on Panama at Fishkill.

During that period, I read Mario Puzo's, *The Godfather*. That's when I knew, when I got out, I wanted a power structure so strong nothing could penetrate it. Well, be careful about what you wish for, as they say. *As I look back, I visited so many prisons and cities, they could've used me for an anti-crime poster, similar to that of the Navy, "Join A Crew and See the World Thru Bars," or "Crime, It's Not Just A Job, It's An Adventure - In Hell." No joke!*

While on my forced vacation in June of 1982, Walter "King Tut" Johnson organized and robbed over three hundred members of the Kingdom Hall Jehovah Witness Church, with his mother and family in attendance. That fucking guy could have been a motivational speaker, his motto "If you can envision it, it will happen."

Chapter Four - Out of Boot Camp

Ready for Active Duty

In November 1984, I was a twenty-one-year-old kid and after serving over three years touring prisons, I was free. I just exited the prison gates. The air was clean- without the smell of a few hundred men with body odor and their foul breath polluting the air. I took in the sounds of cars and the breeze moving through the trees; replacing the sounds of clanging bars, guards yelling out orders or when the lights went out, the sounds of men fucking. I'm out. Thank you, Jesus!

My trip home started with the Metro-North Train from Poughkeepsie to Grand Central Station. I was met in New York by my brother James, Kool-Aid, and mom who were waiting for me in a van. The reunion came just four days before my birthday.

My intentions were honorable; I wanted to become a law-abiding citizen, leaving the criminal life in the past where it belonged. During the first year I had several jobs: messenger, construction, and maintenance, but none were held for very long. Unfortunately, honorable intentions alone are not always enough to disassociate oneself from the negative influencing elements to which one has become so accustomed.

Less than a week after my release, a 21-year-old kid from the neighborhood was on his way to work, about to leave his building at 710 Euclid Avenue when he was approached, shot and murdered; till today that murder was never solved. Nothing to do with me; just saying welcome home. Anyway, my neighborhood was still rough, and I was back in the concrete jungle with four felony convictions; meaning, the next *violent felony conviction* could mean a life sentence for yours truly. *Feeling sorry for me? That's okay, I understand.*

The 3 Strike rule had its good and bad aspects. When paroled in November of 1984, I already had two violent felony convictions. Next would be the 3rd strike and its life. So, you do whatever it takes to stay out. However, the risk for what you do next, including murder wouldn't change the outcome. Why steal if you're going to jail? It's time for the big-time money.

Vices for some may be drugs, alcohol, food, or gambling. My weakness always has been girls, girls, girls, girls, come shout and clap your hands. My addiction was some good ole pussy. I've had my share of women in my days and I am blessed to say I am lucky not getting infected with AIDS. I wasn't Wilt Chamberlain, sleeping with over ten thousand women but I'm not crying poverty.

I recall when I first came home from serving three years and six months, I was on the hunt for the "Punnany" a.k.a. Pussy (According to the urban dictionary: A great way to refer to a female human vagina.) Its kind 'a cute, so the chicks are usually cool when you ask to see their punnany, or touch it, etc. *C'mon baby, let me check out your punnany or Wassup with that punnany, baby?* I just turn 21, fresh out of the penal system and hornier than all of "2 Live Crew" combined. The "2 Live Crew" was a hiphop group from Miami, Florida. They caused considerable controversy with the sexual themes, particularly on their 1989 album, *Me, So Horny.*

When I first came home, I would hang out in my PJ`s with my family, no job, no hustle, and no hotel money. I had to sneak to have sex at home when no one was home. The alternative was to find discreet locations, like in the seventh floor staircase, or the roof -- that was always a good location to bust a nut or two. Man, if only those walls from the Cypress Hill projects could talk --man, sex in the hallway stories. Back then, you'd do it any an everywhere.

Life was getting good again, the streets were calling. I started hustling, being fly and thinking positive. I was getting together with my friends and we partied hard. We went to Disco Fever in the Bronx, Encore in Queens, Bentleys, Red Parrot and Show Time at the Apollo in Harlem. I did not get high, the smoking weed thing was only briefly during High School. No drugs or alcohol for me my high was always great sex, fucking a bad chick. I'd be up all night, sleep all day. Punching my own clock and doing whatever I wanted to do. When in the streets, it was always something that would occur to break your peace, trust and there was betrayal.

Sex in the City

I was able to get a small side jobs and had a few hustles which enabled me to meet some new ladies and take them out and move up from the staircases to the Holiday Inn. My sexual appetite had also expanded. I remember the first time I ate some pussy. Before that bid (previous time in prison) eating pussy was a no-no. Being in prison so long and listening to all of the older cat's telling you, "If you would have been eating the pussy, chances are your girl would still be there waiting for you when you got out. The first young lady I can recall tasting her pussy was KCF, from the Fort Greene section of Brooklyn. I just happen to be in the area with my stepbrother, Country, when I see this dark skin pretty chick with slanted eyes coming my way. It was wintertime, she was dressed nice, with her little dress slacks, blouse, overcoat, dress boots and her hair was in braids. I pushed up on her as she was coming from the store. We conversed, the connection was there, and I asked her out on a date, and she smiled a yes. Friday came, I picked her up and we went to Beef Steak Charlie's, then to a movie. It was late when I took her back home. She invited me up to her apartment, which she shared with her infant daughter, her mother and older sister. I didn't expect it, but she left me in the living room, went to her bedroom, undressed, took a shower and came back wearing only her robe. KCF was indeed dark and lovely. She led the way, started undressing me, all I had to do was take off her robe. She starts sucking on my rock-hard manhood. *Not bragging, just want you get the situation.* As we assumed the sixty-nine position, being a virgin at eating pussy was indeed different, but as I entered my tongue in her fresh vagina and acting like I knew what I was doing. I was amazed it wasn't that bad, I started licking her pussy as if it was a spoon with cake batter. Her movement and sounds ensured me that I was doing something right. As I switched it up and open her pussy wider, I focused on her clitoris and boy that must have been her spot, because she lost it. I must admit KCF was tongue and lip licking good. We were an item, on and off for 4 years.

One lady in particular who had me whipped was Zella from East New York; she was a pretty yellow bone. When I first met her and I was hustling on a minor scale, just making a couple thousand dollars a week in drug money. The first time we hooked up, she came to my Cypress apartment and I undressed her pretty yellow firm body. She was looking like model material, lean and mean. I can recall that day; we started off performing oral sex on each other. Zella was great at handling her business, which was one of the reasons she stayed around for as long as she did. Years later someone who knew us both was telling me that Zella's oldest son looked just like me. She was assuming that was my son – momma's, baby, poppa's maybe?

The more I became involved in the street and hustling fulltime the more females I was meeting and bagging or they were bagging me (don't need to take all the credit) it got to a point where I had females who wanted to fuck me. They were choosing me as if I was a celebrity. I went from fucking on the roof tops to a steady room at the Marriot across the Street from LaGuardia Airport. It's strange; I recollect having a childhood crush on some older chicks when I was in Junior High School. Then the opportunity presented itself and I ran into them during the time my name was ringing bells, it was unbelievable how they were interested. Being a bit older and a little self-sufficient showed me how easy it was to make them mine.

Then there was "B", from Brownsville, short, long hair with blondish streaks, pretty caramel complexion large melon size breast and with a nice bubble butt. I snatch up "B" on our first date in a limo. Her little ass was dressed to a Tee in an expensive dress and heels. After a night of dinning in Manhattan and driving around and enjoying the scenery of Central Park, "B" was the first young lady that utilized her mouth to place a condom on my dick; now that blew my mind. "B" knew exactly what she was doing. I liked when we were both butt naked and I requested "B" to keep on the stilettos. I used to tear that ass up. It was like an extreme infatuation, wanting her badly that once the opportunity presented itself, Wow! I would lose it in that pussy. "B" was an A in my book.

I did not discriminate; if an attraction was there, I'd pushed up on any young lady. They came from all walks of life: working class, college students, some were hustlers that sold drugs, shoplift clothes and some were just your everyday pickpockets.

The one who really had me really whipped (I know I said that already) was Nadine. She was built and dressed like a model, very classy, elegant with a lot of style. This lady was six years younger than me when I meet her at a night club. She was on the dance floor with several of her girlfriends. I noticed this guy I knew who was dancing with her and her friends. I was drooling, couldn't keep my eyes off of her. Finally, the guy I knew came off the dance floor and came up to me. Trying to be smooth, not wanting him to know that I was sweating this particular young lady, I asked him. "Yo! Who is that bitch with the white dress, you were dancing with"? He said, "Come on Glaze that's my sister." My bad! Long story short, we ended up getting together. I am not going to lie out of all the women I dealt with and all of the trials and tribulation that I encountered, except for my wife who was number one. Nadine was special, and when all is said and done, from our conversations, to her attitudes, she was just natural to be around, no drama, and no bullshit. Would it be fair to say, I loved all my ladies?

There have been times, when I was around chicks with $6,000 in small bills. The lucky lady that was with me on that day would receive that bag of money. It's insane, there was a time where I have purchased my girls' cars, clothes, fur coats and jewelry or helped them get a place of their own. Dudes from the street called it *tricking*. I called it, what the sense of making 40,000 dollars a day if you don't have anyone to share it with. *Those were the days, girls, girls, girls. How I loved the girls.*

Dealing with The A-Team

As I initially mentioned, I settled in back home and was being relatively good. However, shortly after returning home, I began hearing a lot about a group called the "A-Team," who was allegedly responsible for a number of crimes in the area, including dealing drugs, robbery, and murder.

A week after my return home, in December of 1984, an acquaintance named, Darren "Be-O" Styles, was murdered while on his way to work in the Cypress Hills projects. After almost ten years nobody has been charged with Styles' murder.

Rumors on the street had it that Be-O was killed, because he was planning to testify against a member of the A-Team for robbing him. Word had it that Be-O and a buddy had robbed some people in Queens and on their return from their robbery spree they themselves were robbed by the A-Team. Be-O and his buddy decided to press charges, and the leader of the group was arrested and charged with armed robbery. Members of the A-Team approached Be-O and his unnamed friend on several occasions, trying to persuade them to drop the charges. They refused and Be-O was murdered. The friend, however, was spared apparently only because he happened to be incarcerated at the time. The friend refused to testify, however, his mother did and the A-Team member who robbed Be-O and his friend were convicted and received a sentence of 12 to 25 years.

Almost all the Cypress Hills residents were afraid of the A-Team. The Fountain and Sutter Avenue section was known to be off limits -- people were simply too afraid to walk through that area.

The original leaders were Da-Wu, El, Sha-Kim, Minister Ref, and Minister Allah, who were one of the First born gang and were a terror on wheels - the typical tough guys. From all over the five boroughs of New York City no one fucked with the A-Team. When they came through any area, people would normally get the hell out of their way. Minister Allah was approximately ten years older than me.

One of my friends, Lannie Dillard "L.D." had an unspecified problem with the A-Team and as a result L.D. and his family were given an eviction notice and told they had exactly 30-days to move. Apparently, the A-Team and the Housing Authority were "under-the-table" partners. A few days before the 30-day deadline I went to L.D. and asked for two guns, saying that I would take care of the problem with the A-Team. I was under the impression that if you killed the chief, then the Indians would go into hiding, meaning, of course, the A-Team and its leader. L.D. refused to give me the guns. Nevertheless, the A-Team had a sudden, inexplicable change of heart, and the eviction notice was lifted.

The local, so-called, tough guys from the projects avoided walking on the A-Team side of the projects. I couldn't believe how everyone was literally afraid to go on that side of the projects. After a while I got to the point that I used to walk on that side just to prove a point. I would normally have my hand on a Smith Wesson 38, waiting for anyone from the A-Team to approach me, ready to enjoy pumping one into their face. *This was a new side of me, thanks to all the love and affection I treasured in prison.*

Well fortunately I didn't have cause to shoot any of them. However, one day in the summer of 1985 when I was by myself, I approached several of the A-Team outside near the corner bodega on Logan and Sutter Avenue. There were between eight and ten A-Team members present as I approached Elson, "El" for short. I was alone and unarmed. I introduced myself to Elson, saying that I didn't have anything against him and had no reason to care what the A-Team did, as long as my family and those I cared about were left alone. This was the beginning of a relatively a close association. Elson told me sometime later how he was impressed by the bold manner in which I approached them. And just like that, the A-Team and I signed a verbal peace treaty and slowly, but surely, we built a very strong bond. *As they say, water seeks its own level.*

When You Don't Want to Be in the Top Ten

I still had one problem with the A-Team, this older dude, Boomer, didn`t forget that I robbed him, on the Q bus, prior to going to prison. Boomer was now part of the A-Team, which came into existence sometime in 1983.

Later I was told by the leader of the A-Team, when I came home from prison, I was on their hit list. They were plotting to kill me for the time I robbed Boomer and the fact that they felt I was a threat. But in a short time, Boomer was no longer part of the A-Team. He had crossed the line by attempting to rape, one of the member's younger niece. He was smart enough to relocate before he was killed. I also found out he was fronting, like he was somebody with money, living the good life and his jewelry was fake, just as fake as he was.

Got a Job in Security for The A-Team

In a matter of weeks after agreeing to a peace agreement with the A-Team, I was offered a position in security for a thousand dollars a week. Even drug crews had strict schedules and my work schedule was from Sunday thru Thursday, 11PM to 7AM. My job was to protect the block workers and customers; making sure everyone was safe, customers got what they paid for and no one got robbed. My additional responsibility was to make sure that some *crack head* was not trying to sell dumbdumb drugs (bad or fake drugs) to any of our customers. During my shift I caught one crack head selling dumbdumbs to one of our customers. I shot him in the ass and he never came back. Trust me he told all of his buddies and none of them came around either. Watching out for NYPD and possible drug bust was also on the top of my job description.

Moochie, Drugs and Me

In 1985, I hooked back up with Moochie, from the Nut Hut, on a drug tip. Moochie, L.D. along with myself and a few others became business partners on a drug spot on Marion Street. L.D. originally had the spot and he brought me in, and we were purchasing our cocaine from Moochie on a small level. Moochie presented an opportunity where he would give us kilos of cocaine on consignment and be our partner. It was a win, win situation.

However, eventually a problem arose, too many chiefs, not enough Indians. We'd argue all the time when bagging up the drugs, and especially when splitting up the money. Any little problem we'd disagreed on that reached a point that eventually I could have murdered one or two of my partners if I didn't leave. At twenty-one I walked away from one of the most money making drug spots in Brooklyn at that time. *Trust me it hurt my pocket, but it saved some friends lives.*

Started Selling Crack and Heroin

As in life, one opportunity ends, and another opens. Wanting to increase my income, I began selling crack and heroin during my Sunday thru Thursday shifts and averaging close to $20,000 per week. But I was greedy always looking for other outlets. The more outlets the more sources for income; more money, my mind was racing. Even though I was rocking and rolling with my hours on the block with the A-team, I was able to get hooked up with an associate to put together another drug location in the Bedford Stuyvesant section on Ralph and Pacific.

It took work and creativity to build up that spot. We took over an abandon building, paid an electrician to run wires for our electricity source, and without paying Con Edison. I sold crack and heroine out of that building. On the first day I only made $1,000 dollars, the next day I did $2,000, until eventually the spot was doing approximately $5,000 dollars a day. Hell of a time, it was 1985 moving into 1986. I had a decent crew and workers. My whole attitude and dress attire changed; I was now wearing $1,000-dollar suits - my favorite shoes were Bally's. We were driving brand new leased Cadillac Sedan Devilles and Ninety-Eight Oldsmobiles. The funny thing, back then most of us all drove without having a driver's license or insurance - *difficult getting insurance when you don't have a driver's license.*

Heroin use during the late sixties and early seventies was very popular in black communities. As a young kid I watched how folks were high on heroin and they'd nod out in the streets and in front of the steps of brownstone buildings. Sometimes they'd literally fall asleep in the hallways of the buildings. Majority of heroin user used needles to shoot heroin into their arms, legs or anywhere they could find a vein that was working. During that period users would share the same needles way before the AIDS Epidemic.

A heroin high produced a sleepy, mellow mood. Personally, I was always against drug use. As a kid I witnessed how drugs destroyed individuals and their families. I've seen user aggressively lead into domestic violence on the streets for all to see. Men would literally beat their wives or girlfriends to the ground, and nobody would interfere. A couple of times I watched NYPD patrol cars pull up and get out of the car and approach these men. A man would tell a cop this is my wife or girlfriend and for the cop to mind his own business and the cop would get back in his car and leave. Crack use is totally different than heroin's mellow high. Crack charges you up, like the energizer bunny, as soon as you smoke crack it you become charged, but the rush doesn't last long. As soon as the high wears off, the crack head is out in full force committing a crime to make more money to cop more crack.

Dealing with The Dominicans

As I sat back and analyzed what was going on around me. I noticed a Dominican group that was running this one block, for a vast amount of time, although, they were not from the immediate area of ENY. With that in mind, I started scheming on how to eliminate them and take over that block. So early 1985, I assisted the A-Team in "dethroning" the Dominicans from one of the drug shifts on Fountain Avenue. This block was selling drugs

24-hours-a-day, 7-days-a-week. Each day was worked in regular 8-hour shifts. Business was good, the average take per day ranged from a low of six-thousand-dollars to a high of almost ten-thousand-dollars during weekdays, and upwards of fifteen-thousand-dollars per day on weekends. *Let's not forget, there will be a tax collector; not necessarily the IRS.*

Not long after this, the original members of the A-Team decided they didn't really want me as a full-fledged member. I backed off and started hanging out with a friend, Sid, and another individual named "Frenchie."

I continued to study the Dominican's every movement and how they arrived on the block, setting up their security, picking up and dropping off money and drugs. It was time to present, EL, the leader of the A-Team with a proposition. The proposition was: We - I would take over the block by eliminating the Dominicans, and the block would be ours. If the A-Team didn't want to get down, then I was going to get my man Sid from BedSty. Sid was one of those pretty boys from Bedford Stuyvesant. He didn't take shit from anybody. We were always scheming and doing whatever it took to get ahead. But it's like this, if I was going to war, I would rather have Sid on my side than against me.

Before we initiated dethroning the Dominicans, it was around 11:00am on a Sunday and I was returning from making sure all was good at the Fountain Avenue drug block. On my way back home, I noticed that a group of Hispanics were watching me rather closely. The first thing which came to my mind was that these would be the people with whom we would go to war for control of the Dominican's drug block. I backtracked, because I didn't want the group of Hispanics following me to know where I lived. I moved against the railing on the side of Building 1230 on Sutter Avenue, when a few of those following me came from the car. They were all dressed liked gang members. At first, they tried to appear almost nonchalant, as if they were only going to walk past me, but a big guy suddenly stopped right in-front of me, saying that I had robbed his father the night before. I hadn't robbed anyone on the street in years, so I knew the big guy was lying and up to no good. My hands were in my coat pockets the entire time, my left one on the .38 snub nose with the hammer cocked and ready. The big guy in-front of him moved, as if he was reaching for a gun, and I fired. I shot through my coat, hitting the big guy in the leg. The big guy fell to the ground and his companions ran away. I ran in the opposite direction. Later, I learned that the big guy I had shot in the leg was supposedly a law enforcement agent, although we never learned which office or agency he was supposedly from; the man never identified himself as law enforcement. Word on the street had it that officials believed it was El who did the shooting that Sunday morning. Neither El nor I were ever arrested, or even charged with the shooting.

Warring over the Fountain Avenue block did continue, and it did involve numerous shootouts with the Dominicans. One morning, after a shoot-out, I-Ref, another friend and I snuck up on the Dominicans. I-Ref and I went to the building where the Dominicans were, and knocked down the door of the first-floor apartment. Once inside we pistol whipped four of the Dominicans, then had them lay face down on the floor. El came in shortly afterwards as we were about to murder the Dominicans, when someone suddenly began yelling that there was "beast" everywhere. "Beast" was the word for the police. I-Ref and Jim-Jim went out the front, while El and I ran up to the fourth floor and on to the roof. The door was stuck. El tried everything, but it wouldn't budge. I stepped back, and then repeatedly rammed the door with body blows, until it was finally knocked from its hinges. I followed El as he jumped from rooftop to rooftop – we were four stories up, but fortunately the buildings were not far apart.

Having distanced ourselves from the scene, El had decided to leave his weapon behind, a pump shotgun, as we made our way back to the streets. I picked up the shotgun, despite El saying not to. El climbed down a fire escape, then jumped to the ground from the first floor, landing safely. I followed, but because I had El's shotgun, as well as the, 45-automatic of my own I lost balance and crashed to the ground, hitting my head and losing consciousness. El saw what happened and returned to help me. Blood was dripping from my forehead and my right-hand was cutup, but I steadfastly held onto the guns.

After coming to my senses and regaining balance, I again followed El. We climbed fences and were in and out of people's backyards, eventually passing through an empty lot before ending up on Crystal Street, where we ran into the projects and then into one of the A-Team's many apartments. El and I got away -- in fact, the only person arrested was I-Ref, who happened to have my .38 snub nose on him. This concerned me more than anything, because the .38 pistol was used only a week before in a shooting that involved a law enforcement agent.

My man I-Ref was caught after we separated and was arrested on gun charges. The cops, showing up, saved the Dominican's lives. They then took them to the 75th precinct to look at some mug shots. I guess they were too scared, because I was never arrested, and we were on our way to successfully taking over the Fountain Ave block. The Dominicans finally gave up, because they did not want any more problems. *Almost, just like that the block was ours.*

The initial result was my crew and I were able to work the block Sundays thru Thursdays, from 11:00 A.M. to 3:00 P.M., while the A-Team took the rest. My next move was to put several acquaintances to work: King Tut, Robert aka"Fat Rob" Frampton, Kevin "Kev-Web" Williams and a few others. Money started rolling in and I was soon taking in several thousand dollars a day for myself. I bought my first car in January of 1986 -- before then my crew and I had been driving rented domestic luxury cars, for which we paid upwards of $700 per week. My first car was a grey and black Cadillac Seville. The money was so plentiful that I even picked-up the largest portion of the cost of Fat Rob's, wedding.

The Original "50 Cent" - Making Assumptions

On my way back from Fat Rob's wedding, it was in January 1986; I was driving one of the rental cars and had parked in-front of my Cypress Apt. on Sutter and Euclid. There at a gas station across the street was "a bunch of guys" from the Bushwick and Bedford Stuyvesant section of Brooklyn. A childhood buddy of mine, Kevin "50 Cent" Martin, informed me that the group parked at the gas station were there to kill me. He then said that he had talked them out of it. *Kevin was the original 50 Cent from whom Curtis James Jackson III the rapper took the name. Kevin was later killed. He was short about five feet two but was tough and nasty.*

The intended hit arose from the murder of an individual known as "Pen," a friend of the bunch from Bushwick Brooklyn. The word was that Sid and I had killed Pen. Sid and Pen got into an argument over nothing according to me, but tempers flared nevertheless, and Pen began making open statements that he was going to kill Sid. I received word of this from Sha-mel, one of Pen's buddies and of course I told Sid. We always took threats seriously and so we got our guns and went looking for Pen.

We drove to Pen's block on Himrod Avenue in Bushwick area. We then stopped to ask a young lady if she knew Pen and where he lived. While Sid was talking to the girl, I looked in the rearview mirror and saw Pen stepping out of his car, with his well-known 44 magnum handgun in-tow. I hollered to Sid to "drive off, drive off," but Sid

couldn't understand why, or what was wrong with me --
until he looked into the rearview mirror. The two cars drove
up the block and a shootout ensued, however, no one got
hurt. *Nevertheless, when Pen turned up dead some
seventeen days later, Sid and I were the prime suspects.*

Almost Killed My Brother

For the period of 1986, at age 22 years old, my
brother James Gibbs (Kool-Aid), and I got into a big beef
mind you he is only eleven months older than me. This
character had a very bad habit of talking down to people
and saying very nasty and disrespectful things. One night
we got into a big argument, he was telling me which one of
my girlfriends at the time I could or couldn't bring back to
our apartment in Cypress Projects. He was telling me that I
couldn't bring my date back to the apartment because he
was dating her sister, and at the same time he was
entertaining another girl with her infant child at the
apartment. Nevertheless, I went to the apartment. I was
alone, and he locked the door with the deadbolt so I
couldn't get in. I was knocking on the door and he wouldn't
let me in. I became pissed and started kicking on the door,
but he still wouldn't let me in. Now, I'm feeling like the
wolf and the three little pigs, I'm really pissed, so I went to
a pay phone and called the apartment. He answered, and I
told him to let me in the dam apartment. This clown boldly
said, "No! you need to take your ass to a hotel." Now, I am
seeing red. I leave the pay phone and run from the corner of
Sutter and Euclid back to our building at 1266 Sutter, apt.
4B and I started knocking again. Then in that moment of
frustration, I took my 9 mm German Luger, fired three to
four shots into our door to no avail. Now, he is really scared
out of his wits. This bitch ass dude decided to call my
mother at 1A.M., telling her that I really lost it this time.
Suddenly, my mother starts paging me from her home
number, using 911 nonstop, but I didn't return her call. As I
waited around, a distance from the building, I saw him
placing his lady friend and the baby into a cab. As the cab

drove off, I waited for him as he headed back to the building. He was looking back and forth and around until he spotted me with my 9mm German Luger in my hand. He took off running, with me on his ass. He ran into 1260 the next building from ours, running up the staircase and he was gone. From the 1st, to the 2nd, to the 3rd, to the 4th, and finally he reached the 7th floor, exiting to the roof. As he was running on the roof heading to 1266, he lost his footing on some pebbles and fell face first. I caught up with him; I had the gun pointed right at him. I was fuming and foaming at the mouth, like a mad dog, yelling, and screaming at him, "You wouldn't allow me into my place. And how could you put that bitch and her baby before me?" I put the gun to his head, as he is pleading and crying and yelling, "Please don't kill me, you're my brother, for the sake of Mommy, I am begging you for my life." As I am about to squeeze the trigger my pager starts going off. It's my mother, and me with tears in my eyes, still foaming at the mouth like a "pit bull" knowing as bad as I wanted to empty a clip into his head and kill him, I knew it would have been like I killed my own mother. I knew my action on the roof would have surely caused her death and I wouldn't have been able to cope with that. I told him he is lucky of the fact that I love our mother more than life itself, and if he ever stepped out of line with me again, I am going to forget we exited from the same WOMB! I thank God now that was one mistake I didn't make. I was devastated by that whole scenario. I came inches away from killing my own brother, all because I lost it. I knew then I needed help and I was heading down a much darker and dangerous road with no return. Fortunately, as time passed my bond with my brother grew strong.

Jacked by Detectives

With the Dominicans out of the way, managing our territory and our people was a full-time job. The streets were like the Wild West, Europe and the Middle East's early days. If you weren't taken over an area, someone wanted to take you over. *And sometimes you just got jacked - like Crimea.*

One late night, heading home from Bed-Stuy, driving my two-toned black and silver Caddy Seville, I was jacked (bad guys being robbed by other bad guys). Being a drug dealer, and to avoid being stopped, I should've been driving a beat-up Chevy, but I didn't. Dead tired, I made a left turn at Ralph and Pacific heading home to Cypress. Man! Timing; I was less than a block and a half from home. They say that's the distance most car accidents happen. Anyway, I was pulled over on Belmont and Euclid by two white detectives in an un-marked car. Thinking I didn't have a license as I pulled over and stopped at the curb. They asked me to get out of the car, which I thought that was too polite. The youngest detective starts searching the car and suddenly, he pulls out a package wrapped in aluminum foil from under the passenger seat. He looks at me, with a grin on his face, and asks, "What this?" To be truthful, I was like Scooby Doo, "I don't know." The young detective opens the aluminum foil and all I could see was pure white powder. S*hit!* One of my associates must have forgotten to take nine ounces of pure heroin out of my car FUCK! This is good for an A-1 felony charge. *I needed this, like I needed another asshole.* With my prior felony convictions, I was automatically facing 25 to life. I can recall the young detective saying, "Sarge, this is pure heroin" Twice, they looked at the dope, then looked at me. The next time they looked down at the dope, I ran as fast as I could into the dark, escaping into the shelter of the Cypress Hill Houses. Inside my apartment, slumped on floor, against the door, I asked myself; *why in the hell did I allow myself to slide back into this predicament, facing life imprisonment?*

I paged Amare, a friend and business associate. My Seville was registered in his name and he was currently living in Tarrytown, New York and working at General Motors. Amare immediately reported the car stolen, while I contacted my lawyer who walked me thorough the process to get my car back -- *thank you Lord for crooked cops*. I came to find out the cops never reported the drugs, claiming to have stopped the car for a routine check and the driver fled. Worse still, I learned that the drugs weren't mine, but planted to set me up if I got stopped by cops. Less than sixty days to the date, the associate who placed the drugs into my car, was found dead on top of the roof of Kingsborough Houses, shot twice in his head by a 45 automatic. That's the way shit went down back then. Again, I'm suspect.

Consequences, there are always consequences. The drug business had its own laws and punishments; probation was not one of them.

Chapter Five - M&M - Money and Murder

Killing a Friend, Not Easy, But Necessary

If someone didn't want to take over your territory, or
if you weren't getting' jacked and setup, you might even be
getting robbed by a trusted friend from your own crew. One
of my spots on Ralph and Pacific was robbed twice within a
month. Okay this is New York and it does not matter who
you are, everyone gets tested in the drug game and that's
exactly what happened. My employee's story was that the
guys who robbed us, were the same guys who robbed us
once before. I couldn't put my finger on it, but I had a bad
feeling. Following my gut, I snatched up my workers one at
a time, took them for a ride and placed a 44. sub nose in
their mouth to get them to tell me what I needed to know.
*Your boss probably never held meeting this way or
confronted you in this manner.* Anyway, they coughed up
the truth, and to only find out it was a friend. He was
somewhat like my mentor, a few years older than me. I will
call him "Crazy Clyde" along with his cousin Ty and
another person from the Albany Housing Projects. The
workers told me that Clyde had threatened to kill them if
any of them told me the truth. I assumed they decided to put
their faith in my hands.

I could not believe it, one time in the past, when
Crazy came home from doing a State bid (time in prison) I
looked out for him, took him shopping and put money in
his pocket. Out of all the many drug spots in the 5
boroughs, why did he need to rob me? Despite he was like
family and I loved him, unfortunately he would have to die
for his bad decision. This is a nasty business; everybody
knows the risks, the rewards and the consequences. *We
have no unions, no mediations, and there isn't Judge Judy
or traffic court, or guilty with an explanation.*

I paged Crazy a number of times from a pay phone
in Brooklyn and he finally called back. I can recount telling

him that the people who stuck up the spot-on Ralph and Pacific previously did it again, just to get his reaction; nothing. I continued by telling him that I want those responsible dead, ASAP! He agreed, and we would meet near Cypress later that night. Amare and I drove across town from the Bedford Stuyvesant Section to East New York where we stopped across the street from Cypress Projects near Sutter and Euclid Avenue, right in front of Manny's Bodega. Amare was a few years younger than me. He was an all-around good kid, with a good job, working for General Motors. He should have left the Projects and stayed away from the streets and me, but he was hooked. Amare's good credit and honest earnings designated him the one responsible to get us rentals and lease luxury cars. He was not the typical street kid, just another lost soul who got caught into the web of money. I was telling Amare that I was going to light Crazy up like a Christmas tree. The nerve of him, out of ten million different illegal drug houses in the five boroughs of New York City, he picks mines to rob.

Before taking care of Crazy, I needed to be sure he was guilty and Boom! There was Sybil, Crazy's girlfriend, and Big Bronco, who I believed were involved with Crazy. Amare and I pulled up to the local bodega and got out of the car. Crazy had them with him, leaving me to believe he was unsure that I knew he was involved. Amare, Crazy and I started discussing the terms of the hit. I told Crazy from my understanding, that there were three people that robbed the drug spot and I am willing to give $5,000 dollars apiece for each of those Mother Fuckers! We discussed that they are most likely from that neighborhood where the stick ups took place. Therefore, I was going to have one of the workers that were robbed, drive through the area with him in order to point out the alleged stick-up kids. He gave no negative reaction, leaving me frustrated. As we are going over step by step of my plan, NYPD cars with their sirens screaming began passing us from opposite directions. I finally asked Crazy if he was strapped. He said, yes. He had a sawed off shot gun, in his car and two handguns. I told him it's too hot out here and he needed to go put his weapons away, then come back and we would go to BedSty, grab one of my workers and canvass the neighborhood. Crazy agreed and he instructed Big Bronco to go with him and told Sybil to get in the car with Amare and me. Now Amare and I looked at each other a bit baffled. We drove off and I requested Amare stop at another store to buy some time to figure my next move. I'm puzzled, thinking why did Crazy have his girlfriend go with us? I am inside the store trying to decide what my next move is going to be, as I purchase a bottle of Perrier water and a pack of double mint gum. Returning, I entered back into the front passenger seat and instructed Amare to drive off. As we drove, we only got to the next block, Pitkin and Hemlock, when I instructed him to pull over by the welfare Center building, 888 Pine. At that time, I got out of the car, the whole area was pitch black, no streetlights. I went around the back of the car and open the door to the back seat on the driver's side and told Sybil to get out. I can see she was scared. She asked, "Why?" Annoyed I said, "You know why." Then, in a very stern and forceful voice, I requested, "Just get the fuck out of the car, now!" At that time, I had my gun drawn and grabbed her. I then asked her, why did your man rob my spot? Looking at me, eye to eye, not flinching, she said, "I don`t know what you're talking about."

What did I expect her to say? "Bitch don't lie to me, you and your man are like the ghetto version of Bonnie and Clyde." I pulled the trigger. The bullet entered her stomach, and she fell and crawled into a fetal position. Right away, I am disgusted at myself. I realize I shot Sybil; now I am going to jail. It was never my intention to do anything to her, only Crazy. But I was filled with so much rage that I bent down and placed the gun to her head and pulled the trigger. Time stopped, I heard nothing, but felt the recoil, forcing my hand to jerk back. I watched the bullet and sensed it travel through her head and then the sound as it exited, made everything crystal clear. I must have closed my eyes, because I never saw any blood as her head didn't seem to budge. It was surreal. Then, being so close, the matter from her brain, head and skull splattered onto my face. I can recall, not thinking, taking my tongue licking the blood from my face and using the sleeve of my hoodie to wipe off the rest. At that moment I realized I crossed over to the dark side. I was a sick soul; an overkill, for the crime. I hopped back in the car and instructed Amare to drive back to Cypress Projects in order to blow Crazy's Mother Fucking head off!

As we headed back to pick up Crazy, we got to Sutter and Euclid which was surrounded by several NYPD blue and white police cars with sirens going. Amare and I are puzzled; we knew that no one could have known about me shooting and leaving Sybil for dead. With that, I instructed him to get us the hell out of there.

We drove back toward Kennedy Airport, threw the gun away and when we got to the airport exchanged the rental. Along the way I discussed the situation, Amare, isn't to say anything about me killing Sybil. He doesn't know anything, and he won't have anything to worry about. I emphasized, we must keep our mouths shut and stick to, "we know nothing". I was truly afraid. After dropping Amare to his girlfriend's place in Flatbush, I continued on to the Ocean Hill Brownsville section of Brooklyn to one of my ladies who I was seeing at the time. I needed an alibi.

Setting Up an Alibi

Driving along the way I was pulled over by one of NYPD's finest. They searched me and the car, which turned up nothing. Again, they didn't seem to care less that I didn't have a driver license. I went on to Betty's crib and to my surprise she wasn't there. There goes that alibi, I said to myself. I did not know at the time that Betty had been admitted to the hospital because she had pneumonia. Normally, I could just pop up to see any of the women that I was seeing un-announced. Next stop was Cathy's house. She lived off of Eastern Parkway and Utica. I got there just before 1A.M. and her story would be I arrived at 11P.M., and we watched Eyewitness News. I didn't leave until I dropped her off to work at 7A.M. that morning. That was my alibi.

After I dropped off Cathy, I tried to get Sybil off my mind by starting my day off by checking on my people in East New York to see how the cash flow was coming in. Then I got a page from Crazy. I called him back, by that time I'm thinking he knows that I shot Sybil, but instead asked me, where she was. I told him, once he and Bronco left to put up his weapons, Sybil went her separate way. He uttered, "That bitch." I didn't know at the time when the police later discovered Sybil's body that they would find numerous bundles of heroin in the lining of her coat; heroin that was stolen from my spot. So, I guess he assumed that when she left, she sold the bundles of heroin and kept the cash for herself. I tried to get Crazy to meet up with me, so I could murder his petty ass, but he blew me off with "he will contact me later". I offered to give him 5,000 dollars up front and that I needed him now. He didn't take the bait. Several days passed by before Amare was picked up at work for questioning. Every day since I shot Sybil we kept in touch at least two to three times a day. On Friday February 28, 1986 I did not hear from him at all. The writing was on the wall. *Would or wouldn't Amare talk?*

Sybil's Revenge

If it's not one thing, it's another. Unsure, of my next move and concerned about Amare, I decided to go visit a childhood friend serving a twenty-five to life sentence at Auburn Correctional Facility, in Auburn, New York. I went to 59th Street and Columbus Circle and caught the Operation Prison Gap Bus to Auburn. Prison Gap Buses were established by family members who came home from jail and knew that type of service was needed to keep love ones in contact with their families who were incarcerated miles away.

On my way back, Saturday March 1st, 1986 the bus made a stop and I called my mother who informed me that a detective *named* Joe Ponzi, from the 75th Precinct stopped by looking for me. I proclaimed my innocence to my mother and told her upon my return, I would contact my lawyer and go to the precinct on Monday. When I arrived to Manhattan at 59th and Columbus Circle, I took a yellow cab to Brooklyn, to meet up with my man Tiny, when Amare's number appeared on my pager. I called the number back and it was the Brooklyn DA's office. Bingo! They had Amare. I'm now in Brooklyn, dialing from a pay phone, on the corner of Nostrand and Fulton, when out of nowhere someone called my name. As I turned around it was this nigger named Pop, pointing a nickel plated 38 at me. A few days prior, Pop and I had a shootout in Cypress Projects because this chump tried to rob me. Nevertheless, now on Nostrand and Fulton, three nights later, he is trying to kill me, chasing me up Nostrand Avenue and I'm not strapped! Nostrand Avenue is a rough area, normally cops are everywhere. As my luck is going downhill, while bullets are flying and crying out, not one of New York finest were in sight. All I remember is running and being out of breath. Exhausted, several young ladies were exiting a cab. I attempted to give the cab driver $900 dollars, all the cash I had in my pocket, to just drive me to safety. The cabby drove off, tires screeching, with the passenger side door open and banging into parked cars. To my great fortune I had out run Pop. As I looked back, the cabby wasn't concerned about the money, as much as he just wanted to get away from the bullets since one hit his side view mirror.

I was able to escape unharmed. Within three hours I was shot at by two different individuals, in two different sections of Brooklyn. Pop was the first; the next would be in the Cypress Hills Houses several hours later by Crazy and his cousin Ty when they open fire on me. Dropping to the ground, I was really pissed off after that failed attempt. I got to my feet, hopped in my car with Tiny to head to one of my places where I lived to get strapped, and put on the bullet proof vest to go looking for my enemies. I knew if I ran into Crazy or Pop or anyone I had a past beef with, they would truly die that night. We drove around for hours with no luck. At 3 A.M. we called it a night.

About noon, Sunday, March 2, we got up and thought about strapping up and going on the hunt, but we thought better of it and placed it on hold. We started our day by going to Hancock and Patchen Avenue in the Bedford Stuyvesant section of Brooklyn. I went by my mother's church to let her know I was alright, and I would be meeting up with my lawyer the following day, to go down to the precinct and get this matter about Sybil's shooting resolved. I always denied any wrongdoing to my mother. I didn't have the courage to tell her the truth about all my terrible deeds. She wanted to believe; mothers are that way.

As Tiny and I drove off from the church, within a couple of blocks an un-marked police car pulled us over. I got out of car, put my hands up and asked Tiny to do the same. The detectives got out of the car and stated it was only a routine check and for us to put our hands down. That was bullshit. Out of no-where approximately ten blue and white NYPD cars with sirens blaring, barreled down on us. They got out of their cars, guns drawn, telling us to place our fucking hands up. I can remember this detective saying to me, either we have the wrong person, or you are in a lot of trouble. I was handcuffed from behind and placed in the back of the detective's un-marked car. At that time, I started to panic and then out of nowhere I had an out of body experience. It was like I was able to step outside of myself, slapping the shit out of myself, and telling myself, don't worry about anything, you haven't done anything wrong. To my amazement - it worked. I became real calm and kept saying to myself that I didn`t do anything. *Didn't change anything, but I felt better.*

They escorted me to the 83rd precinct for the murder of this guy named Jonathan Pen Maxwell. He was murdered back in January of 1986, in the Bushwick, and I was their number one suspect. Several witnesses came down and not one identified me as Pen's murderer. I sat for hours, before two homicide Detectives from the 75th Precinct picked me up and drove back to East New York's lovely 75th Precinct. I was in there for hours in one of their holding cells. My lawyers were able to get in touch with the homicide detective in charge and I was led out of the holding cell to the detective's office. Shocked, he tells me that Sybil was not dead, but was in a coma, and if she came out of it and identified me as the shooter, then they will charge me. I walked out of 75th Precinct on cloud nine. It was Monday morning March 3rd, I felt unbeatable. I now knew how John Gotti felt upon his release after a victory. I was there number one suspect. I was never charged with Pen's Murder due to a lack of evidence. Years later, it remained unsolved. Again, the usual suspect. Can you believe it.

Monday the following day I went to see my lawyer and his partner to hire their firm to represent Amare as well. Sybil had succumbed to the gunshot wounds, so Amare was indicted for second degree murder after a week.
After spending over 10,000 dollars in legal fees for Amare, I was advised to disassociate myself from him. It turned out that a few days after I was stopped, Amare was also stopped, while driving my Cadillac Seville. He was stopped by homicide detectives from the 75th Precinct, who had with them Leroy Mims, Sybil's brother. Amare was taken in for questioning, because, as the detectives recounted, the

last time Sybil was seen alive she was with him and me. Sybil was still alive but was brain dead. The detectives kept pressuring Amare by telling him that "Glaze" was finished, because they knew that I was the one who shot Sybil and that Amare had nothing to do with it. They kept telling him that he had a chance and should take it before it was too late.

Amare was then taken down to Brooklyn Central Booking and given a polygraph test by a Detective Joseph Ponzi who later stated that Amare passed the test with "flying colors." Next, an Assistant District Attorney was summoned, and Amare agreed to make a videotaped confession were he officially implicated me as the trigger man in her murder. He also made a video with the Brooklyn District Attorney giving play by play details of the execution. Afterwards, Amare was formally charged with 1st degree assault and criminal possession of a weapon. That was Friday, February 28, 1986. Just like that I stopped looking out for Amare. Under the law it was Amare's word against mine. He claimed I committed the crime and I deny it. If someone else was there and stated what Amare said, that would have been enough for me to be indicted. Until then I was a free man.

My brother, Kool-Aid, and I tried to visit Amare on Rikers Island, but Amare's mother was there at the time and told the correctional staff that she didn't want either of us to ever see her son. So, I sent King Tut, who was my partner on Fountain Avenue at the time, to see Amare. Amare had my car title, registration, and keys, and knew not only the whereabouts of my car, but also the location of some expensive jewelry. Other than getting back my jewelry, car title, and keys, I didn't accomplish anything by sending King Tut to see Amare. It was March of 1986 and I was planning to buy a new car, because the homicides detectives took my Seville from Amare.

I wanted a white Cadillac Eldorado, so some of the guys from the A-Team, El-son, Supreme, and I went to Langhorne, Pennsylvania, to buy cars. El-son bought two: a black Oldsmobile Toranado, with a black ragtop; and a grey Buick Riviera, with a black ragtop. For myself I purchased a black Chevy Celebrity. I really wanted a white Eldorado, for my brother, but because everyone was telling me that a white car would attract unnecessary attention, I decided instead to buy a brown Oldsmobile Ninety-Eight. The police were after me, so I was already hot enough, without drawing attention, plus there were others who were after me, especially one guy called, Babyface.

Shootout at the O.K. Corral

Enough was enough. My reputation had grown as someone you did not want to cross. However, Sybil's brother and her children's father didn't see it that way - yet. Babyface, the father of Sybil's kids, was from the Bushwick section of Brooklyn and known as a murderer and a bank robber. He was in his early thirties, approximately 6' 2", however bullets don't consider size. He had a light complexion, wavy hair with a baby face, hence the nickname, "Babyface." His kids were now motherless, and I was on his hit list. At the time he was supposedly on the run for a bank robbery and killing a security guard in Long Island, New York.

It was time for a show down, do or die. I went to Sybil's families building on Euclid Avenue across from Cypress Park. If he was looking for me here I am. I am not hiding. I was a hot head, standing out in front of their building, yelling at the top of my lungs, "If anyone wants me, I am here, I'm not running or ducking or dodging anyone!" I was wearing a bullet proof vest, strapped with two five shot snub-nose 44s, with hollow point bullets in my hand. I could see folks in her family's apartment windows and I am doing my best to get Sybil's baby father and brothers to come down. Being they wanted me, I stayed there for ten minutes, which felt like a day before leaving. I guessed they were probably calling the cops.

As I walked a distance back into the park, Sybil's brother, and Babyface were now in the park, coming at me, and shooting from a distance. Keep in mind it was broad day light and grownups, mother and kids were walking along the park paths. Pedestrians started screaming, running and taking cover. I had no choice; fortunately, the path was clear and immediately returned fire. When I started firing, my 44s, it was sounding like cannons going off. I was in attack mode, running towards them, in attempt to murder them both. They retrieved back into their building, knowing deep down inside, they were no match for me, my heart and adrenaline didn't slow down.

Gun Trafficking - Permission to Kill Me

Things calmed down, I put Sybil's family out of mind. I still hadn't been arrested or indicted for Sybil's murder, but I had to keep myself busy. I was living on a natural high, getting high off on making plenty of fast money, fucking plenty of girls and having fun. So, I went back to my day to day hustle making money.

No matter how much money I made, that was as fast I was spending it. Bored, I thought I would get out of town, and avoid thinking about getting shot. I began a past time venture, a new hustle. I started traveling to the Southeast Boarder of Virginia, North and South Carolina, hitting gun and pawn shops; not robbing, purchasing all types of weapons with the help of clean, but not too clean individuals from those particular areas. It was easy; everyone who could use a few bucks had their price. I would meet people in different states, family members or friends of their family. When you're paying these guys hundreds of dollars up front, tax free money, it talks. I was buying Uzis, tech-9 semi-automatic weapons, 9MM, 44s and 45 automatics, 357 Magnums, 38s, and 380 automatics.

Anything that had value and I could use or flip. I would purchase a Tech 9 for $249.00 dollars each, and sell them for $1500 dollars, a $1250 dollar profit off of one piece. *You couldn't call me lazy, and I wasn't taken food stamps.* I was making approximately two to three trips per month and making at least $7500 per trip. I lied back, just cruising around New York City, looking for different locations to sell drugs. I continued to travel out of town, sometimes just to get away and relax, and sometimes to make an arms purchase.

During one of my return trips I met up with my people from the A-Team and they were telling me that Sybil's people had the nerve to approach them asking for permission to kill me. I had to laugh about that. Why? Who needs permission to kill anyone? I never asked for permission, if someone violated and crossed the line and the violation was the cause for the death penalty -- then be it. The rules applied to me too. I guess Sybil's people felt I was protected by A-Team.

I recall El-son telling Shabazz, "You motherfuckers must be crazy, because nobody's fucking with Bugsy!" Elson called me "Bugsy" after the character in the movie, "*Once Upon A Time in America.*"

El-son and a few of the A-Team members came to the front of building 1266 and called me. El-son told me about the message from Shabazz, and then asked, "What do you want to do?" Whatever it was El-son was down with me. It was decided that we would meet with Babyface, Leroy and Shabazz. The three were supposed to call El-son and me from a pay phone in-front of the Laundromat on Sutter Avenue to decide for a specific meeting place.

I was waiting, strapped with a.45 automatic and a 9mm, and wearing a bullet-proof vest under a brown suede suit. As an extra precaution, El-son had girls all over the place, wheeling shopping carts and baby carriages, with guns hidden in them. Everyone was spread out and positioned. It suddenly dawned on me that we were being setup for the police. Everybody immediately left and went home.

Set up for Attempted Murder

If Sybil's people couldn't kill me, they had an alternative plan. Two months had passed since the gun fight with Sybil's family at Cypress Park, but not forgotten.

I had been hanging out with King Tut driving around East New York. We were up all night discussing our situations and business until early morning when we ran into Kevin Williams, a.k.a. Kev Web. He was like a younger brother to me. He was with this character JB, and two young ladies. Kevin asked me to give them a ride to White Castle on Atlantic Avenue. Against my better judgment I agreed -- sometimes you shouldn't second guess yourself. As I arrived at the White Castle parking lot, the place was jam packed. Initially, I stayed in the car as everyone got out for food. After approximately 30 minutes I became impatient and left the car to see what the hold was up. As I approached Web, he told me the food was almost ready and turned to leave when I ran into Sybil's crack head younger brother, Terrence. We stared at each for a moment and then he said, "Glaze...Glaze everyone believes you killed my sister, I don't believe it." He went on to say, that he and his family believed Crazy Clyde killed her. I just nodded my head and walked away, not saying a word. I drove everyone home, thinking my better judgment got the best of me. Relaxed, I went back to my apartment in Cypress Hill Houses for the night.

Attempted Murder - Really?

Monday, two days later April 29, 1986, it was King Tut's day to run the Fountain Avenue block. It was one of those lazy days and I got a late start from my Sutter Avenue apartment. It was about 2:00 P.M. when I just threw on something to wear to the cleaners and too go with Tut to shut down Fountain Avenue shop.

We stopped to pick up my clothes from the cleaners and then drove to the Fountain Avenue side of Cypress Houses. Tut and I got out of the car and went into the projects where we ran into El-son and some of the A-Team members. El-son was upset; some guy from Montauk Street was trying to hit on his girlfriend, Yvette. El-son was going mad, saying, "Come on, and drive me to Montauk so I can beat this dude down with a baseball bat." At the time Yvette's mother, Ms. Marlene, told me to, "Stay out of that bullshit."

El-son, Tut, me and two other members of the A-Team got into the Ninety-Eight, armed only with bats. Bogey was driving when we were flagged on Montauk Street and New Lots Avenue by a group of detectives and uniformed officers from the 75th Precinct. The Ninety-Eight was surrounded by unmarked blue and white police cars. The officers' guns were drawn and cocked. Everybody in the Olds sat still and raised their hands up.

I was asked my name and replied, "Brian Gibbs." One of the officers shouted to another officer, "We got Glaze!" I was handcuffed and placed in an unmarked car. While sitting in the car, several homicide detectives drove by, stopped and applauded my arrest. They eventually arrested Tut, too.

Tut and I were taken to the 75th Precinct and locked in a holding cell. When we were brought to the precinct, everyone applauded and shouted, "We finally got Glaze"! A few hours later Terrence Chilleous was brought in to identify Tut and myself. I wasn't worried, because I never did, or tried to do anything to Terrence; his brother and I had a shootout, but Terrence and I never had any confrontations.

82

Tut and I were charged with attempted murder on Terrence, and criminal possession of weapons. I said, "This only could've happened in America, when a crack-head angel-dust-user goes to a precinct and out and out lies and you to get arrested."

Tut and I went to court, but my lawyer, Leonard Kaplan, wasn't there -- his assistant, Ms. Carol Siegal was. The District Attorney read the charges: attempted murder and criminal possession of a weapon.

Terrence claimed that, on April 27, 1986, at 2:00 A.M., he was on his way to the White Castle when a dark colored car, with tinted windows, went passed him on Atlantic Avenue, then suddenly turned back and headed towards him. He stated that the back window on the driver's side came down and he saw me firing several shots at him. He said he ran so fast, zigzagging across Atlantic Avenue, which happens to have six very busy lanes, three on each side. Terrence then said he ran into a crowded White Castle, with Tut and me running behind him. He added, "Some girls, inside the place were saying, isn't that the guy they call Glaze, the murderer" He also said, Tut an I grabbed him and tried to pull him out of the restaurant, as he began yelling and screaming, "Get off of me! Don't kill me"! Terrence said, I then pulled out a gun and said I was going to kill him, and his family, the same way I killed his sister, Sybil. He continued to say, Tut and I left an after waiting a short time, he ran to a police car and told them what had happened.

Security guards were in the White Castle restaurant, but no report was filed. And none of the employees behind the bullet-proof window called the police. Here it is he is the only witness in a crowded White Castle restaurant. No one heard gunshots or saw a gun or tried to come to his aid when he claimed that he was screaming, "Don't kill me, let me go!"

I said, "The kid was one hell of a liar"! Apparently, he was good enough to satisfy the Assistant District Attorney, who asked for my bail to be set at $100,000 cash, and $75,000 cash for Tut. We were then scheduled to appear in court on Friday, May 3, 1986.

We had to return to court on that Friday morning to face charges. I was dressed to a T: two-piece, navy Ralph Lauren suit, John W. Nordstrom white dress shirt, blue and red tie, and black Johnston and Murphy wingtip shoes. Tut, his wife, and I entered the Brooklyn Criminal Court at Hoyt and Schermerhorn Street. While going thru the metal detector, Tut got into an argument with one of the court officers and they kicked him out of the building.

Tut finally calmed down and they allowed him back into the building. We boarded the elevator and I heard two homicide detectives talking. My eyes fixed on one detective Richard Brew. When the elevator reached my floor, the detectives got off and I noticed a folder in Detective Brew's hand, with the name "Sybil Mims" on it. Brew and the other detective walked into the same courtroom in which Tut and I were scheduled to appear. I slipped to the staircase and ran into my lawyer's partner

Ms. Siegal. Tut, his wife, and I explained the situation to the lawyer. Tut told me that he also heard the day before that Amare pleaded guilty to the lesser charge of manslaughter, instead of second-degree murder, and that he was supposed to testify against me. The lawyer told me not to worry about it and we all went upstairs.

When I went into the court room and Detective Brew and his partner came into the court room looking around for me. Their eyes finally settled on me.

Moments later the court was called to order, the judge appeared and sat down and so did everyone else, except for the detectives who approached the District attorney's desk. My attorney was then signaled over; they all spoke for a moment before approaching the judge's bench. As they spoke, they all turned and looked at me. My gut feeling, and better judgment was talking to me again, which suggested I come back another day. I looked around, noticed the guards slacking, and saw my opportunity to run the hell out of the court room. I ran so fast out of that court room, down the staircase and out of the building. I later contacted my attorney and learned that my gut feeling was trying to tell me that I had been officially indicted for Sybil's murder, exactly two months after I shot the bitch - sorry - poor Sybil. The question that I had to ask myself at that moment was, "Do I feel lucky or run from a possible conviction that would lead to a possible twenty-five year to life sentence?

To Hide or Not to Hide?

Only twenty-two years old and I felt like Jesse James. I had been hiding out for a couple of hours at my ladies' place, when I called up Kool-Aid and asked him to meet me at my lawyer's office. My lawyer and I talked and weighed my options. While there, I placed a call to my mother and explained to her what was going on. She didn't take the news well, keep in mind my mother was my biggest supporter. Once Kool-Aid arrived, we went back and forth deciding what I was going to do. If I ran, I knew it was going to be tough; they wouldn't stop looking for me and I would probably find myself on America's Most Wanted as public enemy #1. We discussed bail, if I turn myself in there was a slight chance I might get a bail of 75,000 to $100,000 thousand dollars, which I could do. With my past criminal record, being an ex-convict, this would be my 5th felony conviction -- if convicted. Being that I had already served state time from July 981November 1984 and still on parole, the chance of getting extended parole again on a murder charge, wasn't looking good.

Decision made; I was going to turn myself in. My lawyer made the arrangements thru the judicial system, that on Monday morning, May 5th, 1986, I would be brought in by my attorney where we would be met by detective Rich Brew at the Brooklyn Criminal Court and I would surrender.

I then drove from my lawyer's office and headed to Albee Square Mall to shop for some items that I would be needing to take with me to jail, to endure the fight of my life. At the mall I ran into King Tut and his wife and a few of his crew. I told him what happen and what I was about to do. At that moment he told me that he heard Amare had pleaded guilty to manslaughter and was going to receive six to eighteen years if he agreed to testify against me. I told Tut that I was going to turn myself in on Monday and fight the case. In the middle of the most popular mall in Brooklyn at the time, he started pleading with me to reconsider.

The mall was crowded, and we are all near the food court when I told Tut it was final; I was turning myself in. He kept trying to persuade me not to; as supposedly two tough guys from Brooklyn in this crowded mall embraced and cried like little babies, saying goodbye. The next couple of days I spent time saying goodbye to family, friends and my ladies. My family was saddened, feeling this could be the end of my freedom forever. *Freedom my ancestors fought and died for*. The odds weren't in my favor, being a career criminal with four felony convictions at twenty-two years of age. Chances were if convicted for this murder, I would receive twenty-five years to life. And even after serving the 25 or plus years, would the parole board ever release me? I also took that free time to have some last-minute sexual encounters with several of the young ladies I was fond of. I had to take advantage of getting some loving, because it might be a very long time before getting anymore pussy would present itself. It wasn't a surprise that each and every one of my ladies begged me not to turn myself in. It did not matter; my decision was made.

My Mother and My Guilt

Most important at the time I was hoping to spare my mother the fact that I was guilty. The trial and its outcome would be heavy on my mother's mind and spirits. I have said often, the most important person in my life was my mother, Dorothy Gibbs. I can't say that enough. She was the best thing that ever occurred in my life. Even during my teenage years when I first started getting into trouble, from getting kicked out of Franklin K. Lane High School for assault and robbery of another classmate. I remember just slapping the shit out of Robert, a student, and demanded his belongings and yes he reported the incident and I was kicked out of Franklin K. Lane. I remember going to a hearing at the Board of Education with my mother. In attendance were Robert and his parents. The charges were read, and Robert actually testified and gave his version and I was suspended from school and the irony of it all, Robert parents chose not to press charges. Looking into my dear mother eyes I could see that my actions had caused her pain and embarrassment. To be honest, never once did I set out to cause my mother the heartache and pain due to my stupidity and reckless behavior. That day as I looked into her eyes after the hearing, all I could say to her repeatedly, "I'm sorry" as I watched the tears roll down her face and that caused me to cry. I wish I could say that would be the last time that my actions were the reason to cause her pain; the truth of the matter that was only the beginning.

My mother taught my siblings and me, right from wrong, but I was that lost sheep that went astray. She always encouraged her children to live life as a good Christian and stay away from all negativity. Being a young follower at the time, I loved my mother with all my heart, but I was in love with the Street and all of the things I thought the streets had to offer. My mother would sit down with me and discuss my behavior and actions and for the life of me I couldn't be truthful with her. If she heard that I was involved in any criminal activity that went on in the neighborhood, such as someone being robbed, or someone's home being burglarized I would lie to her. I couldn't find the courage to tell her the truth.

As time went on, I became "Glaze." I was a criminal, I was a stickup kid committing armed robbery, I was a drug dealer, and I was a killer. How could I, one of the most important individuals in her life, her baby boy be such a total fuck up (my words), who had gone completely astray? But trust me when I say that my mother knew what she was hearing about her son Brian "Glaze" Gibbs was true. Call it a mother's instinct, but she knew.

Yes, my mother knew I was "Glaze." I can recall one night I was on my way to our apartment in Cypress Hill houses, and these two guys from the Crown Height section of Brooklyn tried to rob me. It was late winter of 1985 or early 1986, when they caught up with me in front of 1260 Sutter Ave., building. I knew one of them; it started out with small talk asking me several bullshit questions that had nothing to do with anything which gave the indication these chumps were looking to rob me. I had about $1500 in cash and wearing over five thousand dollars in jewelry. As it became obvious of their intention, I told them to give me five minutes that I had to pick up a couple thousand dollars from my man on the third floor. Now these assholes were just being greedy. Instead of going to the 3rd floor, I continued to the 7th floor, to the roof, and then over the roof to my building, 1266 Sutter Ave. Running down to the 4th floor to my apt 4B. My mother was still up at about 10 P.M. as I went and hugged my mom and told her, "I love you" as she was on her way to bed, and already prepared for work the next day. I then went to my stash and grabbed one of my many guns, a Colt 45 automatic. As I left our apartment in search of these two knuckleheads to put a bullet in their asses, they were no longer at 1260 Sutter. I ran into them on Sutter and Euclid Avenue and I just went into attack mode, allowing my 45 to talk for me. As I was shooting at them, they were shooting back at me as they ran off into the darkness.

The next day my mother confronted me by saying that all night it was peaceful until I came upstairs and went back out and then it sounded like the 4th of July. I played dumb and told my mother, "You know how bad this neighborhood is, it could have been anyone out there shooting." *My mother just looked at me saying, "Yeah, right." It was black and white.*

Welcome Back Glaze

Bright and early Monday morning, two days later, May 5, 1986, I woke up a little stressed. I went to my lawyer's office. We went to court to reappear for the scheduled court date which I ran out on the Friday before. I was arrested by Detective Brew and his partner. They drove me to Central Booking, where I was processed, fingerprinted, and strip searched. I was charged with the murder of Sybil Mims and criminal possession of a weapon. I went to court and was remanded without bail. I was back at Brooklyn House of Detention for the second time within a week.

From May 5, 1986 until June 22, 1987 I spent time in the Brooklyn Houses of Detention and Rikers Island suite C-95 HDM (House of Detention for Men). Not feeling too optimistic, facing life imprisonment, I really had that, "I do not give a fuck attitude," and I didn't. I was causing major havoc in Brooklyn House and Rikers Island. I was unintentionally and unreasonably ruthless when it came to any misunderstanding and would usually stab up my enemies or bust them upside their head with a mop ringer. I couldn't take much with me to jail, but they allowed me to walk around with over $5,000 dollars' worth of jewelry: a

14k gold link chain, with a big round medallion and gold nugget watch that was most inmates bail money. Yes, the jewelry was an overkill. I know, a little obnoxious, but that was then. *Not a soul attempted to fuck with me. I guess if they wanted to go for the Gold, they would have to compete for it. Fuck, it wasn't the Olympics.*

Terrence and Amare Must Die or Torture

Killer logic, under my circumstances, dictated that I placed a hit out on Amare and Terrence (Sybil's brother). I had to drown my conscience. Without Amare and Terrence my case would be dismissed. The district attorney scheduled a hearing to have Terrence testify and to be crossed examined by my lawyer. The district attorney and I must have been on the same page; he had Amare videotaped, believing anything is possible before the trial. Two of my workers, Fat James Gibbs and Little Darrell, who I felt were seasoned killers would complete the job before the hearing. These two cartoon characters Fat James and Little Darrell said they tracked Terrence down for days to kill him and when they caught up with him, they couldn't kill Terrence because he was with another guy. Another guy? I went off on those two bitch ass mother fuckers. I told them if the roles was reversed, I wouldn't have cared if there was a hundred witnesses, I would have killed as many witnesses as possible, even if I only killed ninety nine witnesses and got busted during the act. At least I would have been locked up with them, and looking in their eyes telling them both, "I killed ninety-nine and was trying to hit the last one." Obviously, I was upset. That was the difference between me and those two bitches, Fat James and Little Darrell, they were the type who preached and talked that mafia Don shit but did not live up to it. Unfortunately, Little Darrell was shot several times by Delroy Uzi Edwards and was near death as I was fighting this murder case.

Mission not accomplished, and considering my state

of mind at the time, I was forced to torture Andy who was in Brooklyn House with me at the time. He claimed he was Delroy Uzi Edward's brother. As a couple of my follower's hog tied him and basically beat the living shit out of him, using a long wooden scrub brush and a wet towel. Andy finally coughed up Uzi's, East Islip, Long Island address where he was in hiding after he shot and nearly killed Little Darrell. When I gave Fat James the address, this chump told me that they were not going out to Long Island to get Uzi. Even once little Darrell recovered, he refused to go after Delroy. It showed me that Fat James and Little Darrell were not cut from the same cloth as me, Tiny, Tut, Ref or the A-Team. At the end, Fat James and Little Darrell gave themselves a big party once Delroy Uzi Edwards was sentence to a seven to life sentenced, in Brooklyn Federal Court for six murders, seventeen assault and drug charges on December 1st, 1989. Not so lucky. I guess they found justice in the legal system. I still had to deal with Terrance and Amare.

C-95 Police Brutality

I was having some difficulty with other inmates, so I spent some time in The Tombs. The Bronx, and Queens Houses refused me -- H.D.M. and C-74 did too. The only place that accepted me was C-95 – "police brutality." I arrived back at C-95, Dorm 2.

I hated dorms, big rooms which contained about 50-75 beds. There was no privacy. It was scorching hot, and I lasted about a week before being transferred to 14 Upper.

I stayed there for a few days, and then was transferred back to Dorm 2. I was going to court almost every day for pre-trial hearings for Sybil's murder, because the District Attorney's star witness Amare changed his mind and now refused to testify against me. The hearings were conducted in order to determine if there was enough evidence to take me to trial.

The Corporate World Call It Networking

While awaiting trial protected behind bars, I made and built some great bonds and friendships with a lot of the five borough's most ruthless violent criminals of all nationalities. You wouldn't have wanted them as enemies. However, some of their qualities you may find in the corporate board rooms. It was these connections that would entrench me into the drug business and making 40,000 dollars a day.

While still in prison, believe it or not I did make enemies, since I was facing murder, kidnapping and etc., if anybody got in my way, I would try to kill'em. I would stab them with an ink pen, it didn't matter; *although, I wasn't able to write any letters for a while.*

Among my friends there was Pappy Mason, a sturdy Rastafarian, with long dreadlocks and gold teeth, one of which has a shamrock carved in it. Pappy was described by a Sergeant McGuiness as stupid and brutal. Pappy was thought to be a little more than crazy. [1] Louise Coleman, Fat Cat's mother, said Pappy once hung his girlfriend by her legs out of a moving car and dragged her along the pavement. I assumed until dead.

Viola, the sister of a Lorenzo Nichols, who you will get to know, was jokingly named Pappy Mason's girlfriend, although she was a member of his gang, the Bebos. She worked directly for Pappy, bagging crack. Viola was a crack addict and an exceedingly plump one, which is unusual for a crack addict. Mason would refer to her as his "overweight lover." She would snap back, "I ain't no overweight lover, you motherfucking, dreadlock-wearing son of bitch!" One-time Viola smoked $10,000 worth of Mason's crack, and Fat Cat had to make good, by giving Pappy a free kilo of coke. She never lost a pound. Pappy's crew, all of them for the most part, practiced the Rastafarian way of life, such as dreadlocks, eating no red meat or pork, showering but not using deodorant. For the most part as far as I was concerned, the Bebos were definitely about business. Made their money and took care of any problems that came their way.

Another acquaintance which I built a relationship with was with Lorenzo Nichols, a.k.a. "Fat Cat". The Nichols' organization terrorized poor and middle-class black neighborhoods with public murders and wanton violence. He was also described as being cunning and ruthless. In a future article it was written, "Many members of Nichols' crew were close family relatives, including his mother and two of his sisters. Brian "Glaze" Gibbs was another trusted associate, so blood thirsty that Fat Cat had to restrain him."

Fat Cat ran a drug trafficking gang in the Jamaica, Queens Neighborhood of New York City along with his friend Howard "Pappy" Mason -- each running their own crews. Their gangs sold drugs and grossed as much as $200,000 per week in profits. Fat Cat's heroin and cocaine operation took in an estimated twenty million dollars per year. He was not hard to spot, stocky, wearing fur coats and gold jewelry. With only a ninth-grade education, his brain kept turning, and ready to torture or murder anyone who betrayed him or stepped in his territory.

Fat Cat's Big Mac Deli Raided

[1]

Lorenzo "Fat Cat" Nichols was born on December 25, 1958, in Birmingham, Alabama. During the 1980s, Lorenzo Nichols became one of the top drug lords in New York City. He got his nickname "because of his linebacker thick neck, a head so big it nearly blocked out his friends' faces in snapshots, and his rangy beard," according to Ethan Brown's book *Queens Reigns Supreme: Fat Cat, 50 Cent, and the Rise of Hip-Hop Culture.*

While still in prison awaiting trial and prior to me meeting Lorenzo "Fat Cat" Nichols, he and several others were arrested on July 29, 1985 on drug charges when police raided the Big Mac Deli in South Jamaica, Queens; a business he and his wife Joanne took over from her father. They found over $200,000 dollar in cash, a large amount of bagged up heroin and cocaine and several guns. Within a couple of days, Cat went to court and was out on seventy thousand dollars bail. Several days after his release Cat reported to his Parole Officer Brian Rooney and told him that he was just visiting friends and had no idea it was a drug location. Parole officer Rooney did not buy the story and felt he violated his parole from a previous armed robbery conviction in 1976 and was remanded back to prison to complete his sentence. Cat was furious and now a drug and weapons charges could carry a life sentence in prison, which didn't sit well with him. Having been a millionaire and one of the three largest drug dealers in the five boroughs, he had no intentions of going from living in heaven to being stuck in hell for life. From jail he ordered subordinates to "hurt" his parole officer, Brian Rooney, for reporting that he had violated his parole.

On October 10, 1985 Fat Cat's parole officer Brian Rooney was shot and murdered after being set up by twenty-seven-year-old Perry Bellamy on orders by Pappy Mason. On Sunday October 27, Perry Bellamy was arrested, and on Monday October 28 Howard Pappy Mason was also arrested for the murder of Fat Cat's parole officer. When Perry Bellamy was arrested, he foolishly gave a video confession implicating all who were involved in the murder including Fat Cat. Perry Bellany would have to be eliminated so that he would not be able to testify in court. To be continued.

Fat Cat and Pappy

Fat Cat and Pappy, met for the first time in 1976, on Rikers Island. Cat was charged with armed robbery and was serving a sentence of 0-18 years, and Pappy, who was convicted of attempted murder, was serving a sentence of 0-7 years.

During that time Rikers Island was a rough place. Not a day went by without an inmate being critically wounded or killed, or forced into homosexual encounters, and watching guys getting their asses whipped and robbed for their sneakers or commissary items. But during that time Cat, Pappy, and a guy named Jug Head had become friends. Cat was the fighter and whenever he had a problem with another inmate most of the time it resulted in a fight. Cat was five-foot-seven and weighed about 230 pounds, and he won his fights about 80% of the time. Cat would also get into fights, because he used to look out for the weaker guys. He looked out for Jug Head on a regular basis, and even showed him some pointers on how to fight. So, since Cat was quick to whip somebody's ass and knew how to put down the knuckle game, he gained respect and earned a reputation as being a person not to be fucked with.

Pappy was well known, because the majority of the guys on Rikers Island at that time had been in one of the juvenile detention centers with him. Pappy had been in trouble with the law since he was 7 or 8 and was sent to Spofford Juvenile Detention Center on several occasions. The older he got, the worse his crimes became, and he ended up being sent to several juvenile detention centers in upstate New York. During that time, which included his membership in the Brooklyn Jolly Stompers, Pappy also established his own reputation as being someone not to be fucked with. It became a known fact that if you had a problem with Pappy, then you had to attack him before he got to you, because he would be coming after you. Pappy was tall and slim, five-feet-nine and about 140 pounds, but during his stay at Rikers Island he started setting examples right away; he hit several guys alongside their heads with a metal mop wringer and those who escaped the wringer treatment received a knife from Pappy.

When Cat and Pappy went to start their sentences in upstate New York, Cat was considered a model inmate; he never ran into problems with either staff or inmates when assigned to a program.

As for Pappy, well, you name it and he was into it. When Pappy started serving his sentence upstate, he rebelled against the system from day one until his release. Pappy developed hatred towards all staff members and ended up spending most of his sentence doing time in the box for violating prison rules and regulations. Pappy was constantly fighting with correctional officers. If one disrespected or got out of line with him, then he'd just punch them right in the face. One time, in Clinton Correctional Facility in Dannemora, New York, he kicked an officer down a flight of stairs. Pappy went from Rikers Island to Elmira to Attica to Auburn to Comstock to Clinton. All of those facilities have a Maximum A security rating. An "A" *rating doesn't really have a positive connotation to the prisoners, unless it's a restaurant.*

On a positive note, Pappy was known for going to the aide of other inmates. Hearing that Pappy had been beat up by prison guards inmates reacted during the evening meal by starting a major riot in the mess hall. The officers were outnumbered by inmates and every officer in sight was subjected to being assaulted. Tear gas had to be shot from the guard towers for staff to regain control. The whole institution was locked down for almost a week before the investigation was completed and the ones responsible were taken to the box. When the institution is locked down, the inmates remain in their cells all day and their meals are brought to them. *Not exactly room service.*

Still Awaiting Trial - Amare Must Die

Sunrise, sunset, thirteen months and seventeen days passed fighting inmates. While waiting to go to trial, jail life wasn't easy, surprise, surprise. My typical day, when not battling, was spent on the phone and in the visiting room scheming on ways to get to Amare. He was the key witness that could actually place me with the gun in my hand, pulling the trigger that put Sybil to rest. Being that I was facing a possible life sentence if convicted, I was still seeking to make dough to build up my stash.

I was continuing to give King Tut ideas and planning moves on things he could do to maintain our cash flow. Unable to sit still fighting this case, I was wired, and tearing shit up. They, the system, considered me to be a menace to the New York City Penal System, labeled me a

(CMC) Central Monitoring Case. My chart and how many people I was separated from were like an army roll call. I was always into something from stabbing, piping, fighting and causing havoc for anyone that opposed me. *Looking back, drugs like valium should have been mandatory, could have saved a lot time and money.* Anyway, I spent a lot of quality time in the hole. I was in there sometimes twenty-three to twenty-four hours a day and maybe I would get out to take a shower, or go to the recreation area. But most of my time was spent in total lock down. I did a lot of reading, research and soul searching. So, when I was in the box, doing some critical thinking, again, I realized what I needed to survive once I was out was a good power structure. To my surprise, the answers would present themselves to me.

Prior to my trial and I had checked things out and saw how the older guys were operating the telephones. They had something called "slot time." Different guys would use the telephone at different periods throughout the day. The average guy would be lucky to get ten minutes on the telephone in the morning and a ten-minute call at night. There were dominating inmates who had control of the telephone, using it for 30 minutes to an hour at a time. I felt ten minutes on the telephone wasn't enough and I needed it to change.

Lucky for me, Nathaniel "Az" Kelly was transferred to the eighth floor with me. Az had received 25 years to life after a murder conviction and was awaiting transfer to upstate. Az and I had attended Redirection High School and were on Rikers Island and Coxsackie together back in 1981. Az told me, "Glaze, we're not in C-74 adolescent on Rikers Island anymore, we're dealing with adults. So, the main thing here is the phone. So, when you go from floor to floor, get yourself established immediately on that telephone; as soon as you come through those doors, right then and there." So, Az and I got busy taking over the eighth floor's A-Side. We were making power moves, beating guys down, stabbing them, or burning their cells. Within a week-and-a-half, with the help of Az, the eighth floor's A-Side was our domain.

Az was later transferred to upstate New York, to start serving his sentence. I felt sorry for Az, because I liked him. I also had "Prince," and Ronald "Born" Jefferson transferred to the eighth floor. We had it sewed up. I would give other inmates two-and-a-half minutes on the telephone. When the last thirty seconds of a call was left, I would sing to them, like the old Mouseketeer song: "Now it's time to say goodbye to all your lovely friends. M-I-C, call you real soon. K-E-Y, why? Because your time is up, M-0-U-S-E."

My reign on the eighth floor lasted a little over a month; inmates on the A-Side were telling on me. "All the stand-up guys were telling on me." The captains and several of the correctional officers escorted Born and me off the floor. As I was leaving, an officer, named McDonald, started singing to me: "Now it's time to say goodbye to all your lovely friends. M-I-C, see you real soon. K-E-Y, why? Because Glaze, your time is up, M-0U-S-E." Born was transferred to the sixth floor and I to the ninth.

As I came through the door, on the ninth floor, the first thing I wanted to know was who had control of the telephone. An individual, named Kev, said that he was in charge of the telephone. So, before I even got settled in, I stepped up to Kev and informed him that I had to have ample time on the telephone. Kev said, no problem.

I was cleaning my assigned cell, when Kev, who was about six feet tall and solid muscle, made his move. He snatched my gold chain and cross pendant from my neck, then repeatedly punched me in the face. We both fell to the floor. I landed on top of Kev and got up first, trying to kick Kev in the face. Then, two guys grabbed me, shouting, "Correction Officers are coming!"

Now, a lot of guys on the A, B, and D-Sides were telling Kev that he was going to get it for fucking with me. Kev was a big guy, but he was now scared shitless. He gave me back the chain and kept the cross, but I lost a ring in the process. All of these guys on the C-Side were asking me if I remembered them, but I didn't remember any of them. I was telling them that I needed a shank. Well, this guy gave me a bullshit-ass shank – but beggars can't be choosy.

So, I took the shank, with a cup of boiling hot water, mixed in a couple of soap balls and went into Big Kev's cell. I threw the boiling, soapy water into Kev's face. Next thing I knew I was up in the air; this guy body slammed me to the floor and my head hit the toilet. As he was going for the shank, I bit his hand, grabbed the shank, and then began stabbing him. I caught him in his side, his chest, and his neck. He ran out of the cell and I was right behind him. As always, as I was about to close in for the finishing touches, officers came, and I disappeared into the crowd. They carried Kev out and for some reason the captains and guards called me up-front. They rushed me and were throwing punches as I was just covering up to protect myself.

They allowed me to stay on the ninth floor. The word on Kev was that he was paralyzed, but when I saw him six months later, on Rikers Island, he looked healthy to me -- and big as ever. But we did resolve the matter. He said that he didn't want any more problems with me.

I lasted less than a month on the ninth floor, because other inmates were jealous of me. One evening, while in the law library, studying up on my case, someone threw a match in my cell, to burn me out. Someone with whom I was friends put out the fire, before it had a chance to spread. I believed these guys named Wallee Comer and Frazier put out the fire before it could do too much damage.

Upon my return from the library Wallee and Frazier told me that somebody was trying to burn me out, which meant automatic transfer off the floor. But because Wallee and Frazier put out the fire before anyone noticed, the movement never occurred. I had twenty-seven guys from which to choose when trying to figure out who was responsible for the attempted burnout.

I started thinking back and asking myself which one of them had the best reason for wanting me out. After thinking about it and weighing the situation, the finger pointed to one guy, and that was the guy who gave me the shank to stab Big Kev. To sum it up, he didn't like the way my power increased among the inmates. We fought I stabbed this guy several times. I had him on the floor and he kicked me in the face, but I shook it off. This guy was fighting for his life and you can't back a scared opponent into a corner. All I knew is that I jabbed at him with the shank and he bit the shit out of my left thumb. So, I stabbed him in his face, and he let my thumb go. He ran up-front, yelling for the officers, and they took him to the doctor.

The officers were having a fit and one officer in particular made a little speech. He was talking to all of us, but I asked him why he was making his speech to everyone while staring at me. One word led to another and we got into a heated argument. I told him to crack the gate and him and I could lock asses together, but he never unlocked the gate. About half-an-hour later, I asked the officer, his name which was Waterman, to come inside the dish room. He did and I told him that I didn't have anything against him and wasn't looking for any problems. However, if he had anything against me that he felt he'd like to get off his chest, then that was the time and place. He told me that he didn't have anything against me and didn't want to fight. From then on, I never had a problem with him.

Who Stole My Gold Watch

I was waiting to go to the third floor to do Bing time for stabbing the guy on the ninth floor who threw the match in my cell. (Bing time was solitary confinement; prisoners would spend 23 to 24 hours a day inside a small cell with only a mattress and a toilet-sink combination.) While I was on the eighth floor, I was wearing a $1,500, 14k gold nugget watch. I believed someone stole it from my cell. I had twenty-nine fellow inmates in the dayroom strip searching themselves looking for my watch. I came up empty-handed.

"The D-Side was closed down, because they were installing new windows. I sent word to Joseph Sherman and a few other guys on the B and C-Side, to conduct a search, just in case a guy from my side had passed it to someone on another side. I searched all the cells -- fifteen upstairs and fifteen downstairs. I had two homemade knives, ripping up people's mattresses and going through their cosmetics. It was during noon chow time when correctional officers Proherb and Robinson were on-duty. They heard that I was on a rampage, because of my missing gold watch. They knew I had a knife and told me to hand it over and I wouldn't get into any trouble. I gave up the knife, and as soon as they left, I pulled out another knife and continued my search. As I continued the search, a deputy warden and captain came through and asked me who the fuck I thought I was, ordering a search. I addressed them in a respectable manner; told them my watch was missing, and all my fellow inmates wished to show their innocence by suggesting they search themselves. The deputy warden and captain took me outside, in-front of the officer's desk, where Officer Robinson came out with my watch. He said he found it in my basketball sneakers. Then, it occurred to me that I placed it in there because I was going to wash some clothes.

Right then and there they wanted to place me in C.M.C. (Census Monitor Control) to be able to know and control my every move. Fortunately, Big Joseph Sherman convinced the deputy warden to allow me to stay on the eighth floor and put me on his side because I was his little cousin. He told them that he would be able to keep me out of trouble. Joseph was about six-feet-four, solid build and weighed between 290-300 pounds. The deputy warden agreed, and I was moved from side A to side B. On the B-Side there was Big Joe and my man Christopher Arthur, a.k.a. Ra-hem, I knew them both from the Albany Houses in Brooklyn.

Every Jamaican who came through either Rikers Island or the Brooklyn Houses caught hell from me. I would either stab or bust them over the head with a pipe. In the Brooklyn Houses the guards started calling me "Don Glazeion" which only made things worse by further inflating my monster ego. My last rampage got me kicked out of the Brooklyn Houses and transferred to C-95 at Rikers Island, where it's known for its "police brutality," where the guards had no qualms about jumping on the inmates. I lasted about a month in C-95 before being transferred to H.D.M.

While there I was jumped by ten to fifteen officers, after another inmate was jumped by some guards in the mess hall, and me and two other guys went to his aide. We were overpowered and beat down. Out of all the jails in New York, C-95 is the only jail I know that is really run by the Correction Officers. They control that place; the inmates get only a little slack.

False Assassinations

Passing time until the Sybil murder trial made the street seem like child's play or at least it ran a close second. I went to H.D.M. in December of 1986, and before long I was doing whatever I wanted. Kevin "Reenie" Smith more or less helped me get into such a good position. When I arrived on the B-Side of 2-Block, Reenie was pretty much in control of things. I benefitted by knowing Reenie; eventually over time I took over the reins from him.

I'll describe H.D.M. as being wide open, with unobstructed access to heroin, cocaine, marijuana, liquor, knives, guns, and a whole host of other illegal contraband. Actually, several people overdosed and died while I was in H.D.M.

Two individuals, Stacey Lewis and Lil' Sha-Del, were shot -- that incident was rigged. Stacey and Sha-Del smuggled in a .25 automatic and had one of their buddies shoot them, Stacey in the leg and Sha-Del in the hand. They setup the shooting to try and get some leverage in their cases, claiming someone tried to assassinate them. I said that if anyone had ordered a hit on them, they would've been dead. H.D.M. was a place where everything goes - a real live jungle. A gunshot wound to the hand and leg would not have been classified as an assassination attempt.

To make incarceration more tolerable, one of my fellow inmates, called Scooby, would help smuggle in drugs for me, which my crew on the outside would provide. Drugs and money are one and the same on Rikers Island. I would then sell the drugs inside H.D.M. for cartons of cigarettes.

At one point I had several hundred cartons spread throughout the cell blocks. I would also send free cigarettes to those I liked that were in the Bing. To make life a little more pleasant, I also had a mess hall "contract" for myself and Lorenzo "Fat Cat" Nichols; we would receive various fresh vegetables and fruits, and vegetarian sandwiches.

One day Scooby tried to rip me off over one of the drug packages. I wasted no time, immediately pulling out my knife, clicking it, and launching at Scooby. His shirt was slashed, and he ran down the stairs, screaming for the officers, who escorted him from the block. About two hours later, during the 4:00 P.M. count, several guards rushed into block 2. They searched my cell, as well as my brother's, Kool-Aid's, and Reenie's. A few other cells were searched, but nothing was ever found. Another supposed to-be-tough guy told on me. A few days later, during a poker game, Reenie and I got into a dispute, not over the card game, but because I had my brother and several others transferred to my block which didn't make him comfortable. As well as I had some clout with certain captains and officers, and perhaps Reenie was jealous. In any event, one word led to another and Reenie soon found himself on the business end of my 007 knife. I split open the right side of Reenie's head and had cut him another two or three times, before Kool-Aid could intervene and pull me away. The riot squad rushed in and took Reenie to the hospital where he later received stitches and hauled me to a separate holding cell. I remained in the holding cell about an hour before being stripped searched; neither weapon nor blood could be found, so I was allowed to return to the block.

A couple of days later while Kool-Aid, and a few others were returning from visits, Kool-Aid and I were met by two captains and several guards. Apparently, quite a few inmates had gotten together and written a letter to the warden and security captain; a man named Benjamin. The inmates claimed they feared for their lives as long as I was there. Kool-Aid and I were escorted to 1A, side B, where Fat Cat was located. The move occurred during count time, so I couldn't get to anyone involved in bringing about the transfer – but I did rip out the telephones before leaving.

Cat and I were cool on the strength of Pappy Mason. On December 26, 1986, Cat and I were together in the bullpens; he was waiting to go to Queens Court, and I was waiting to go to Brooklyn to see my lawyer. While we were there, Cat asked how much my bail was. I told him that I'd turned myself in and bail hadn't been set. He asked, if I got bail set, then how much did I think I could make? I told him probably up to a hundred and fifty-thousand dollars. Cat told me if I received bail and it was higher than that, then he'd take care of the rest. We also talked about Amare, the witnesses in my case. He said that being the witness was in jail, we could get one of the street girls to visit him a few times and slip some poison in his soda or sandwich. Cat added, "Mercury from a thermometer would be the best and quickest."

In January 1987, Pappy Mason was on trial for the murder of Fat Cat's parole officer; Brian Rooney. Fat Cat had the police report on the whole case and while returning from a visit, he told me that other inmates presently with him in H.D.M. had made statements regarding the case. He told me to find the inmates and have them come down to the clinic during sick call the next morning. I did what was requested of me and the following morning the other inmates came to sick call to see Fat Cat. He talked to them and showed them all the statements that had been given to the police about the Rooney murder. He then told each to give me an affidavit, stating they knew nothing about the murder. Everybody signed statements and then Fat Cat told me as I stood armed, with a shank, to leave them alone.

Kool-Aid, Fat Cat and I all got along well during our stay together in 1A. We had plenty of telephone time, food, and just about anything else we wanted. Although, our comfort didn't last very long. After about two weeks, both Kool-Aid and I ended up in the Bing. The reason was unclear.

A few days after going to the Bing, I was scheduled to make my court appearance on the Sybil's murder charge. Reenie, who had been transferred, was also scheduled to appear in court on the same day and before the same judge, Francis Egitto of the Brooklyn Supreme Court.

Both of us had been locked up on murder charges. I was the first to arrive at the court holding cell. Rennie was among the second group to arrive. The two of us were separated by gates, but Reenie told me we would resume from where we left off.

As soon as I was locked in I changed clothes, replacing my sport jacket and silk shirt with a sweet hood. I had a cookie box I brought from Rikers Island. Although I was searched, the cookie box was not, as the box appeared to be unopened. The point is that I used it to smuggle out half of a pair of scissors;

As soon as Reenie came into the holding cell we went at it. Reenie began swinging and I pulled out the scissors. Reenie was surprised by the sight of the weapon. I felt I had nothing to prove, because I stabbed Reenie earlier, but Reenie rushed me, and I had no choice but to stab him again. He was holding me, trying to grab my arm with the weapon. While he was trying to get the weapon, I had it in my mind to stab him in the neck, but common sense told me not to. I was in a position to kill Reenie, but knew it wasn't worth it. Insane! All I kept thinking about was going in front of Judge Egitto that day hoping to get bail and to add another murder charge which probably wouldn't sit well with him.

Not Allowed Back to Rikers Island

Getting back from court, when my time was up in the Bing, either C-95 or Rikers Island didn't want me. So, I was kicked off Rikers Island and sent to the Brooklyn House. I arrived back at Brooklyn House of Detention with a mellow attitude. I was strictly low profile. All the officers and inmates were surprised, wondering what came over me and why the change.

However, it was short lived; a few days after my return I got into a fight on the reception floor, because some guys on the house gang disrespected me. I was then transferred to the eighth floor's D-Side. El-son, the A-Team leader, was on the B-Side. As always, I established myself in order to receive ample time on the telephone. But otherwise I basically kept to myself. I knew a lot of the guys on all sides of the floor, so they would come out on the bridge and talk to me.

I was back and forth to court almost every day. One day I arrived from court and an officer pulled me to the side. It was a female correctional officer for whom I had a great deal of respect. She told me, "Glaze, somebody threw a match in your cell and set it on fire." She said that none of my personal property was burned, and told me, "Glaze, you know I'm supposed to move you according to policy."

She asked me to promise her that I wouldn't do anything to anyone during her shift. I promised and kept my word. The whole eighth floor was waiting to see who was going to be the victim I would send to the hospital for setting my cell on fire. My man, Puerto Rican Apache, gave me a shank, and I went to the law library until the officers changed shift. While I was at the library, a move was made. Several guys who were tight with me didn't want me to catch a new charge and took care of the matter for me by beating down the culprits. By the time I came back the problem was taken care of and the culprits were in the infirmary.

One Friday evening, during "Mr. Magic's Rap Attack" on either WBLS or 98.7 KISS F.M. everybody started yelling: "Yo, Glaze, did you hear that?" I asked what they were talking about and was told that King Tut had a song dedicated to me, called *Public Enemy #1*, by the group Public Enemy. But I was cooling down. I attributed the change to fact that I was getting married soon - while still in prison.

Kidnapping, Little Respect among Drug Lords

While I was back in Brooklyn House, during Memorial Day weekend of May 1987, Channel 7 News flashed a lady's picture on the screen. I thought the woman looked familiar.

With Fat Cat still in prison, the competition thought it was a good time to take advantage of the situation. On the weekend prior to Memorial Day, 1987 a lady left her home in Elmont, Long Island. She was driving her brand-new Mercedes Benz, going shopping to prepare for several cookouts for the Memorial Day weekend, when she was pulled over by two individuals posing as N.Y.C. detectives. They were driving an unmarked car, supposedly investigating the murder of parole officer Brian Rooney. This innocent woman was Joanne "Mousey" Nichols, the wife of Lorenzo "Fat Cat" Nichols. And for that she was kidnapped off the streets of Long Island in broad daylight - go figure.

Blind folded and placed in the back of a dark colored van with no windows, she was tied up and taken to an unknown location for several days. Still blind folded, she was tied to a wooden chair, and guarded by a large, vicious, growling pit bull. *She was told on numerous occasions that if their demands were not met, they were going to have the pit bull bite off her breast, one breast at a time before they killed her.* Mousey was more horrified by the thought of not ever again seeing her kids, parents, family and friends, and a good chance that her family would never find her body to give her a proper funeral. This was a bad move; street rule 101, never kidnap someone and involve the parents who have nothing to do with the street. However, this rule was occasionally broken when whole families had to pay for one family member's fuck ups.

The kidnappers made contact with Mousey's family and instructed them on their demands, which included a hefty ransom and instructing that no law enforcement contact whatsoever. Of course, they contacted the police; they were taxpayers and even criminals need to be protected. Eventually Cat also solicited the help of Gerald Prince Miller. Prince was the nephew of Kenneth Supreme McGriff and the only one available at the time. Prince was seeking to broker the deal on behalf of Fat Cat as he was able to talk directly to his wife's kidnappers. Gerald Prince Miller is now serving a life sentence for the Feds. Prince was responsible and convicted for ordering the death of several Columbian cocaine suppliers from his Rikers Island jail cell. Four to six Columbians were robbed of a large sum of cocaine and their bodies were chopped up and disposed of.

At the end all Cat had offered the kidnappers were his cars and jewelry, including a Mercedes Benz, BMW, and a Porsche. He never offered them any cash or kilos of heroin or cocaine, which was a major setback. At the end Joanne's parents came up with $77,000 dollars cash to secure their daughters release. No one had a clue who the kidnappers were, but felt it wasn't gang related. Anyone who wanted a large sum of money, the best way to get it is to go after someone who is into an illegal activity. Prince dropped off the money to a location that was chosen by the kidnappers. Once the money was dropped off, approximately thirty minutes later one of the kidnappers came by and snatched up the $77,000 cash. For the life of me, I never understood how the cops who were supposedly observing and video tapping the pickup, couldn't follow and catch the kidnappers.

Fortunately, Mousey was released on Sunday, May 24, 1987. A King Allah and his partner Richard Frejomil, after additional surveillance and tips, were finally arrested on June 28, 1987 in Baltimore, Maryland for their part in her kidnapping. Although arrested, King Allah would threaten Fat Cat's Family if Mousey testified against them in court. To be continued.

The Forming of The Round Table

Lorenzo "Fat Cat" Nichols was one hell of a master mind. After the kidnapping of his wife Mousey in 1987 there was the home invasion of his number one girlfriend, Carolyn Lynn-Tyson's home. As Jug Head and Bo-Bo dropped off approximately 219,000 dollars in cash, for Fat Cat, these guys Ron-du from the Bronx and a couple of his guys appeared at her home and were hiding out in the bushes near Lynn six bedroom, aristocratic styled home in Dix Hills, Long Island. Cat had purchased it for her along with a brand-new navy Mercedes Benz 300. Lynn was one of a few that Cat trusted with his money, another one was his eighteen-year-old niece Cookie. She had her very own home in Farmingdale Long Island, along with her brand-new black coupe BMW 633csi. Back to the home invasion that night, as Jug Head and Bo-Bo were dropping off the loot, as she had become accustom to doing, they were ambushed by a masked Ron-du and his crew. They came out of the bushes with their automatic weapons drawn and pushed them all back into the house and took both BoBo's and Jug Head's guns and made them lie face down on the floor and hand cuffed them from behind. For one reason or another they pistol whipped Lynn seeking more money, drugs, and jewelry. They got another $335,000 in cash before tying Lynn up and leaving. During the ordeal, Ron-du lifted up his mask not knowing that Jug Head who was lying flat on his stomach was able to recognize him from a mirror that was situated on the wall. Jug Head remembered Ron-du from their juvenile days at Spofford (a correctional facility for youths) and their adult bid, up north in one of New York State many correctional facilities. Rondu was a career criminal, a killer and was a stick-up kid - you name it. Once everything was over and they left Bo-Bo was able to maneuver, knocked over the phone, and dialed 911 for help.

111

Lynn was taken to the hospital where she was kept for observation due to a concussion. Fat Cat was furious and was seeking answers and wanted blood. First of all, only a few and I mean a few, knew where Lynn lived. So how in the hell did a guy like Ron-du know of or was able to get to Lynn's doorstep? Something wasn't right with that picture. And why didn't Ron-Du and his crew not kill everyone? It didn't take long for Cat to realize it was Jus-Me, of Fat Cat's own crew, who set that robbery up. But Jus-Me made Ron-du swear that no one would die. Within days Cat gave the order to eliminate Just-Me, RonDu, and any of his known associates.

Within a short period of time Issac Bolden aka Just-Me was murdered. Next a van pulled up near the Claremont Public Housing projects in the Bronx an area where Henry Bolden aka Ron-du grew up. Inside the van Tu-Bar, Bo-Bo and Slim waited for days before one night when Ron-du came out of hiding and they spotted him coming out of his old building in the projects. As Tu-bar, Bo-Bo and Slim used walkie talkies to stay in contact. Ron-du being who he was, a notorious stick up kid, with several "beefs" with folks he robbed and shot, was on point watching his ass as he traveled through the dark.

Slim was the one who had the best shot of taken Ron-du down, but call it a six sense, Ron-du was on point as Slim went in for the kill. As Ron-du was walking his hand dropped to his side to what appeared to be an Automatic colt 45. At that time Slim just start firing at Rondu and he started firing back. Bo-Bo came from the other side and start firing at Ron-du, emptying his clip from the opposite side. Fortunately, Ron-du got away with his life. Unfortunately, as Slim and Bo-Bo got back into the van Tu-bar went off on them both, yelling and screaming, "How in the hell did you botch that hit? We had him, and you allowed this dangerous mother fucker to get away. Fat Cat isn't going to like this." Based upon Ron-du's reputation Slim and Bo-Bo were both out of their league and in my opinion, you can't send a ticket scalper or a young cat with no experience after someone like Ron-du. Tu-Bar popped all of that shit, but his big ass didn't get out of that van to go after Ron-du.

At that time The Round Table was formed by Fat Cat while we were still in prison; only Cat, Pappy, Supreme, Prince were members. The Round Table was formed on the belief that based on each of their own positions of power, because of their reputation and respect from many of our criminal peers and admirers; it would prevent further attacks on their families, friends and themselves. Unfortunately wishing doesn't always make it so.

When I first Met Pappy Mason

In retrospect, I first met Pappy back in October of 1985, just before Parole Officer Rooney was killed and I was in South Jamaica Queens, visiting Jug Head. I'd met Jug Head back in 1982, when we were both incarcerated at Coxsackie.

Jug Head and I were talking outside about a large package he wanted to give me, so I could start hustling. While we were talking, Pappy drove up in a black Jeep Renegade. A person by the name Lamont was with him. Both got out of the Jeep and came towards us. Pappy and Lamont were both dressed in black fatigue suits and wearing dark shades. I remember Pappy was wearing a large rope chain which had a big square gold piece with a man on the inside and the name "Be-Bo" in large diamond letters. Lamont and I started talking about the days we spent together on Rikers Island and then Pappy and I were introduced. I continued my conversation with Jug Head and told him I wasn't established and therefore not quite ready to move a large drug package. I told him that when I felt I was ready, then I'd get back to him.

A few days later Parole Officer Rooney was murdered and a couple of weeks after that Pappy was arrested and charged with Rooney's murder. When Pappy was arrested by homicide detectives he was with Raphael "Ruff" Ruffin they were in Pappy's black Jeep. Ruff had started practicing the Rastafarian ways shortly after Pappy did and so both had long dreads when they were stopped. At first, Ruff was pretending to be Pappy. The detectives didn't really know who was who and were about to take Ruff in, when Pappy spoke up and said that he was really Howard "Pappy" Mason.

Ruff and Pappy loved each other like brothers. When Pappy was serving the 0 to 7-year bid, Ruff was there for him. Ruff used to visit Pappy on a regular basis, going from jail to jail. He would buy food packages for Pappy and bring them to him during visits, and even smuggle marijuana to Pappy in small balloons. Ruff was Pappy's family and pretty much the only one who was there for him and when Pappy was in Clinton, it was probably Ruff's constant contact with him that kept Pappy from getting murdered when he was raising so much hell.

The next time I saw Pappy was now at Brooklyn House of Detention for Men, while both of us were awaiting trial for murder.

Fat Cat's Introduction to the Drug Game

To keep things in perspective, a few things you should know about Fat Cat. Back when Cat was paroled in 1980 for criminal activity, he took his time getting into the drug game. The drug game was something totally new to him and he was selling small quantities of heroin -- dime bags -- with the name "Pink Shade" stamped on the bags. Cat was doing his best to be a good hustler, but things weren't going so great. He was barely making ends meet and was living off his wife, Mousey, in a one-bedroom apartment in the basement of Cat's mother's house, in South

Jamaica Queens. In late 1982 or early 1983, Cat started progressing in the game. He started making major moves, buying several kilos of cocaine at a time. Back then a kilo of cocaine was going for between $25,000 and $35,000.

A guy named Old Man Danny oversaw 150th Street and 107th Avenue drug blocks. He was the man making all the major moves in that area. But in the drug game you have your ups and downs and that's what happened with Old Man Danny. He killed a guy who had beaten him out of a large sum of money. A fellow by the name of Perry Bellamy witnessed the whole thing. Perry worked for Danny at the time and so did Cat. But Danny wouldn't let Cat sell the same product at the same price as he did. For example, if Danny was selling $10 and $20 bags of cocaine and heroin, then Cat had to sell $3 and $5 bags of cocaine and heroin. At the time, Cat was making between $30,000 and $50,000 a day.

Old Man Danny was arrested and charged with the murder of the guy who had beaten him for that large sum of money. Danny awaited trial on Rikers Island, and once he went to jail Fat Cat took over the 150th Street and 107th Avenue drug blocks.

When Danny went to trial, the star witness for the Queens County District Attorney was Perry Bellamy. Rumor had it that Cat paid Perry a huge sum of money to take the witness stand against Danny. Cat felt if he were to be acquitted on the murder charge, then Danny would return home and take back the drug blocks. If that would've happened, then Cat would have had to put a hit on Danny in order to keep control of the blocks. But Cat, being the master of the game, knew if Perry, who was already a known police informer, testified against Danny then Cat, would be relieved of the problem without having to get his hands dirty.

Only a chosen few knew exactly what happened with Cat's involvement with Perry testifying against Danny. Things became more obvious after Perry testified and Danny was convicted. Danny called Cat and told him that Perry had testified against him, and he wanted Cat to have him killed. Danny's request went unwarranted and Perry was constantly around the block. Pappy never liked Perry and wanted to kill him. Pappy hated a snitch and he used to tell that to Cat all the time. But Cat used to tell Pappy to leave Perry alone. Danny was sentenced to life and died in jail in 1987 or 1988 of cancer.

Cat soon started making real money. His daily income increased to around $100,000 a day and he had a lot of guys working with and for him. Just before Cat got really large, a childhood pal, named Chase, came to see him. Chase was into robbing armored cars and he had set up a move but was short one gunman. So, Cat contacted TA and asked him to come to the block. When TA arrived, Chase ran down the plan to him and he was impressed and became part of the move. Chase's plan worked out to the letter. The move was a success and Chase and his crew made off with over half million dollars. Out of loyalty, Chase paid homage to Cat by giving him a nice portion of the loot. But someone tipped-off the New York Police Department and Chase and TA were arrested and charged with armed robbery. Word had it that TA left between $150,000 and $200,000 with Cat, and those were the funds Cat used to really get established in the drug game and he never looked back. The rest, as they say, is history.

Cat told me that from Sunday to Wednesday he used to make anywhere from $100,000 to $200,000 a day selling bagged-up heroin and cocaine. From Thursday to Saturday he would average between $200,000 and $350,000 a day. None of that was counting the money his workers or crew members owed him from receiving cocaine on consignment. Cat liked it when the price of cocaine was as high as $50,000 a kilo; it eliminated some competition.

During 1983 Fat Cat's name was being heard all throughout the Metropolitan area of New York City, including in the upstate New York State correctional facilities, as one of the biggest drug dealers in New York City.

When Pappy Joined Up with Fat Cat

When Pappy went to Queens to see his good friend, Fat Cat, which he met on Rikers Island back in 1976 he gave Pappy about $5,000 to help him get back on his feet; then Pappy told Cat that he wanted a position in his organization. Cat told him the only position he had available was a security position. Cat explained that position meant that Pappy had to be strapped with a gun at all times, make sure none of Cat's workers got robbed, and if anybody got out of line, including customers, then it would be Pappy's job to put them in their place. Pappy was told that he would have to patrol 150th Street and 107th Avenue, and be able to protect Cat's people, and surrounding areas 12 hours a day, six days a week. Cat said the job paid $1,000 a week. After laying down the job to Pappy, Cat was surprised when he accepted.

Pappy arrived on time the very next day, just as if he were reporting to a regular 9 to 5 job. Each and every day Pappy was supposed to be at work, he was there and on time. That impressed Fat Cat.

When Pappy came to Queens, he gave Cat's organization the brute force it was lacking and made Cat a person not to be fucked with. Cat had several workers who would just disappear with drug package or owing him money, or both. Pappy would go out, find them, and bring them in. When someone was "brought in" after fucking up or trying to beat Cat for drugs or money, it meant being

117

taken at gun point sometimes being thrown into the trunk of a car or in a van and taken to one of Cat's stash houses. Once there, the person would be stripped naked and chained or otherwise tied up in the basement. Next came the beatings with Billy-clubs and leather straps and fed only dog food and water. There was no doubt that Pappy was brutal, but he got the job done and was the best security enforcer Cat had at the time.

After about a month or so, Cat suggested to Pappy that he bring out a few more guys for security. Cat found out that Pappy was knocked out, sleeping on the pool table several times and began feeling sorry for him. The 12-hour days, six days a week, plus Pappy's after work activities began to take their toll. Cat sympathized with Pappy; he knew his job was rough and he liked Pappy a lot at the time.

Pappy Starts the Be-bos

Pappy continued as Cat's top security enforcer for about a year-and-a-half, making about $10,000 a week. He went from $1,000 to $10,000 a week before Cat sent him out on his own, in 1985, to start his own organization.

Word had it, the reason Cat gave Pappy his blessings to start his own organization was because Pappy was bringing too much heat on Cat, and he knew that would eventually bring him down. Pappy and his people were always into something and what Cat hated most was that Pappy always used violence to settle everything, and Cat didn't really agree with the philosophy of absolute violence. Besides several guys from Queens who lived there all their lives hustling told Cat that he needed to calm Pappy down. Since he'd arrived with his Brooklyn crew the murder rate had really increased.

A lot of guys in Queens hated Pappy, but none of them would tell him that to his face. It might sound silly, but guys from Queens didn't like guys from Brooklyn. Brooklyn and Queens were prejudiced against each other, because they lived in different parts of the Metropolitan area. I know it sounds crazy but it's true -- and sad too.

The bottom line was that several guys in Queens didn't like the guys from Brooklyn coming to their area and making moves: scaring the shit out of them and having sex with the girls. Most of the drug crews from Queens just didn't like Pap, but they respected him, as they all knew he'd kill them without blinking an eye. It was really more fear than respect.

Cat was the only one who could control Pap and make him listen to reason. Jug Head could talk sense into Pap too; as Cat, Pap, and Jug Head were real close. They had been that way since the days on Rikers Island in 1976. Plus, Jug Head was an original Brooklynite.

Pappy and his crew, the Be-Bos, were "hustling backwards," as Cat put it. He said, Pap and his people weren't making any good money on the hustling tip, because Pap's bag-up crew used to put very little product in the bag or capsule. In New York City there's entirely too much competition from other drug dealers, which allowed customers to buy a decent bag or capsule of cocaine or heroin. Therefore, many people refused to buy from Pap's workers or at his spots.

At the time, Pap's headquarters was a rundown game room on South Road and 107th Avenue. Pappy was getting about five kilos of cocaine at a time from Cat on consignment. Cat would buy between 30 and 50 kilos at a time and in the drug trade the more you buy the cheaper it gets. So, when Cat gave a kilo of cocaine to anyone on consignment, he usually made between $10,000 and $15,000 profit. Cat gave coke on consignment to plenty of guys, as well as different quantities of heroin on consignment. Pappy, Jug Head, AB, Bo-Bo, Luke, Fat Jeff,

Pea Nut, and many more were getting cocaine and heroin from Cat on consignment.

Married in Prison

Well, back to me. What was I thinking; my murder trial was only a few months away. In all reality when I think back to April 13, 1987, the day I jumped the broom and got married at Rikers Island, I was doing the woman I loved a disservice. I was 23 years of age, incarcerated, fighting for my life, seeking to beat a murder, attempted murder, kidnapping and weapon charges and I was guilty as sin. I was young and reckless and didn't know a dam thing about marriage and being a good husband, and to be governed by the bonds of matrimony. I was fateful while in prison.

Tamia James was the girl I married. "I knew Tamia for about 15 years. I started a relationship with her in December of 1985. I was sexually involved with a lot of girls during the time. I guess I was spreading my oats. On May 5, the night before I turned myself in for the murder charge, Tamia was the last woman I slept with.

New York State has a law; if you have a life sentence you are considered to be legally dead. I happen to have a funny feeling about the word, "dead," especially if it's in reference to me. I always try my damndest to avoid that area. With the thought of being legally dead on my mind, I started talking marriage. I asked damn near every girl I dealt with, and didn't deal with, to marry me and they all said yes except one, Sasha Baylor, who told me to wait until I was released and then she'd marry me.

I ran down my list and gave it some thought, because, in New York State jail system, when you're married you get conjugal visits with your wife for 48-72 hours. She gets to sleep with you in a mobile home.

After weighing the facts and who I knew the longest, I decided to marry Tamia. I truly loved her. I guess I was more attracted to her, because she was and still is so gorgeous, and she truly loved me. When I was putting the marriage game into effect, Sasha changed her mind and decided that she wanted to marry me. But it was already too late. Everything that was needed was already put into motion and I was just waiting for the day to come to say, "I do."

The day came. It was Monday, April 13, 1987, at about 9:40 A.M. I was nervous, and it felt like butterflies were flying around in my stomach. Two other guys besides me got married that day. My sister was our witness. I gave Tamia the money to buy her own engagement and wedding ring; I didn't want a wedding band. When I got married, I sent out the jewelry I was wearing to Tamia. I stopped all the other girls from coming to see me. I stopped calling and writing them, and I decided that I was going to be a faithful and a dedicated husband. To this day, I honestly believe that Tamia wasn't ready for marriage. It seemed like she married me just to have something to do. She had a lot of pressure on her, her friends were telling her not to marry me, because I was only marrying her because I was facing life in prison, and that I still had a bunch of girls coming to see me. Her friends would ask her why I'd only let her visit me one day a week, when there were three days allowed for visits every week. They would remind her of the times when I was on the street, all the different girls that she saw me with. During our visits she would bring up these thoughts. I would tell her, "First of all, the majority of your so-called friends are a bunch of renegade females who have never been and will never be loyal or faithful to any one man." I had to sit back and allow her to see reality for what it was. For the whole thirteen months and seventeen days of incarceration, I took care of her. Her phone was shut off and I had the bill paid, plus the penalty to have it turned back on. Every time she wanted money to go clothes shopping for her and her son, I arranged for her to receive money to take care of it, and when she wanted a fur coat that was taken care of. When Christmas and birthdays came around, she received a nice sum of money. Other times, my man, Herman, dropped off $10,000 to her.

Once I was married, I lost contact with all other females, by choice. I felt that my wife would be able to take care of my business for me, visit on all three of my visiting days, and come to court as she'd always done.

The Sybil Murder Trial

Married and with the jury selected my trial for the murder of Sybil started the week of June 15, 1987. My attorney was Murray Cutler, his son Bruce Cutler, was John Gotti's well known attorney. My new wife, family and friends were at the trial to support me. Sybil Mims' family was there, too.

The coroner took the stand and said that Sybil had died from gunshot wounds to the head and body. Sybil's sister took the stand and testified that she had been the one who identified Sybil's body, and had received a telephone call from Crazy Clyde, who said that Sybil was last seen with Amare and me. She also said that Clyde told her that he had done something to me and I must have found out and that is why I killed Sybil. She was crying through her whole testimony. The District Attorney and Cutler both cross-examined her. I thought he was doing a superb job. The arresting officer, on the attempted murder charge, took the stand and repeated a statement that Terrence gave him. Cutler "ate him up" on the cross-examination, by asking him if I, Glaze, went into a crowded restaurant with over a hundred customers present, and tried to drag Terrence out of the restaurant while he was shouting, "Don't kill me! Don't kill me!" then where were the witnesses? And where was the physical evidence, such as the handguns and casings, and photos of the crime scene? Cutler also said that if everything happened according to Terrence's statement, then why the White Castle security guard or other White Castle employees, who were protected by bullet-proof glass didn't call the police? A valid answer couldn't be given. Cutler then explained to the jury that a valid answer couldn't be given, because the crime never occurred, and Terrence made up the whole story. When Terrence finally took the stand his hostile and disrespectful attitude supported Cutler's claim, that he was a drug addict and could not be trusted.

Detective Richard Brew, the arresting officer for the murder charge, took the stand. He said that he was assigned to the case and was at the murder scene after the crime. He testified that he and his partner canvassed the area and went door to door to see if anyone had heard or seen anything. He said a lead from the family and Clyde Gibbs claiming that Sybil was last seen with Amare, and that was the basis for picking up Amare for questioning. He said Amare confessed to be the driver and fingered Glaze as the trigger man. But when my attorney, Cutler, inquired as to Amare's whereabouts and asked why Amare had changed his mind about testifying, Detective Brew could only say, "I don't know." The District Attorney and Murray Cutler finally gave their closing arguments, and after Judge Egitto charged the jury, they were sent away for deliberations. Other witnesses, including Clyde also changed their mind about testifying.

By Monday, June 22, 1987, my case was in the hands of the jury. I must admit I was scared to death and honestly did not know what the outcome would be: life without parole for the murder, and up to twenty years imprisonment for the attempted murder.

After several hours elapsed, I was taken from the holding cell into the Brooklyn Supreme Court to stand in front of Judge Francis Eggitto; my lawyer, my mother, and family sat, waiting anxiously. The judge looked toward the juror's box and asked the foreman, "How do you find the defendant on the first count of murder in the second degree?" The foreman responded by saying, "Not guilty." I can still remember hearing the loud sound of my mother's cries of joy. They found me, not guilty on all charges. I broke down and was crying as I was on my way back to the holding area with the rest of the inmates, until I was to be released.

As I got back to the holding cell several inmates wanted to console me. They were all under the impression that I blew the trail. I had to tell them that the tears running down my cheeks were like a bride's tears of joy -- acquitted on all charges.

Less than an hour expired before my paperwork was processed and I was taken back to the court room and released where I met up with my lawyer, family, and friends. I said, softly, "Free at last, free at last. Thank God Almighty; I am free at last." But how long would my freedom last? *Obviously, I believed many reading my story may see my verdict as another example of "Blind Justice," but if you believe in God and wonder why people like me keep getting another chance? Well, I wonder myself, but I'm not one to second guess God.*

Viva Atlantic City

After the acquittal the opportunities that I would be offered were based on my brand called "Glaze." But before thinking about employment, my wife and I took a cab and headed to Cypress Hill Houses where I showered and put on an outfit she had purchased for me. I called a limousine and we went to Atlantic City to celebrate. We enjoyed dinner at a fine restaurant, and polished off a bottle of Dom Perignon, headed to our room and made love until falling asleep holding hands. The next thing I knew, it was morning when I received a wakeup call from the front desk. I showered, got dressed and took the limo back to Cypress Hills, dropped off my wife and headed to Rikers Island to visit my man Tiny, Cat, Pappy and a few others. I received a greeting as if I was a big celebrity; all the inmates and a few guards who knew or heard of me greeted me with respect and admiration. *Not your world, I understand.*

Myeshia - Pushing-Up on Amare

During the visit I ran into a young lady, named Myeshia, and her son, T.C., which stood for "Top Cat." Myeshia was on her way to visit Fat Cat. Pappy Mason also had a visit that day, a young lady, named Lisa, who was a correction officer at Queens Houses. My identification wasn't really in order, but I was allowed in just the same, as the officers knew me, but they did tell me to get the proper identification. Fat Cat and Pappy told Myeshia to take me to get proper identification, and for me to come back to see them for the Thursday visit. Fat Cat was at the time was still married to Mousey with Myeshia on the side. Little did I know then, that in the near future, I would be responsible for Myeshia's execution.

I also went to see my brother, Kool- Aid, at C-95, and my man, Black. Then I went to see Fat Cat, Pappy, and Rennie -- yes, Rennie. Despite the fact I stabbed Rennie, when previously we went at it in the court holding cell, me and Rennie became cool again. When Amare was brought down from Coxsackie, preparing to testify against me for Sybil's Murder, I wrote Rennie and told him that he could help me and I could help him, and to put our beef to the side. I apologized for stabbing him and I didn't want to pursue the issue, and if he helped me by pushing up on Amare, to make sure that he did the right thing, then I'd take care of the main witness against him, who was still on the street. Rennie saw Amare, with my man, Wallee Comer, and pushed up on Amare to make sure that he corrected his mistake of fingering me as the trigger man in Sybil's murder. Amare also received a large sum of money and was more or less told that if he would've taken the stand against me, then his mother would've received numerous gunshot wounds in her face. With all those thoughts and that money package, plus a lawyer was hired for him, he refused to testify. Amare told me that he was shocked when Rennie approached him, because I'd tried to kill him -- and he was still going to bat for me, by pushing up on him and telling him not to testify. I felt I owed Rennie.

While visiting with Pappy Mason, he wanted me to get down with him and his crew the "Be-Bos". Pappy's crew purchased drugs from Fat Cat and I thought, why should I work for Pappy when I can work for Cat? I decided to take a few weeks off to think about it and left New York.

When I arrived back in New York, a female friend picked me up from the airport. This particular young lady offered to buy me a 1987 Mercedes Benz 560 SEL, if I would get a divorce, and said that I didn't even have to marry her. Her family had money, but I never was into letting a female do anything for me. If I wanted something, then I would buy it myself. I didn't want anyone, especially a woman feeling that she could buy me.

I was spending a lot of time out of town with a young lady, named Tatyana. Yet, I always returned to New York to be with the other girls I knew, including Tamia – my wife. Sorry Tamia, if you are reading this.

During Christmas 1987, I stopped by Tamia's aunt's house and gave her a mink jacket and something for her aunt. That's when I learned Tamia was carrying my child. This was the first turning point in my life in crime. There would be another person that my life on the street could and did affect.

I wanted Tamia, my child and myself to live somewhere safe. So, I'd given Tamia several thousand dollars and she went with my brother, Country, to find either an apartment or a house. She had an apartment set up, but the owners changed their minds, saying the money was drug money. This occurred on numerous occasions. Finally, I decided to buy a house in Elmont, on Long Island. The price was $120,000. I put $27,000 down and paid someone who would take care of it. Unfortunately, I was at war with several different crews at the time and an associate, L.D., advised me not to buy the house in Elmont. He told me the individuals with whom I was warring were very dangerous and would think nothing of driving to Long Island and suggested the safest thing would be for her to leave New York and maybe even move down south.

Chapter Six - The Corporate World

Gangsters Inc. A Free Agent

With the acquittal for the murder of Sybil Mims, attempted murder, kidnapping, and weapon charges I was on cloud nine; a free man after lying up for thirteen months and seventeen days fighting that case -- free at last. *I don't think that was what Martin Luther King meant.* Anyway, *I was free. I don't know if it was subconscious or upfront in my mind, but with my record, filling out a job application wasn't going to guarantee me a management position in the corporate world. However, possibly in a multilevel marketing company; which is what the illegal drug distribution is really all about. However, unlike Mary Kay's we won't be caught dead in pink Cadillacs.*

I beat the system which is rare; the chance of any defendant beating a state case is only 20%. It's 93% for the federal government verses 7% for the defendant. The risk verses reward ratio is extremely high. I was one of the chosen few, who were guilty as anyone could be; rolled the dice and won -- that pissed off a lot of people. Now it was time to see how my life in crime would continue and who was going to be my new employer. Options, options, options...

Several days after my release I was receiving offers to become part of the most prominent and well-established drug organizations. I literally felt like a free agent being recruited for a basketball, football and or baseball team.

Like in the corporate world, offers included a generous, cash sign up bonus. Stock *options weren't an option, unlike the big drug companies*. The most profitable were bidding for my service. They all wanted me to be an important member of their team, all because of the brand I had built and being a seasoned living veteran of my trade, which included the following:

(1) A ruthless murderer.

(2) Career criminal with 4 felony conviction.

(3) To date in and out jail a total of 5 years and known as a one-man wrecking crew.

(4) Proven and tested via the judicial system.

Beside Fat Cat, a.k.a. Lorenzo Nichols, and Pappy Mason and several other crews, one in particular's offer stood out was Baby Sam, a.k.a. Samuel Edmondson. He was originally from East New York and had one hell of a reputation and a number one crew.

Baby Sam came to Cypress Hill Houses personally to recruit me. Sam was the real deal and truly not a person you would want to be enemies with. When Baby Sam contacted me, he pulled up across the street from my 1266 Sutter Avenue apartment in a silver Cadillac limousine. The funny and surprising part about the whole encounter was that Sam was actually driving the limo. He got out wearing a tailor-made suit, with a bulletproof vest. His pitch was, I didn't have to do much for $10,000-$20,000 dollars a week. In the corporate world, you would need more than a high school diploma to accomplish that. I would be his right-hand man; to be there during all large drug and cash transactions. And whenever there was serious beef and enemies had to be eliminated, I would be there, ready, willing and able to kill at will.

Despite the offer was tempting and he had numerous drug spots in Brooklyn at the time. Some of his crack locations were generating approximately $100,000 to 150,000 thousand a week. I'm not sure if even a Mary Kay or a Coca Cola distributorship could generate that kind of income. My feeling then, why would I want to be down with Sam and his crew, when the majority of his crew was all leaders and were capable of running their own crew. There was Johnny Ray, Victor, and Big Amar' and Kyle. My thoughts were too many would-be chiefs and not enough Indians. Plus, I wanted to be my own boss, build my own brand and run my own crew. That was one good decision. On March 2, 1989, Sam and his crew were arrested and indicted on a 70-count indictment including: drug racketeering, 9 murders, 7 attempted murders, and several assaults and weapons charges. The arrests stemmed from his involvement in the murder of a New York housing cop, searching for a missing child when he walked right into a drug deal that cost him his life. Eventually, Sam and his crew all received several life sentences.

It's ironic, I never saw Baby Sam again, although over time I was getting heat from some of their crimes that he and his crew were later convicted of committing. On March 31, 1988, in the Bedford Stuyvesant section of Brooklyn in the Glamorama Beauty Parlor, the shop owner James Hamilton Sr. and a beautician, Shirley Bibbs were victims of a hail of 9 mm bullets. During the investigation a pregnant woman went to the Brooklyn DA's office claiming to have witnessed the whole incident from a distance. She sat down, went thru the mug shots, and picked out the one they called GLAZE as the shooter. Joe Ponzi, a Brooklyn detective and his team weren't convinced that I was involved, feeling they needed more evidence. *I couldn't be the only murderer in the five boroughs of New York City.*

As I said I had the opportunity to be a part of Pappy Mason's organization, the Bebos, but passed it up. He wanted me to work alongside him as his number one guy. Honestly, I was not a fan of his present number one guy, "Ruff," aka Rafael Ruffin. In my eyes, he was a coward and he got away with a lot of shit; if it wasn't for Pappy, he would have been murdered a long time ago. Ruff used to set up shop in unauthorized areas that members of Fat Cat's crews were operating - not cool. At one point in time Ruff entered into one of Fat Cat's top workers' areas and he came so close to Cat giving me the order to murder Ruff, but again he was spared because of Pap and I didn't doubt that Pap knew Ruff was stepping on the other's toes.

Later it was Ruff who made a deal with the Federal Government and finally helped solve the murder of a rookie Parole Officer, Brian Rooney. He informed the US Attorney that it was the Lucas Brothers, Lamont and Randy who pulled the trigger on Parole Officer Rooney. Ruff later ratted about the involvement of Fat Cat, Pap, Jug and Bo.

If Pappy was home and not in prison probably being a part of his crew would have been a bit more appealing. More disturbing to me was that his crew was a bunch of wannabe Rastafarian and that was not my style. I could identify with Pap, although it was also hard for me to identify with the Bebos - we didn't share the same values. Ruff even wanted to be down with me, but he was a clown. The bottom line, his crew the Bebos was too un-organized for my liking; so I kindly declined.

Joining Up with Fat Cat and My M&M Crew

It was shortly after I turned down Baby Sam's offer to work for him, that I received a message that Fat Cat wanted to talk to me. My life would change, believing it would be for the better. I got away with murder, more than once; unfortunately, that made me start to feel untouchable. I had established a relationship with Lorenzo "Fat Cat" Nichols that would drag me into the opposite direction of the Lord our God and toward the creation of my crew, M&M, Money and Murder. We did not have colors, gangs had colors, blue for Crips, red for Bloods; we would be a money-making crew.

I was offered that opportunity when Lorenzo "Fat Cat" Nichols, the largest drug dealer on the east coast of the United States, gave me the Key's to his organization. He was running what was left of his organization from prison. This would be a win, win situation. *He was still in charge of his operation, the CEO Chief Executive Officer and I was to be CFO, Chief Financial Officer, and responsible for hiring and firing - literally.*

Receiving the opportunity to run one of the Largest drug empires on the East Coast was an opportunity that I could not pass up. It was too good to be true. Unfortunately, no stock option or 401K program was included. Cat was the major supplier for most of Queens and Brooklyn. Anyone who wanted a large weight of cocaine or heroin, one way or another, it came from Lorenzo "Fat Cat" Nichols. I must give credit where credit is due. *Lorenzo was probably one of three most intelligent people I met, but not enough, to not get caught.* A great mentor, if only for the right reason and the right cause, life would have been so different. All through the years before Fat Cat made his position at the top, the positions and their crews changed as soon as any drug organization got too big. Then the quality of employees degraded, errors in judgment, arrogance and just dumb black men without loyalty or common sense would get caught and "flip", snitch to go free or cut deals to lessen their sentence. *It's relative; not intended to be hypocritical.*

During October 1987, just about everyone who Cat could really depend on was either in jail or addicted to drugs. Cat felt time was running out and that he needed somebody who was reliable. *Eventually, I became involved to the point that I was overseeing anything that Cat was involved in, anything involving the business, or violence.*

At the time I took over Cat's crew, it was falling apart, and needed someone to manage it on the outside. Pappy was in jail due to parole officer Brian Rooney's murder and a weapons charge. Jug Head, was another player from Brooklyn. He, Cat, and Pappy went way back to Spofford correctional days. Their bond was like a brotherhood especially since Cat did not have any brothers, only older sisters. Jug Head was one of Cat's top guys until late 1985 when he went on the run after his name was implicated in Parole Officer Brian Rooney's murder and finally caught a drug case in Baltimore. Luc was another solider working for Cat, who was in jail and Cat didn't trust him because he was always getting high. There was a cat named Bo-Bo who had been dealing forever, but as Cat would say, Bo-Bo was a fuck-up. So, when I got home, I was in the best position to get the job done right. I was now in charge of the largest drug organization on the East Coast and would build my team M&M. Fat Cat and I was an easy choice by far.

Back then, before Bo-Bo disappeared, he and Cat had one of those love-hate relationships. One day Cat loved Bo-Bo like a brother, then, the next thing you know, Cat wanted him dead. To me, Bo-Bo was a good dude and he kept people laughing. Bo-Bo wasn't the violent type. He was more the slick type; someone who would run a con game on a person. Cat held him responsible for the drug raid of July 29, 1985, which resulted in Cat receiving a prison sentence of 25 years to life. Cat felt that if Bo-Bo would've told him that a worker, who worked for Bo-Bo, had been arrested, then Cat, would have been prepared for the raid; knowing the worker would fold under pressure and eventually try to set him up to take a fall.

Bo-Bo, at a moment in time, owed Cat about a million dollars, because, when Bo-Bo was in charge of the operation, he was constantly messing up by playing "Big Willie", living beyond his means; spending not only the money he was making for himself, but also spending Cat's money. He spent money on different girls, gave money to both his and Cat's family members and friends, gambled, and lost large drug packages – just to name a few things, but he was really funny.

One time, Cat gave Bo-Bo $30,000, it was April 1987. Bo-Bo was supposed to place a $20,000 bet on the Las Vegas boxing match between Marvelous Marvin Hagler and Sugar Ray Leonard. He was supposed to bet on Sugar Ray to win. The other $10,000 was Bo-Bo's; for his plane and hotel expenses, and pocket money. However, when Bo-Bo went to Vegas he got on the crap table and lost the whole $30,000 -- always playing a big shot. Hagler lost the fight, so Bo-Bo tried to run a con on Cat by telling him that he thought Cat wanted him to put the money on Hagler to win. Unfortunately for Bo-Bo, a lot of other New York hustlers were at the fight and word got back to Cat that Bo-Bo lost about $30,000 on the crap table.

Bo-Bo was in a position to become a millionaire. But because he was always playing the big shot, gambling, getting high and just plain fucking up, he never realized his potential. One thing I can say about Bo-Bo is that he was loyal to Cat. Fat Cat put a murder contract on Bo-Bo's head a number of times, but Bo-Bo usually got wind of it and disappeared for a few months, until Cat calmed down.

The last hit Cat put on Bo-Bo was in October 1987. Cat gave me the order to kill Bo-Bo on sight. During that time I was visiting Pappy and told him that Cat wanted me to kill Bo-Bo. Pappy told me to tell Cat to nix the hit on Bo-Bo, because he knew that he was a funny motherfucker. Pappy told me all of that in Pig Latin language because Pap was at the Brooklyn House of Detention at the time. The next time I visited Cat, on Rikers Island, I told him what Pappy said and Cat called off the hit. But Bo-Bo still stayed away for about two or three months.

Unwelcomed by Cat's Family and Crew

Initially, my arrival to Queens as the new man in charge of operations was not welcomed by Cat's family and crew. I had to win them over and that wasn't going to be easy. However, after several incidents occurred around 107th Street and 150th Avenue, a couple of Cat's hand to hand dealers were shot and robbed by a local stick up crew. An opportunity to turn them around then presented itself. Fortunately for me and unfortunately for the leader of the stick-up crew who came up missing and weeks later his dead body was found in a boarded up abandon building, next to an empty box of Glazed donuts. After that nothing was said, however Cat's family and his workers attitude was totally different towards me and my authority was no longer questioned. *Welcome to South Jamaica, Queens.*

My days were spent running around Brooklyn to Queens, providing security for large purchase transactions of kilos of cocaine and heroin and taking care of the business at hand. I opened up new shops in Brooklyn; selling crack cocaine and heroin in Fort Greene, Coney Island, East New York, Bedford Stuyvesant and anywhere I could, and I did. I was being creative as far as selling more for less and it was definitely a new challenge. I was selling crack that other dealers were selling for $10 dollars, I was selling for $5 dollars, and what they were selling for $5 dollars I was selling for $3 dollars. The heroin I was purchasing was so good it had me moving so much of it that I was in the position to purchase larger amounts of kilos of cocaine. To cook cocaine and sell it as the substance called crack. Crack has been the #1 drug of choice since the early 1980s. I have seen so many people fall victim to the pipe, that the street named it "*the glass dick.*" It was a shame how so many people had lost their lives, freedom, family and livelihood by sucking on that glass dick. That chemical was so addictive and powerful that each and every one who indulged could not help

135

themselves, but to be caught up into the wonderful world of CRACK! New users were blind to its destruction of drugs, seeing didn't been believing. I never understood it, I just supplied it.

One example that really freaked me out was the story of Darlene new to the drug game. She entered her friend's Rachel's apartment looking to shoot some heroin after finding one more excuse to use again. When you shoot enough heroin, you reach a point where you aren't shooting it to get high; you're shooting just to take away the sickness. There is no high, but your body craves more and more and more. It's an endless roller coaster.

Darlene entered this filthy apartment which looked more like a crash pad than a family home. There were newspapers all over the floor, bits and pieces of clothing lying on chairs, overflowing ashtrays, discarded food wrappers, and three sets of works sitting on top of the TV. Darlene asked Rachel's husband, "Where is she?

Entering Rachel's bedroom Darlene stood transfixed. Rachel's son is sitting next to her on the bed with a tray of ice cubes, shoving them up inside her vagina. This was something she'd seen before. Rachel had overdosed, and the ice cubes helped somehow. Rachel's son, continued with the ice, looking at Darlene, commenting, "She over dosed; Dad and I are bringing her around." Darlene nodded, unable to speak. As she hears Rachel's husband calling out, asking if she would like a cup of coffee. Darlene didn't answer. She couldn't believe it. She'd heard that ice cubes helped greatly, and she could even see her husband treating her, but her son? It really disgusted her. If she didn't need drugs so badly, she would have walked out. Instead she offered to help. Little by little Rachel came around. With that Rachel's son looked at Darlene and said, "She's okay now com'on, share a bag. We all need to relax."

Back to Business

Managing Fat Cat operation and M&M business was awesome. I was now making over $40,000 per day. I was ghetto rich and in position to do whatever I wanted, and whenever I wanted. I didn't allow anything or anyone to interfere with the tasks at hand, meaning if anyone opposed, crossed, disrespected, or did anything that violated any of my people, family, friends, friends of the family, the penalty could and normally was death.

At that time, as I reflect upon it now, I had a lot of things on my plate, running my day to day operation, and overseeing the largest east coast operation. The key to my success was largely due to my ability to manage. The main criteria was TRUST, I had to be able to trust each and every member of my crew who was going to be around me and Fat Cat's Operation. I selected family members, guys mostly from the neighborhood, brothers I knew from when I did time, and those with strong referrals. I built a very strong crew. A crew that was willing to do any and everything from A to Z on my command, without hesitation. I had murderers working for me and guys whose job was to just pick up and drop off drugs and money. *But it seems that most everything has an expiration date. I understand the earth as we know it has one as well.*

Push it

If you're going to be drug dealer, you will need your own brand. *Taking a marketing course, maybe very helpful.* When there are a million and one drug spots throughout the five boroughs, how does anyone compete? It's like having a liquor store on every corner. Why should someone purchase from you verses the next drug spot. In the drug game you must be creative to have your customers know that they are receiving a quality product at a bargain price. I would get my heroin from Fat Cat. The first package of heroin, he told me to put a 1 or 2 on it, but I was greedy and put a 6 on it.

For example it's like taking a kilo of heroin and cutting it with 6 kilos of Bonita and Quinine (these are cutting agents for heroin) combined, so instead of 1 kilo of heroin you now have 7 kilos of heroin. If the heroin is good, and it can handle the cut, chances are you will make a lot of money. But if the `heroin can't handle the cut, it will take you forever to sell your packages. Nevertheless, I learned a valuable lesson after it took me forever to sell the package. I never made that stupid mistake again.

The next package that I received Cat told me to put a 1 on it. So, I mixed the kilo of Heroin with a half of kilo of Bonita; it was selling out like hot cakes. That product was so hot that I name it "Push It," after the song by the girl rap group, Salt & Pepper called *Push It Real Good*. I made so much money off of that title I literally couldn't stop selling it, the name of the product was so popular that other drug dealers were going to my spots and buying "Push It", only to re-sell it. There was nothing like having and selling the best product in town.

Setting Up Shop - Tricky Business

The areas where I set up shop, my personal spots, in my early days were mostly in Brooklyn: Bedford Stuyvesant, East New York, Ocean Hill Brownsville, Coney Island and In South Jamaica, Queens. The guys at my drug spots were given heroin and crack drug packages on consignment. They would receive $1500 worth of drugs at retail, and they would owe me a $1,000, the rest was their profit. During that period, it was important to lay down the foundation for doing business, by setting example of anyone who got in my way or showed any form of disrespect.

When opening up shop in a new neighborhood it could be a little tricky and difficult. At times you would get into a conflict with other drug dealers within a close distance, which could and often led to violence, including death. We would try to eliminate any potential problems by talking it out and agreeing to whoever, my opponent or me, had the best heroin or the best crack, that was who the addicts were going to buy from.

My marketing strategy was simple, when everyone was selling $5 dollar crack vials; I was selling the same thing for $3 dollars. Even people who got high looked for a deal; as if they are grocery shopping. You would be surprised what customers would bring to the drug spots to purchase crack: food stamps, jewelry, TVs, VCRs, stereos, and cars with their titles. You'd see it all; so many women would easily sell their body for a high.

I competed for customers with guys like the Corley's, a group of brothers that were selling drugs for years. I believe, I met, Peter Corley at Auburn Correctional facility in 1985 when I went to visit an associate. Also, at one point before I start making some serious money, I was hanging out in Queens with Frenchie. We met in Coxsackie, NY State correctional facility when I did my state bid from 1981-1984. He was known for robbing Queens' drug dealers and at that time if he could set up a couple of quick moves to generate 50-100 thousand dollars, I was not going to say no.

For several nights we were sitting on James Corley's wife and his number one man at the time seeking to snatch either one or both up and force them to take us to the cash and drugs. I went out with him for about a week with no luck. I hated wasting time, so I went back to my regular activities trying to find ways to make some fast money as Frenchie stayed on his grind and eventually robbed a member of Supreme Team for about fifty thousand dollars. The Team knew it was Frenchie, but out of respect or to prevent an all-out war with Frenchie's brother, Born, Frenchie was given a pass. About one year later Born was shot and murdered due to another matter, shortly after Frenchie was murdered by the Supreme Team for an old robbery. *Are you still in for $40,000 payday?*

The Creation of The Round Table

As mentioned earlier, The Round Table originated from those main 2 incidents: Mousey's kidnapping and then the break-in of Lynn's home. Cat decided to form The Roundtable. It was made up of Cat, Pappy, Supreme, and Prince. Again, his purpose was, they were all one team, one family, one unit. His mind set was, if they were all under the same umbrella, based upon each one's name and reputation from the street and jail, people will think twice about going against them.

During Christmas of 1987, Cat gave Bug-Out and me our Roundtable Rings. Mine was a 14k gold and diamond studded pinkie ring. A person had to be voted into the elite club and all newcomers had to be approved by the senior members. The front of my ring was designed like a roundtable. On top of the ring were letters that spelled out "Round Table" and on one side there was the letter "G" in diamonds, and on the other side was the initials M&M, also in diamonds.

Everyone who was a part of the Roundtable felt, if everything was properly established, then we could have a power structure so strong that no one or thing could penetrate it. It was a safety mechanism; before anything adverse could occur to us, it would be brought to our attention and we could put a stop to it in its early stages. With such a power structure, we would've been so strong that no enemy of the Roundtable could have possibly survived in any of the five boroughs of New York City. Our enemies would not have been safe even in jail, not only within the New York Metropolitan area, but anywhere in the whole State of New York. Plus, we could encourage young black males and females, who didn't have criminal records, to become police officer, correctional officers, as well as F.B.I. and D.E.A. agents. If accomplished we would have full access to any investigation involving any of our people, including names of informers, and if it became necessary, to help our people escape from prison. We had to have our people in the right positions legitimately for everything to work as we intended it to work. *What a concept.* But it's been said, many good plans are doomed to failure.

Every member of the Roundtable had their own separate crews and was basically on their own. Pappy and Bug-Out had between 20 and 30 guys under them, and I had between 10 and 15 guys under me; but all three of us were under Cat, meaning that our crews combined made up part of Fat Cat's crew. Supreme had anywhere from 50 to 100 guys under him, probably more, and were known as "The Supreme Team." Prince, Supreme's nephew, had his own crew, too, which consisted of between 25 and 50 guys. *To a degree, everybody was under Cat; it was more or less, pretty much Cat's show, running through me.*

Cat loved Supreme like a brother. Whenever Supreme needed assistance, regardless of what kind, Cat was always there to lend a helping hand. Supreme would be up one minute and down the next; he would be a millionaire, then the next thing you knew he'd be down on his luck from getting high. Supreme spent the money, too. He'd buy houses and all kinds of expensive foreign cars, including Mercedes Benz, BMWs and cars and jeeps for all his workers. He even had a cab stand where he used nothing but Lincoln Town cars. Supreme had a rule for his workers. *If they decided to leave the Supreme Team, then they would leave the same way they came in. What Supreme meant was that if they came in with nothing, then they would leave with nothing.* He would make a crew member leave everything the cars, jeeps, jewelry -- everything had to be left behind.

In August 1987, Supreme was out on an appeal bail. His conviction was from a 1985 arrest; he and several of his workers were arrested and charged with possession of drugs and drug paraphernalia. The case occurred in South Jamaica

Queen's House, and the arrests and seizures were carried out by the Queens Narcotic Detectives. So, the case was transferred to Manhattan Criminal State Court. Supreme made bail on that case, as well as a kidnapping case. While he was out on bail, he was indicted and had to appear before Judge Rothwax, in Manhattan Supreme Court. Judge Rothwax was known for being a rough and tough kind of judge.

Supreme was known for being a fly guy, the pretty boy type. When Supreme walked into Judge Rothwax's courtroom, he was accompanied by one of his many female companions and several male members of The Supreme Team. Supreme was dressed sharp; he was wearing a grayish silk suit and black alligator shoes. But Judge Rothwax wasn't impressed. When the clerk announced, "The State of New York Manhattan Supreme Court versus Kenneth McGriff," he should have read it: "Rough and Tough Judge Rothwax versus Fly Guy Supreme." Judge Rothwax revoked Supreme's bail and remanded him to jail. Supreme stayed on Rikers Island almost a year-and-a-half before pleading and receiving a sentence of 9 years to life on the advice of his attorney, David Cohen.

Nobody on the streets, or in jail for that matter, understood Supreme's move to plea. But Supreme kept saying that he was going to beat it on appeal, based on a legal technicality. However, he should have known that you lose your right to appeal once you plead guilty. But in August 1987, Supremes' conviction was reversed, and he received an appeal bail and went home. However, that was short-lived. In October 1987, the F.B.I. and U.S. Marshal Service raided the Baisley Housing Projects and arrested Supreme, along with several of his crew.

Supreme wasn't arrested on a new crime that occurred while he was out on the appeal bail. He was arrested on the original charges back in 1985. The feds believed Supreme had paid-off someone higher up in the judicial system.

Supreme was charged under Section 848 of Title 21 of the United States Code -- Continuous Criminal Enterprise -- and Sections 846, 843, and 841, of Title 21 -- conspiracy to possess with intent to distribute heroin and cocaine.

While fighting his case, Supreme stayed at the M.C.C. New York. He was willing to fight it all the way and go to trial that is until the federal government arrested Fat Cat, Pappy and several others on August 11, 1988. That's when Supreme decided it was better for him to plead guilty and move on. So, that's what he did. He ended up receiving a 12-year sentence and a $500,000 fine. With that sentence he should have been be released in 1993.

Supreme made one hell of a deal, because, when he pleaded guilty, he pleaded guilty to all known and unknown crimes. This meant that he couldn't be charged with anything from the past. Supreme felt that once Cat was indicted, the government would hit him with a superseding indictment with things that he and Cat had been involved in. So, when the opportunity arose, Supreme decided to take his number and run with it.

As for Supremes' nephew, Prince, it was no secret that Prince and Cat didn't like each other. It was outta strength, love and respect that Cat had for Supreme that they continued dealing with each other, and it was on that same strength that they dealt with each other long before Supreme made his plea in 1988.

During late 1986 and early 1987 Cat depended a lot on Prince, because damn near all of Cat's crew was in jail and Jug Head was on the run for the murder of Brian Rooney, the parole officer, as well as the drug case that he, Cat and several others were arrested on together. Prince did

143

whatever Cat asked of him. For instance, when Fat Cat's wife, Joann, was kidnapped during the Memorial Day weekend of 1987, Prince was with Cat's family, comforting them. Prince was also involved in the negotiation with the kidnappers. He was also the one who dropped off the $77,000 cash ransom. It's a known fact if Prince was granted the opportunity to find the kidnappers, there was no doubt that he and his people would've tortured and murdered them for Cat.

Also, Prince was trying to find Ron-Du and the other guys who were responsible for pistol whipping Lynn and robbing her in her Long Island home, where they made off with almost a half million dollars. Prince would've loved to have found both groups and killed them all, because he knew that Cat would've been in his debt big time. If Prince would've ever run into Ron-Du and his people in the upstate New York Correctional Facility, then Ron-Du would've murdered him on sight.

I can recall a time, during April or May 1988, when Prince was locked up on Rikers Island. I received word from this girl, Bunny, that Prince had told her to tell Cat that he needed a couple thousand dollars. When I went to visit Cat at Shawangunk Correctional Facility in Walkill, New York, I told him I was going to give Prince a couple G's. I still remember Cat's exact words: "Man, fuck Prince. He's my man and everything, but I'm not going to be giving him money for him to take care of some bitch."

At the time most of Prince's crew was either in jail with him or on the run from state charges and the people he did have working weren't making any real money on the drug tip. So, I ended up giving Prince the money he'd ask for, and on several other occasions I assisted him by dropping off a few thousand dollars here and there to his people; we were all supposed to be representing -- the Roundtable.

144

I started liking Prince, and it got to where he was calling me daily. I always told him that if he ever needed my assistance, to let me know and I'd be more than glad to do whatever I could to assist him in his cause. I also told him that I could relate to how it was to be incarcerated, and unable to take care of things that had to be done.

When Prince was on the street he lived like a Prince. You name it and Prince had it, including a bulletproof Mercedes. In fact, Prince made sure that not only himself, but his entire crew had bullet-proof vests, hats, and T-shirts. He was also tight when it came to security.

Falsely Accused

At one time I was feeling pretty ill with the flu. Everybody came to my apartment in East New York -- my mother, sister, cousin -- all came by and tried to nurse me back to health. Cat's niece, Cookie, as well as a number of my other female friends came by, too. I was miserable. I remember, during that same week I was in my apartment, trying to stay warm to get better when Cat called and wanted me to meet with some of Prince's people in Queens. Word was that several people went into Prince's area and shot up some of his workers. Prince, who was in jail at the time, had received word that Tu-Bar and I were behind the moves in order to take over his areas. I told Cat he knew the rumors were all bullshit and that Tu-Bar and I didn't see eye-to-eye enough to even get along most of the time, let alone enough to try to take over any of Prince's drug areas. Even though I was sick, I left my apartment on the strength of Cat and went to meet up with some of Prince's crew, at Cat's game room, to squash the rumors. Prince called while I was in the game room.

The more I learned about Prince my feelings toward him changed. Prince had done a lot of rotten shit I didn't like. For example, he and his crew would get a girl and bring her to their apartment and have sex with her and use a

145

hidden video camera to record it. After finishing, Prince would usually allow his crew to come in and run a train on the girl. What I mean by "running a train" is, there would be several guys, sometimes 5 to 10, waiting in line to fuck the girl without her consent. They used to beat up, torture, and rape girls on regular basis, and that's why it's not hard to find even today over 200 girls who hate Prince and his crew. It was like once Prince and his crew received a little power; it went to their heads. Just imagine, a girl consenting to have sex with one guy, then being turned around and raped and sodomized by several others, as well as being made to perform oral sex on them. What was even more insulting, and humiliating was that it was all recorded on tape. No wonder so many girls hated them.

I believe that, if Prince had stayed on the streets when I was out there, then I would've killed him myself and castrated him. I guess one of the main reasons I felt so much hatred towards Prince was because of what he had done to a girl I later became involved with. That was during the summer of 1987.

Prince had his people kidnap this girl Mary, on Fat Cat's orders and with Myeshia's assistance. Mary was with Myeshia on the pretense that Myeshia was supposed to have gotten Mary a sample of heroin, so she could give it to some other people and if they liked it they would be interested in buying a large quantity. If a deal was made, then Mary would've made a nice profit for herself. So, Mary and her daughter were with Myeshia, standing on a corner near a telephone booth in front of the housing projects in South Jamaica Queens. Myeshia had just hung up the telephone talking to Prince and gave him their location. Prince sent his people to the corner where Mary, her 4-year-old daughter, and Myeshia were waiting. It was in broad daylight when a dark-colored van approached with three men. The driver stayed in the van with the motor running and the other two got out, grabbed Mary, blindfolded her and threw her into the back of the van.

During several days of heavy interrogation, Mary was blindfolded, stripped, raped, and tortured. Prince used a hot curling iron to repeatedly burn her across her legs. Fat Cat and Pappy kept calling there to question Mary, too. What Cat was trying to find out was if she had any involvement with either Mousey's kidnapping, or the robbery at Lynn's house. Mary was being tortured, because she was friends with this girl, named Cee and Cee's boyfriend, Ron-Du, and Ron-Du's people, were responsible for robbing and pistol-whipping Lynn. Also, Mary knew another female, who was sexually involved with King Allah, and as mentioned King Allah was behind kidnapping Cat's wife, Mousey.

After several days of interrogation Cat and Pappy concluded that Mary didn't know anything. Although they were debating about letting her go, because they feared she might go to the police. They talked about killing her, but Mary swore she'd keep her mouth shut. So, they let her go.

Prince gave Mary $1,000 and let her leave. But he gave her some "rules and regulations" she had to live by. She had to make sure she kept her mouth shut and Prince said that he would be assigning this guy, named Baby-Wise, to stay at her apartment and keep an eye on her.

During that whole ordeal, Myeshia took care of Mary's daughter. Mary knew from the very beginning that Myeshia had set her up. As I think about things now, I should've hated Cat and Pappy right along with Prince, since Prince was taking orders from them.

Mary lived under Prince's "rules and regulations" for about three months. As soon as the State of New York arrested Prince on murder charges and started locking up a lot of his people, Mary packed up and moved to Virginia Beach, Virginia.

Parole Officer Brian Rooney's Murder

One of my missions/assignments was during December 1987. Fat Cat was still awaiting trial for the murder of Parole Officer Brian Rooney and still looking for satisfaction against his wife's kidnappers.

Prior to my taking over Fat Cat's operation, Earl "Tu-Bar" Frazier was supposed to be head of Cat's security.

Cat and Pappy had put up around $7,500 each to bail TuBar out of jail. Tu-Bar made bail from Rikers Island during the latter part of June or the early part of July in 1987. TuBar was granted to take care of a certain matter for Cat and Pappy. He was to find and murder the people who were involved in kidnapping Cat's wife, Mousey during that Memorial Day weekend, as well as those involved in the robbery at Lynn's house. He was also expected to find the whereabouts of Perry Bellamy's mother.

Perry Bellamy, again, was the guy who made a videotape confession implicating Cat and Pappy's involvement in the murder of Parole Officer Brian Rooney. Perry had already been convicted for his involvement in the murder and received a sentence of 25 years to life. Both Cat and Pappy thought Perry was going to be the state's star witness against them, for ordering the assassination of the parole officer. Once Tu-Bar located Perry's mother, he was supposed to have killed her. The reason was so that Perry would be brought to the funeral home, so he could be killed before being able to testify against Cat and Pappy. Perry's mother was an evangelist and Tu-Bar kept saying that he couldn't find her.

A plot had to be devised to kill the witnesses that would save Fat Cat from a life in prison for the murder of his parole officer. During one of my daily visits with Cat, we discussed ways on how to erase Perry Bellamy off the census. This was not an easy task considering Perry was in an upstate New York maximum security facility under protective custody. Our first and most unconscionable scenario was to get Perry released for one of his family member's funeral. Then, once the death and funeral were arranged, most likely Perry would be escorted there by two to three New York State Correctional Officers, with the possible assistance from NYPD. The initial target again was Perry's mother. We went back and forth until Fat Cat eliminated that plan, because she was a preacher. The next target discussed was to tag his father, who resided and worked in Queens. After weeks of discussions the final decision was made, Cat gave me the green light to murder Perry's father. At the time my man, Juneau Wilson a.k.a. Sty, was currently on the run in South Carolina for a murder that occurred in the Cypress Hill Houses. I sent for him and during the next two days we went thru the area several times where the hit was to go down. We needed to familiarize ourselves with the area to figure out possible escape routes.

The only crimes I personally knew Tu-Bar to be a part of was Jus-Me's murder and the shooting of Ron-Du a number of times but missing. Jus-Me was the one who set up the robbery at Lynn's home. Tu-Bar fell off a lot by sniffing P-funk -- that is heroin. And because of his drug habit, Tu-Bar wasn't on top of his game and was irresponsible in his duties. So, Pappy wanted me to kill TuBar, because he felt Tu-Bar was bullshitting him. But Cat nixed the Tu-Bar hit and told me to find out everything TuBar knew about Perry's father's location.

During visits and telephone conversations Cat didn't want me to do the hit myself but wanted me to get somebody else. He said to have the hitter go into the Laundromat and ask for change and the person who made the change would be the target. Cat said the most important thing to do was to be sure, that the killing appeared to be the result of robbery attempt.

Cat said once the hit was made on Perry's father, and he was pronounced dead, for me to keep Tu-Bar on the job and have him find out where the funeral was to be held. I was to observe the surrounding area and make plans for the move on Perry.

I was to get with Tu-Bar and have him get with Gerald "Prince" Miller. Prince and his people were supposed to give up several tranquilizer guns. I would then get several dirt bikes, which I had to buy, and my people and I would wait for Perry to show.

Perry being a C.M.C. prisoner, again it was likely he would be escorted by two correctional officers and two police officers. We were to be on point and as soon as they brought Perry around, we were supposed to shoot the officers with the tranquilizer guns. The tranquilizers we were using were thought to be strong enough to knock out an elephant. Once the officers were out, we were to kill Perry, then use the dirt bikes to make a fast getaway using police scanners to make it even easier.

Cat kept saying that with the move on Perry we would make history. He wanted us to use the tranquilizer guns on the officers, because he felt law enforcement agencies would have a great deal of respect for us, because we chose to tranquilize the officers instead of killing them. If we couldn't get the tranquilizer guns, then Cat wanted me to use three separate snipers, all from different angles and on different rooftops, to hit Perry.

I would visit Cat three to four times per week and talk to him via the phone several times a day. Cat depended on me because I was loyal, and I got the job done quickly without excuses. I was dedicated to the cause and probably more dedicated to him than he was to me.

The plan was in place and the day arrived. It was Friday, December 4, 1987. It was three days after my 24th birthday. It was a sunny and a chilly thirty degrees outside. Between 1:30 A.M. and 2:30A.M., Tu-Bar and I left the game room on 150th Street and 107th Avenue and went to Wilken's Laundromat on Linden Boulevard in Laurelton Queens. Tu-Bar was showing me where the target was and how we were going to make the hit and get away. But as Tu-Bar and I were checking out the scene, I noticed that someone was in the Laundromat, despite the fact it was closed, and the steel gate was down and locked. Tu-Bar said that it was Perry Bellamy's father, Maurice Bellamy.

We returned to the Laundromat about an hour later and told the trigger man exactly what his task was to be. The trigger man was to walk into the Laundromat and ask the intended target for change. At that point he was to hit the target and make the murder look as if it occurred during a robbery. He was to then walk, not run, out of the Laundromat, turn left and walk up a short block and get into a waiting getaway car.

So, this is the way it eventually went down on December 4, 1987, around 8:00 A.M., Tu-Bar, the triggerman, AL, Philip "Marshal" Copeland and me all met in Cat's game room, on 150th Street and 107th Avenue. Tu-Bar laid down the game plan. I gave AL some money and told him that he was to be at the nearby bus stop, acting like he's waiting to catch a bus. If anyone attempted to stop the triggerman after he made the hit, it was AL's job to kill them. Tu-Bar and the triggerman left in the getaway car, and AL and I left with Marshal in his Jeep Cherokee. We parked about three blocks from the Laundromat and got out of the Jeep. AL left us and walked to the bus stop, right in front of the Laundromat. Marshal and I went into a store and I bought two quarts of orange juice, and a copy of The New York Daily News.

When we left the store, we looked up the block and saw the triggerman enter the Laundromat. Then we heard shots and saw the triggerman exit the Laundromat and go around the corner. Shortly afterwards the bus came, and AL got on. Marshal and I got into the Jeep and drove away. As we drove away we saw several blue and white police cars, from the 103rd and 13th Precincts, coming from different directions just like Tu-Bar said they would. By the time the police reached the scene of the crime, the triggerman and getaway driver were long gone.

Both Cat and Pappy were happy when they learned of the hit. But there were two problems that upset Cat: 1) that the triggerman didn't make it look like a robbery; and 2) that Perry's father wasn't dead.

Cat instructed Tu-Bar to keep us updated on Perry's father's condition, so we could be prepared to do what needed to be done when the time came. A few days later, Tu-Bar told us that Perry's father was on the critical list and would most likely die. He was brain dead and surviving only by means of life support systems.

Phase Two, the plan was in motion. As we were waiting on information for the location of Perry father's funeral, I had purchased several high-powered rifles with scopes. Once I had the address we were going to find the best apartment or roof top that we could use to execute Perry. We had tranquilizer guns, along with different dosage to use based on the weight of the targets.

With all that planning, the move never happened. When Perry's father finally succumbed to his death, Perry was escorted to court. I attended the hearing and listened as Perry told the judge he did not want to attend the funeral, and wanted to be escorted back upstate ASAP, believing the hit on his father was a setup for his demise. Killing Perry's father Maurice Bellamy was a waste of time, resources and a life. Again, sorry.

In an ARTICLE FROM NEW YORK TIMES 10-5-1989 Mr. Nichols revealed while he was in prison, he ordered the murder in November 1986 of a drug rival, Isaac Bolden aka Just-Me. He told Judge Korman that Mr. Bolden and others had robbed people in his organization.

Happy Mother's Day

Killing doesn't take a holiday. Aside from running my M&M crew I was still an assassin without a conscience.

On Saturday evening, December 20, 1987, less than three weeks after the assassination of Maurice Bellamy I got the call that Myrtle "Myesha" Horsham, the mother of Fat Cat's son, T.C., was cleared for execution. When I received the phone call that Myesha had to die, it was not a surprise, as it was in the making for quite some time. Her penalty stemmed from dishonesty and thievery. I guessed Myesha felt that Fat Cat was married, had other girls on the side, and he was in prison, so she felt that she could do what she wanted to do. That included staging a robbery at her place of residence and allowing several kilos of cocaine to disappear along with a couple hundred thousand dollars. *This was against company policy and highly frowned upon.* Word on the street was that she was giving Fat Cat's shit to this dude she was fucking behind his back. Myeshia had also messed up about $60,000 worth of Cat's money and he was just fed up. To add insult to injury, Myeshia was spending his money on another man, also named Brian.

My triggerman and I ran around for about a weekand-a-half, trying to locate Myeshia and Brian. Neither of us had the slightest idea what our target, Brian, looked like. One night we got with Marshal and a few of the Be-Bo's crew. Marshal provided my triggerman with a handgun, and we went through Forty's Houses, in Jamaica Queens, trying to find Brian. We stayed around Forty Houses for about three hours before we left and went to a house in Queens, which Brian was supposed to be sharing with some other girl. We staked out the house for several hours every day for a whole week, but no Brian.

Trying to find Myeshia and Brian in order to accomplish the hit was fast becoming a headache. We must've spent between 10 and 16 hours a day trying to find them. I even called Myeshia's mother, sometimes up to 15 times a day, but always got the "she isn't home" response. I even pushed up on some of Myeshia's female friends to try to locate her, but no luck.

The next day my triggerman and I were back around the Forty Projects, trying to find Marshal and his crew, so they could point out Brian to us. We were there about 30 minutes before finally running into Marshal and his people, but Marshal was having his own problems.

Two of their drug spots had been raided and a few of the workers were arrested. That meant they took a loss for already bagged up packages of drugs and some money. Marshal wasn't one to handle pressure well and having to answer to Pappy made matters even worse, as Marshal already owed Pappy quite a large sum of money from constantly messing up. Therefore, Marshal wasn't into helping me find Brian that day. But what really pissed me off was the fact that, if Pappy would've been in on the Myeshia and Brian hit, then they would've been into it100%.

The plain and simple fact was that most of the BeBos hated Fat Cat. But for the love and respect Pappy had for Cat, they did show some respect -- but that was the only reason. I personally hated that and started to really dislike the Be-Bos, feeling they were a bunch of bitches anyway. Pappy was my man but fuck his crew, they didn't have any balls and weren't loyal.

Cat and I spoke about the lack of support I was receiving from the Be-Bos in helping me to identify and locate Brian and about the general lack of enthusiasm towards his cause. I let him know that the only reason they weren't assisting me was because it had nothing to do with Pappy. At that point Cat pretty much said fuck the Be-Bos and realized that Pappy was the one who mattered.

Cat turned over $10,000 worth of guns to me and instructed one of his men to locate and point out Brian. He did. It was a Friday evening. The triggerman entered the Forty Houses building where Brian lived. As he approached Brian, he put the gun into his face and pulled the trigger. The only thing that could be heard was Brian screaming in a state of shock. The triggerman ran out of the building a couple of minutes later and made his way to the getaway car.

Brian came out of the building, screaming at the top of his lungs like a woman. "Help me! Somebody help me!" I went around the crowd that was already there and I heard Brian say that a guy came up in the building, put a gun to his face and pulled the trigger several times, but nothing happened. Brian said, his whole life flashed in front of him, and thought he was a dead man.

I left and went to the game room on 150th Street and 107th Avenue, where I ran into the triggerman. He told me the gun misfired and that's why Brian wasn't killed. Plus, the driver in his getaway car caught a flat tire as they were leaving the scene. Brain was getting a real taste of the drug business.

During that time, from November 1987 to January 1988, I was going to Queen's Supreme Court in Kew Garden every day, because Cat was on trial for drugs and weapons charges. I was in attendance to show my support; as well as take care of any matters the lawyer needed, assistance within reference to Cat's case.

I used to try to assist the lawyers with strategy by trying to find a few jurors who were willing to be paid off for a not guilty verdict. I would also foot the lunch bill and make sure Cat got his vegetarian sandwiches from the lawyer.

Cat had another reason for wanting Brian dead. Myeshia gave birth to a baby in 1985 and claimed Cat was the father, but word on the street was that Brian was the father. After that hit on Brian was botched, Cat said to forget it and concentrate on Myeshia, knowing Brian would no doubt be leery and go into hiding.

So, that Saturday night, I believe it was December 19, 1987; I was talking to Cat and Luke at the game room, when Cat instructed me to make sure to get with Dave McClary, seeing that Dave was going to find Myeshia.

Luke called from Rikers Island and informed me that his son's mother, Gidget, was babysitting Myeshia's son, and that Myeshia was supposed to stop by Gidget's sometime that night to pick up her son, T.C.

My driver and I hopped into my Seville and drove from Cat's game room to the Rosedale Projects in Queens. We picked up Dave McClary and his man, James McCaskill. Dave showed us how to get to Gidget's house. It was around 11:45 P.M. when we parked up the block from Gidget's house and were in clear view able to see anyone entering or exiting the house. Dave McClary was a good guy and all, and I don't mean any disrespect towards him, but he was funky. I guess he had a serious attitude when it came to soap and water. He always smelled like a monkey's cage. A skunk had nothing on Dave.

So, we sat and waited with the windows down, even though it was on a winter night. I dozed off to sleep until someone in the car woke me up, and said, "There's Myeshia. There she is." The driver and I sat in the car and I went over the plan with Dave and James. Myeshia had to die and, unfortunately for Regina, her friend and witness, she had to die, too. It was also made very clear that Myeshia's and Cat's son was not to be harmed.

Myeshia got out of the car and Gidget brought T.C. to the door. Myeshia picked up T.C., took him around to the passenger's side of the car, opened the door, and put him in the backseat. After she closed the door, she went with Gidget inside of the house for a moment.

When Myeshia went into the house, Dave and James got out of the car and bent down. James then got up, walked straight across the street and bent down behind some high bushes at the corner. Dave followed, doing exactly the same thing. They were about four houses from where Regina had parked the car. The streetlights were on and I remember seeing James crawling on his belly across the grass and concrete until he reached the nearest car. He then raised himself up a little, and crept past two or three parked cars, until he reached the passenger's side of the brown Oldsmobile Regina was driving. James opened the passenger's door, climbed into the backseat, and held Regina at bay with a 380 handgun, instructing her not to scream or try to tip-off Myeshia. Regina was noticeably shook up. Dave then got up and with the same moves as James, made it into the backseat of the Oldsmobile. Both then slouched down in the backseat.

Myeshia came out of Gidget's house about 5 minutes after James and Dave reached the car. I had a strange feeling when Myeshia left Gidget's house, since Gidget didn't wait at the door or look out the window to make sure Myeshia got into the car and left safely -- something people usually do when someone leaves their home. I had a funny feeling that Gidget knew what was going down; after all it was Luke, the father of Gidget's children, who told us that Gidget was babysitting T.C. and that Myeshia would be stopping by within a particular time frame to pick him up. Myeshia was about to get into the car, when she saw Dave's foot and screamed and started running. Dave made hot pursuit and caught her before she reached the end of the next corner. He snatched her by her hair, picked her up, and put his 9mm pistol in her side and returned to the car. They got in and drove off. We followed close behind. I remember passing August Martin High School just before getting to where we were going. I wasn't that familiar with Queens, so I don't know exactly where we were, except to say that we were somewhere in the vicinity of 180th Street and 106th Avenue. It was a dead-end block and I remember seeing a lot of different parked cars and trucks. Dave and James drove to the very end before stopping and turning off the car. My driver and I stopped, turned off our lights, but kept the engine running.

I saw the gun's flash and heard the noise. I know at least 6 to 10 shots were fired. We were only about 25 or 30 feet away. As I watched the flashes of light and smoke from the rapid gun fire in the car in front of me, I momentarily closed my eyes, made the sign of the cross, and asked God to forgive Myeshia, her innocent girlfriend and take them into heaven. I didn't ask for any forgiveness. It was safe to assume that Myeshia and her unfortunate driver were dead - it was part of the no witness rule. Most important to Fat Cat was, *"Be very careful, nothing should happen to my son." The fact that the kid wouldn't have a mother didn't much matter.*

Both Dave and James got out of the brown Oldsmobile. Dave was carrying T.C. who was crying, so I grabbed him and started hugging him. I then looked into their eyes and asked Dave and James if they shot both Myeshia and Regina in the head several times? They said they had and that both women were dead. Yes, was the word. They claim both ladies begged for their life, Myeshia told them that she had a total of $475,000 cash that she would give it to them if they didn`t kill her, her son, and friend. She didn't realize, no amount of money in the world could have lifted her death sentence. Looking back, $475,000 was a lot of money.

We left and drove to 155 and Sutphin Boulevard, an address I had become familiar with. With T.C. in my arms, I got out of the car and walked up the block. I opened the gate, walked into the yard, placed Myeshia's and Fat Cat's son down and banged on the door several times. I left T.C. there, making sure the gate was securely closed. I then walked up the block and called Myeshia's house for the final time. I wouldn't be asking to speak to Myeshia anymore. When her mother answered, I asked her to immediately get up and get the baby out of the yard. *I had to hang up when her mother sensed her daughter was in serious trouble and cried out, "Where's my baby Myeshia?" I cruised past the house for the last time; to be sure the boy was safe in his home.*

We dropped off Dave and James in front of Fiesta's, an all-night diner and grocery store on 116th Street and Sutphin Boulevard. I told both to keep their mouths shut and to get rid of the guns. They said they'd do both. I then told them that I'd see them later that day and pay them for a job well done.

My driver and I left and went back to the game room. We stayed there for about a half hour before going home and hitting the sack. Fat Cat called me bright and early that morning and I started singing to him in harmony: "Nobody beats the Biz. Nobody beats the Biz" is short for "Busy" - another name for Cat. Cat was talking to me in Pig Latin and asking if Myeshia was dead. I broke it down into little codes and gave him the details, letting him know that Regina was with Myeshia and that she got it too, I then told him how I put T.C. in the yard and made the telephone call.

Cat was really happy and he told me to pay Dave and James. I gave them $5,000 cash and 250 grams of cocaine and both were satisfied. I took the opportunity to ask if they got rid of the guns. They said they did.

The very next day Cat called me and told me to get a copy of the Monday newspaper. I sent one of my troopers to get a copy. The paper had the story about Myeshia and Regina, but there was a problem; Regina had survived. The story said that they had been shot by some unknown assailants. Regina had dragged herself out of the car and started crawling on the dead-end street when someone spotted her and came to her aide. Cat was worried about Regina still being alive, as she could identify Dave and James. And if Dave and James were arrested, they were subject to fold under pressure and implicate Luke, Cat, and me. Cat figured the only way for him to be indicted for giving the order to murder Myeshia would be for them to get to me, since the order came through me.

I first caught up with Dave and when I did I screamed on him. James was his man and James had lied when he told me that he'd hit Regina with at least two shots in the head. According to the newspaper, Regina suffered gunshot wounds only to her body. So, we talked about the possibility of going inside the hospital to finish her off. Dave assured me that if James was snatched up by the police for killing Myeshia and attempting to murder Regina, he would keep his mouth shut, because I had seriously considered killing James mostly on account that he had lied to me.

Cat got back with me and told me to nix the hospital move, because Regina wasn't going to talk, and as far as I know to this day she still refused to cooperate.

I became ill over the next few days and I was out of it. My glands were swollen and irritated, and I was burning up with a fever. I was sick for close to a week. But Cat's calls kept coming in. I remember one conversation we had where I was telling him how sick I was, and he was telling me that he was sick. I then went on to tell him that I felt so sick, I thought I was going to die, and that I started thinking Myeshia's spirit was probably haunting me. Cat burst out laughing and told me that he was thinking the same thing.

Fat Cat and Bug Out

Bug-Out was another individual I would get to spend time with. From late 1986 to 1988, Cat gave BugOut 20 to 30 kilos of cocaine and anywhere from 1/2 to 3/4 kilo of heroin every month. Bug paid back $600,000 to $800,000 to Cat every month. Bug was one of the most reliable people Cat had. The business relationship between Cat and Bug-Out was going well; Cat supplied the drugs and Bug-Out always paid on time.

Bug's loyalty and consistency to Cat is what earned him his Roundtable Ring. Bug-Out had started out by working for Bo-Bo when he came home from Rikers Island after being acquitted on a murder charge. Bo-Bo used to fuck up big time and blame it on Bug-Out and his people and for a while Cat went for it. Bo-Bo used to beat down Bug-Out and his crew on a regular basis. But Cat eventually found out after Bo-Bo went to jail to do a six-month bid during the end of 1986. Around October 1986, Cat found out that Bo-Bo was the one fucking up his money and drug supply. So, Cat gave Bug-Out and his crew the opportunity of a lifetime. Bug-Out didn't disappoint Cat. Bug-Out had a crew of between 20 and 30 men, with a guy named Mustaf as his right-hand man.

Cat would depend on Bug-Out to make money for him. But he couldn't depend on Bug-Out to provide security for him and his organization, because Bug-Out wasn't a violent person and didn't have that physical force. From December 1987 to January 1988, Bug-Out had a problem with Pappy's associate, Ruff. The problem was that Ruff was setting up drug spots in Bug-Out's area and that was totally against the grain, since Bug-Out was down with Cat, and Ruff was running Pappy's organization at the time, and all of us were supposed to be down together. The matter got totally out of hand. Ruff and the Be-Bo's bum rushed Bug-Out's spots and pistol whip the workers and rob the spots of all the drugs and money, then turn around and firebomb the buildings. Bug-Out and his crew started retaliating by doing the same thing. The matter was really out of hand and Bug-Out was losing lots of product and large sums of money because of it. Cat was getting pissed off. The longer the feud went on the more aggravated he became. At the time Fat Cat was still on trial for the drug charges in Queens State Supreme Court in Kew Garden. He had been arrested on July 29, 1985.

The Intervention Between Bug-Out and Ruff

About three weeks into the feud between Ruff and Bug-Out I was talking to Cat on the telephone. I was at his niece Cookie's house on 139th and Van Wyck Street in South Ozone Park. During the conversation, I knew Cat was pissed off, as he kept calling Ruff every dirty, low life name possible. From that conversation, I knew that if it hadn't been for Pappy, that Cat would've told me to kill Ruff.

I was waiting for him to give me the order and I could hear it coming, from all the things that he was saying, but he ended the conversation by telling me to make sure that I contacted Ruff as soon as possible and resolved the matter between Ruff and Bug-Out. Cat told me that he'd already sent word to Pappy, who was on Rikers Island at the time, that he needed to get in touch with him as soon as possible. Cat at the time was in the Brooklyn House of Detention for Men, Maximum Security. So, I left Cookie's house, with my brother Country, and looked for Ruff all throughout South Jamaica Queens, but was unsuccessful. I finally got to my apartment around 3:00 A.M. and went straight to sleep.

Bright and early the next morning I got a call from Pappy, we were close at the time, but Cat called me more frequently than Pappy did. Pap usually called me once a week straight, then I wouldn't hear from him for a month or two, unless I saw him on a visit, or he wanted me to take care of something for him or he was seeking information.

One time I was half asleep when I answered the telephone. Once I realized it was Pappy, I woke right up. He was talking in Pig Latin and I still remember his exact words: "You know, GLAZIE AZIE, you are my man and I love you like a brother, but you know how I feel about Ruff. Ruff is more of a brother to me than a biological brother." He went on to say, "You know, when I did that whole seven years, Ruff was the only one visiting me and taking care of me, making sure that I was alright." He also said that since his present incarceration, Ruff had taken care of his family and his business. Pap told me straight up, "You know, GLAZIE AZIE, I can't accept anything happening to Ruff, under any circumstances." He then changed the subject and went to other things. But during our conversation that morning I came to realize that Pap, to a degree, had given Ruff the okay to go into Bug-Out's area and sell drugs. Pap knew that Bug-Out and his people wouldn't dare attempt to kill Ruff. Pappy felt, and in fact knew, that if a move was to be made on Ruff, then it would come from me. So, the call I received from him that morning was telling me that if Cat gave me the order to kill Ruff, for me not to do it. At the time, if somebody would've killed Ruff, and I had nothing to do with it, Pap would've still felt that my people and I did it.

But, in all honestly, if Cat would've given me the order to kill Ruff, even though I had a great deal of respect and love for Pappy, then Ruff would have been deader than a doorknob - nothing personal, strictly business. My loyalty was to Cat.

163

The problem between Ruff and Bug-Out started when Ruff was about to go away and do 1 to 3 years in an upstate New York correctional facility. Ruff knew that Bug-Out's areas were goldmines, generating a large cash flow on a daily basis from cocaine and heroin sales. Bug-Out was generating between $150,000 and $300,000 a week, but most of the profit had to go to Cat up front, since Bug usually owed Cat somewhere between $600,000 and $800,000 every month for the drugs he received on consignment. Plus, Bug had to pay his crew of 20 to 30 men salaries ranging from $250 to $5,000 a week.

Ruff, on Pappy's orders, tried to takeover Bug-Out's areas and move in the Be-Bos, so that Pap and Ruff could continue to earn a decent percent of the profits while they both were in jail. Plus, Ruff, and probably Pap and a lot of other guys, were jealous of Bug-Out, being that he had one house in Queens, two houses in Long Island, and two brand new Porsches, and just about all of Bug's crew had jeeps, cars, and nice jewelry. In the drug game you'll always find jealousy and envy amongst the dealers from different organizations, especially if one person is doing extremely well. Besides, Pap and Ruff knew that Bug-Out and his crew weren't violent and felt Bug-Out didn't deserve what he had.

Cat and Pappy met and talked in the bullpens at Kew Gardens Queens Supreme Court. Cat was on trial for drug and weapons charges, and Pappy had arranged for his lawyers to call him out to court for an attorney visit, but the real purpose was for him and Cat to talk about the situation between Bug-Out and Ruff.

The result was for me to be the mediator. I decided for a sit-down meeting with Ruff, Bug-Out and myself, to come up with a reasonable solution to the problem. We were to meet at Bug-Out's house. If I remember correctly, it was the first week of January 1988.

All Bug-Out's crew was there, heavily armed with MAC-10, MAC-11 semi-automatics, Uzis 9mm and .45 caliber handguns; and all wore bullet-proof vests. It was around 3:00 P.M. when I arrived, and Bug's people let me through the heavy steel door; they looked like they were ready for World War III. I was escorted to a large bedroom in the back of the house, where Bug-Out, Ruff and Mustaf were already talking. Ruff was sitting in a chair, leaning back and holding a 380-automatic handgun, with his leg across one of the chair's arms. Bug and Mustaf were standing up, each with a bullet-proof vest on and their handguns in their waistbands. I found the whole situation hilarious. There was Ruff, in Bug-Out's house, surrounded by Bug and his people, with the odds totally against him, and he was sitting back all relaxed and pretending to be a gangster, which he wasn't. Ruff was a girl and a lot of people wanted to whip his ass, and even kill him, but their fear of Pappy was why nothing ever happened to Ruff.

When I came in, we all talked, and I told them both that I was there on the combined strength of Cat and Pappy, and I wasn't about to play favoritism to either one of them. I asked both to explain their own side and they did. I decided that both of them would be able to live with Bug-Out and Ruff taking turns selling drugs. In other words, one-week Bug and his crew would be able to hustle, and the next week Ruff and his people would be able to sell drugs in that area. Bug and Ruff both agreed to that idea and said that the move sounded good. The meeting ended on a good note. Ruff embraced all of us and left very happy.

After Ruff left, Bug-Out and Mustaf explained to me how Ruff was really carrying on before my arrival. They said Ruff was telling them that Cat didn't give a fuck about them and if a war came, then Bug and his people would dic, because Cat would side with Pap. They continued saying that once I arrived Ruff's whole outlook and attitude changed and made a complete 180-degree turnaround. He'd become a totally different person right in front of their eyes. The fact of the matter was that Ruff knew that I wasn't to be fucked with, and that if he pushed my button the wrong way, then I would've killed him and dealt with Pappy later.

Bug-Out and I are Made Partners

After the meeting I spoke with Cat and explained the week-in week-out deal between Ruff and Bug-Out. Cat said, "Hell no!" He wasn't going for it -- and he didn't. Cat and Pappy met again, and I don't know what was said, but the result was that Ruff was out of Bug-Out's area and for insurance, Cat made me Bug-Out's new business partner.

With all of the problems between Bug and Ruff, and all the loses Bug was taking as a result of the raids by police in which large amounts of drugs, money, and guns were seized at his spots, Bug was going down the drain really fast. When Cat made me Bug-Out's partner, Bug was in debt to Cat for over half a million dollars; but he couldn't get a credit card. Bug had a hell-of-a-lot of problems. Due to the large amount of money he owed Cat, he cut Bug-Out's supply down to 5 to 10 kilos at a time; trying to help Bug get out of the hole he was in.

During the first month or so of my new partnership with Bug, I sacrificed right along with Bug and his crew, to help him get out of debt with Cat. However, Cat told me not to do that; it was Bug's responsibility for his own mishap and not mine. Bug-Out was supposed to be in charge of taking care of all business matters and I was in charge of all security matters. I liked it that way; security was right up my alley. Bug-Out started out by introducing me to all his crew, then took me out and showed me all our drug spots. We had one drug spot in the back of a grocery store. A bodega; it had a steel door to the storage room in the back of the building. Behind the door were the drugs and the workers. When a customer came to the door, they rang a bell and the worker would look through the peephole as the customer told him what they wanted and slid their money under the door. The worker then slid the bagged–up product back under the door. That spot was located on Sutphin Boulevard and 109th Street. The other spot was in a rundown apartment building, in a second-floor apartment, on 150th Street, several blocks from Cat's game room. Bug showed me several areas where workers were selling out in the open, face-to-face and hand-to-hand with the customers. It was February and things looked good for Bug-Out and me and then Pappy made bail.

Pappy made a reduced bail of $300,000, for the Parole Officer Rooney Murder. He lasted only about two weeks on the streets after Assistant District Attorney, Kelly, and his colleague, Tulman, were getting desperate and they rushed Pappy to trial on the weapons charge. When Pappy was arrested for the Rooney murder, he was striped searched at the police station and they found a loaded .22 caliber derringer in his shoe. So, since Kelly and Tulman didn't have enough evidence, or strong enough evidence to bring Pappy back to trial for the Rooney murder, they decided to move on the weapons charge.

Pappy's short-lived freedom on bail seemed like a whole year, because of all the traveling he did, and I was with him a great deal of the time. Ruff was already incarcerated and had started serving his one to three-year bid, and Pappy and I were running, from jail to jail, visiting our friends and putting money into their accounts.

I barely saw my new partner, Bug-Out. During the weekdays, from 9:30 A.M. until 5:00 P.M. Pappy was in court attending his trial for the gun charge. After court I'd meet him on 150th and 107th, at Cat's game room. Damn near everybody would gather around and wait for Cat's calls. We'd also meet at Viola's house, Cat's sister, to wait for his calls.

I remember the first meeting Pappy held. Nearly everyone who held a major position in either Cat's or Pappy's organization was there. We were sitting in the living room when Pappy started laying down the game. Pappy picked up a newspaper and said, "Do you see exactly what they're saying about me? They're saying that I'm an enforcer and they guarantee that I'm going to turn New York City into a bloodbath, and that people are going to start dropping like flies especially out in South Jamaica, Queens." He then went on to say that he definitely was a true enforcer and that he wasn't looking for anyone else to be an enforcer for the organization but was only looking for straight up hustlers who were ready and willing to take drugs on consignment, and immediately open up shops and get busy. He also chastised those individuals who had been fucking up here and there for a long time.

He was really hard on Bo-Bo and another kid, named Junior. Pappy said that he didn't want any weak individuals down with us, and that anyone who was always a part of our group had to be able to stand on their own two feet -- on the street and in jail. Pap was more or less singling out the fuckups who were there, but he also praised those who were doing a good job. He spoke highly of Bug-Out, saying that Bug was a loyal individual and did a hell of a job, despite the problems he was having at the time. Pap also spoke about me, saying, "Don Glazieon is my man. Glaze and his brother are from Brooklyn, where they've been hustling and making money since they were kids." He said that since I had joined forces with them, their organization had strengthened.

Pappy was also speaking highly of Marshal when Viola called me to the back of the house, then handed me the telephone, saying that it was "Biz." I got on the telephone and said, "Nobody beats the Biz." Cat replied with: "What's up kid?" He then asked me what was going on with Pappy and the meeting. I told Cat what had just taken place, including Pappy chastising the ones who had been fucking up and praising the ones who were doing a good job. Cat told me that Pappy and I should've let it be known that everybody should know who is who and who's been doing what, because only a certain few had been chosen to represent the Roundtable. He said that Bo-Bo and a lot of others had been with the organization since its beginning, and still none of them had earned the right to wear the Ring. Cat said the Ring wasn't for fashion but was strictly for the ones who were true to the game. I will say this much, I was already well respected, but the Ring put a few more notches on my belt; a lot of people throughout the Metropolitan area, both male and female, would see my Roundtable Ring and idolize it -- strange as that might sound.

During Pappy's short stay on the streets we tried to take care of a lot of things, even a night on the town. The singer, Stephanie Mills, was scheduled to perform at the Apollo Theater on February 12, 1988, so I bought between 20 and 25 front-row-seat tickets. Unfortunately, a snowstorm hit that night and several of the people I had purchased tickets for couldn't make it. Aside from Pappy, I, and a few others who made it were: Quick, Lynn's sister; Cookie, Cat's niece; Michelle, Cat's girlfriend; Dave McClary; and Bo-Bo. Dave and Bo-Bo were heavily armed, because they were security for the night. Just before the show I found myself trying to give away the remainder of the tickets from those who couldn't make it. But the weather was so bad that even giving away the tickets was a difficult task. The show was worth it; Stephanie Mills sung her ass off. After the show we took some pictures and sent some to Cat.

I was disappointed when Pap was remanded back to jail. Regardless of how anyone else perceived Pappy to be, as far as I was concerned, he was a damn good person, showing compassion towards the people he cared about and loved. *In life there's always a gray area, some things are just not black or white.*

Having Friends On the Inside

We weren't paying off any cops or politicians, but we had our resources. Prior to talking to Sweet-L, I remember an incident at Cypress Hills that made me believe Baby Sam and his people were out to kill me. Around 2:00 A.M. one morning I had sent Country to pick up, my wife, Tamia from her aunt's house, and then come back so we could go and spend the night in one of my places in Queens. Bug-Out, and about seven of my people and I were waiting downstairs for Country and Tamia to return, when I realized I'd left something upstairs. I took a 9mm from one of my guys and then Bug-Out and I went back upstairs to get whatever it was I'd forgotten.

When we got upstairs I noticed that several guys were entering the project from the Fountain Avenue side. I checked them out but didn't think anything of it at that moment. Although, upon returning downstairs, I saw the same guys leaving the project and heading back towards Fountain Avenue. I asked my people what was up with those guys and one of them told me that they acted like they were trying to sneak up on them. But as the strangers got closer, my guy told me he spun around and let them see the Tech-9 pistol hanging from a strap around his neck, with his finger on the trigger. The rest of my people were on their toes for any funny moves. My guy went on to say that one of the strangers asked him about a building 13 and the name of some girl. After hearing all of that, I knew something wasn't right, because there was no building 13 and no girl by that name.

After taking everything into account, I concluded that those strangers were part of Baby Sam's crew and that they had come to whack me. So, I gave the order for my people to go and kill them. Bug-Out and I were at the corner of Sutter and Euclid, still waiting for Country and Tamia, while four of my guys went to take care of my order to hit the strangers.

Two cops in a blue and white Suburban drove past my people as they were walking fast towards their intended targets. The cops drove about a block from where Bug-Out and I were standing, then made a U-turn on Sutter and Pine and headed back towards us. My people were just over a half-block from us and about to hit the strangers, not realizing the cops were headed back in their direction. I tried to call it off, but it was too late. The targets were getting into a red and black Chevy Blazer and some other American made car. When my people started cutting loose on them, the two cops brought the Suburban to a screeching halt and watched the gun fire. When my people spotted the cops, they immediately stopped firing and started running through the Cypress Hills Projects. The policemen were chasing them in the Suburban and trying to run them over. Bug-Out and I left the corner and went back to the apartment. During the chase, the cops in the Suburban called for backup. Squad cars and unmarked cars were all in the projects in no time at all.

Bug-Out and I were in the apartment for about ten minutes before two of my people returned exhausted. Less than five minutes after my two guys had arrived at the apartment, the front of the building was suddenly surrounded by police cars, both marked and unmarked, and several cops were in front of my apartment on the fourth floor. I was standing in the bathroom at the time, on top of the toilet bowl, ready to drop a load of drugs and 20 guns down a hole where a vent was supposed to be. I was waiting for the cops to start knocking on the front door, but to my surprise, the sound of the walkie talkie and other noises signaling the presence of the cops disappeared. The next thing that I saw was the cops getting into their cars and driving out of the projects.

After about twenty minutes after the cops had gone, the two members of my crew that I thought had been arrested made it to the apartment. They were completely exhausted but explained just how close they had come to getting arrested.

The next day we found out from a 911 operator who received the call about the shooting also happened to be a friend of ours. And that the police officers told her they believed that the shooters were in apartment 4B, 1266 Sutter Avenue and wanted her to send backup. She told us they said, "It's Glaze and his boys." They wanted her to give them permission to kick in the door and enter the apartment, but since she knew it was me she wouldn't do it. She said they tried 3 or 4 times, but she refused to give them the go ahead. She then told them they had another emergency call in the Brownsville Section, so they had to leave. I made sure one of people greased the palm of that 911 operator, because she saved me a fortune.

Better to give, then receive. Not sure that was what momma meant. If anyone looked out for or helped me or any of my people, then I made sure they were well taken care of. When I went out to eat, I left big tips, whether I was on a date with a girl or with my people. A big tip was mandatory. I tipped everybody. I tipped the dry cleaner, the gas station attendant, auto mechanic, and even girls after sex. I felt, what good is it to have money, if you don't have anyone to share it with? I can remember giving girls anywhere from $200 to $2,000 after sex.

Dead Mouse and Bullets

It had been almost a year since Fat Cat's wife Mousey was kidnapped.

Mousey was in Virginia, and Cookie, Fat Cat's niece, who was living in her Long Island home had forwarded a package to her. When Mousey received and opened the package, she fainted. Her mother, Mrs. McClinton had to use smelling salts to revive her.

They emptied the package's contents on the living room table and neither Mousey nor her mother understood the significance of the three bullets -- that is until they picked them up and read the children's names on them. Both then became hysterical as they held each other.

Mousey's brother was summoned from her video store, and after that all I know is that Cat's sister, Viola, Cookie, and Lynn, had left word at my place for me to call them as soon as possible -- that was in addition to all of them beeping me too. I returned all their calls and each one told me the same thing. Cat wanted to see me the next day, which was a Friday. They all told me that it was an emergency and that Cat wanted me to put everything on hold, including my own business and personal matters. At first, I wasn't going to go, because my brother was being released from Sing-Sing and I was to take a limousine, which I had already paid for to pick him up, take him home, and then go shopping. I rearranged things and had somebody else take care of picking up my brother.

Friday morning, I arrived at LaGuardia Airport about 6:45 A.M., paid for my ticket and boarded the 7:00 A.M. flight to Buffalo and landed around 8:00 A.M. Once in Buffalo, I climbed into a cab and told the driver to take me to Attica Correctional Facility. Cat and I reviewed who we thought was responsible for sending the package. Again, we concluded that Kevin "King Allah" Dove was the one responsible. His intention was to discourage Mousey from testifying against him regarding her kidnapping. At the time King Allah was still awaiting trial, while two others had just been convicted for the involvement in kidnapping. King Allah was being held in Nassau County Jail.

Cat, at first, wanted me to go see King Allah and remind him that he also had a mother, wife, girlfriend, and children, and that they would all die if he ever pulled another move like the one with the dead mouse. Cat went on to say that I was to tell King Allah that if he wanted to make a deal, Cat, would make sure that Mousey didn't show up to testify against him, regarding the kidnapping. In agreement that King Allah was also to return all Mousey's jewelry, especially the diamond wedding ring, taken during the kidnapping. Then after King Allah's release, he was to visit Cat and decide to pay Cat for the jewelry he no longer had and for the money that Cat's mother-in-law gave in the kidnapping.

Cat really was going to make sure Mousey couldn't be found to testify against King Allah. Cat's main motivation for wanting King Allah and his co-defendants to beat the case was so when they got home it would be my responsibility and my people to kill all those involved in the kidnapping and the firebombing that soon followed. Cat wanted me to advise King Allah that he knew his mother still lived in the Red Hook Houses and that his wife and kids were in Maryland, and the girlfriend, who worked for the Parole Division resided in Queens.

I found out when King Allah's next available visiting day was, and Country and I went to see him. When we got to Nassau County Jail, we checked in and waited for King Allah to show. After about 15 minutes, a fragile looking guy, about 5'6" tall, with a freckled complexion and reddish-brown hair came out. He sat down and said, "You must be Glaze." I told him I was. With that King Allah said that he had been calling all throughout Brooklyn and Queens, asking people about me. He said that I had one hell of a reputation on the streets and that was good and bad news. He didn't need to explain.

I got straight to the point about the package containing the dead mouse and three bullets, but he tried to deny his involvement. So, I disclosed what Cat had said about his mother still living in Red Hooks Houses, his wife and kids living in Maryland, and his girlfriend, who worked at the Parole Division. King Allah tried to give the impression that he cared about absolutely nothing, including his mother, wife and kids, and girlfriend. He tried to make me to believe that their wellbeing didn't matter to him. But all during our conversation I looked him dead in the eyes and I could tell that he loved his family and definitely didn't want anything to happen to them. He just didn't want me to know his weakness, so he tried to deceive me into believing that he was the most ruthless person on earth. Ruthless! He was nowhere near ruthless, not even close. I also mentioned that Cat was going to make sure that Mousey didn't show up to testify against him. King told me that when they were arrested and charged with the crime, he told his people not to worry, because Mousey wouldn't show up at the Grand Jury and so they wouldn't be indicted. However, he was wrong, because all of them were eventually indicted and now he was next.

I gave King Allah my telephone number and told him to let me know ahead of time when the trial was about to start, so Cat and I could make sure that Mousey couldn't be found. King Allah told me he knew that I knew how it felt for someone to have his back against the wall, with the strong possibility of never getting out of jail. I told him he was right, because during my past predicaments I did whatever I had to do in order to win. King Allah related that I should understand why, by any means necessary, one must do whatever he has to do in order to win. So, by the way he spoke, I knew he had been the one responsible for the package with the dead rat and the bullets. But what King Allah failed to realize was that he was dancing with death and had no idea how close he was. The visit ended and King Allah went back inside and Country and I left.

I flew up to Buffalo the very next day to visit Cat at Attica. I ran down everything that took place during my visit with King Allah. I told Cat that he was going to keep in touch via telephone and that he was definitely going to let me know ahead of time when the hearing and trial were going to be conducted. I could then make sure that Nassau County wouldn't be able to snatch Mousey to testify; because Cat, would've decided for Mousey to be out of reach until the case against King Allah was dismissed. Cat said all we could do was wait. Cat really wanted King Allah and his co-defendants. He wanted those scumbags to pay and I knew that if they would've been released, then they would definitely be killed.

That was just another lesson in being a drug dealer. Knowing that, not only are you risking your own life, but all those that you love and love you. Fortunately, and unfortunately, I learned if I wanted to keep the ones I loved safe - living in the world of violence wouldn't protect them. I hope those of you reading this story that are in or want to get into the drug business, have someone to love and those to love you -- if not change your ways.

Again, Fat Cat had every intention of getting the charges dropped against King Allah, knowing we would have dealt with him on street terms after the trial. Until that time came, one of King's people would call my Cypress headquarters, one or two times every week to ensure we are all on the same page.

Security Breach and a Pregnant Wife

Running the M&M Crew kept me on the edge. Playing two sides of the fence has a death as a consequence. Every business has security issues; in the corporate world they hack into computer system by breaking through the electronic firewall. When employees and customers don't feel safe or secure they lose their trust in you. Every aspect of the business always presented new challenges.

On April of 1988, it was a quiet Saturday morning, and I was knocked out lying up in bed with my lovely pregnant wife. We were living in my mother's newly built, baby mansion in South Carolina, when I was awakened by the ringing of the phone. Gathering my thoughts, I sensed trouble. It was my number one lieutenant, calling from my headquarters in Brooklyn at the Cypress Hill Houses. He informed that one of our crew, I'll call him "A" was visiting at Rikers Island and gave up info on our operations and the run of my security at the Cypress Hills House headquarters to some of my known enemies.

I had let it be known ahead of time that anyone caught leaking information from my crew would die, and that anyone attempting to play both sides of the coin would die. After speaking with Derrick, I got off the telephone and contacted Rick and explained to him the situation about "A". Despite "A" not being part of my crew, he was a close friend who I trusted and was in a position to set me up.

The way security was set up, no one came to see me without prior approval. Once you arrived you would be escorted from your car, cab or the street by four heavily armed crew members. Anyone who entered the building was searched. If you made it past those levels of security, including four to six heavily armed men wearing bullet proof vests, then before entering the apartment, your shoes came off. Every defense against the element of surprise was eliminated. This was before 9-11.

After being informed about the breach in security I felt betrayed and gave the order, "The next time anyone saw associate "A", *he is out of here.*" By 11:00 P.M. Saturday morning, less than 24 hrs., "A" came to my Cypress Hills House headquarters and knocked on the door. Entering Shorty G, Sty and Beaver, greeted him with, "What's up, A?" His response was, "Do not never disrespect me again; my name is 9 Bodies Artie." They all started laughing, they knew the protection blanket was off and he was about to get whacked. My guys came up with a story that they were about to go to the Red Parrot Night Club in midtown Manhattan. "A" stated that he wanted to go, but first he had to get dropped off to change and pick up his jewelry. Once again Shorty G, Sty and Beaver started laughing to themselves as 9 Bodies didn't have a clue that within the next 10 minutes the life he knew would be snuffed out. As the four of them left the Cypress apartment and walked across the street, "A" sensed he was no longer part of the team when someone from a distance called his name. Slowly he turned around to see who was calling him, Sty and Beaver at close range shot "A" in the back of the head on my orders. "A's" body violently fell to the ground while Shorty G, Sty and Beaver walked to their car as if nothing just happen. They drove to Coney Island Amusement Park and rode the roller coaster. Looking back, I'm surprised how in such a short period of time I took some guys from the neighborhood that typically spent their time robbing people in Midtown Manhattan to becoming part of my M&M family. *My crew had become a carbon copy of me, killers with no remorse.*

"A" in less than 16 hours was gunned down in front of 148 Doscher, between Sutter and Belmont Avenues. I wasn't anywhere in New York when the hit occurred, but when the homicide detectives on the scene started asking questions and not getting any answers, one of them said, "None of you have to tell me who did this. I know who it and you knew who did it, too. Glaze did it. Glaze murdered this guy. Glaze is the one who's responsible for all the murders that occur around here."

I had a lot of individuals who were following me for all the wrong reason. But somehow, I felt I was still human. Arriving back to New York, I meet with Fat Cat and literally cried and told him that I didn't want to do this anymore. Who was I to say who lived and who died, I wasn't God? I had so much power at the time; my crew would do any and everything I wanted them to do, with no question asked. Money corrupts. Again, I was making $40,000 cash every day at twenty-four years old, and I was one of the most feared criminals in New York City. *Nothing my son is proud of today.*

By this time, it must be obvious, that among the people in the drug business, that killing people was a daily, accepted occurrence. Not justifying it; just want those who are interested in making $40,000 a day to know, the odds are that you probably never live to enjoy it.

I didn't go to "A's" funeral, I was too depressed. He didn't have any kids and now he was deprived of his legacy. I really hated myself. I stole "A's" life. How could this once upon of time church boy turn into a blood thirsty Killer? I beat myself up until reality set in; however, I continued to be a product of my environment to survive.

If you are in power, you must be vicious. The more brutal and savage, is a level that others can't demonstrate, so you win by default. It's like politics, it seems those with the strongest stomach can handle running for public office, not necessarily the most honest and possibly more competent.

The result of killing "A" was that he was a part of Baby Sam's Crew and if they were sure I was responsible for killing him, they would soon want revenge.

May 6, 88 Here Comes Baby Sam

After "A" was hit, word on the street was that Baby Sam and his crew was going to kill me. The biggest problem with Baby Sam was that I didn't know what all of his crew looked like -- although I did know what Baby Sam, and Johnny Ray looked like.

I was in Orlando, Florida, during "A's" funeral, with one of my female companions, celebrating her birthday. We left New York, LaGuardia Airport, Friday, May 6, 1988, and returned the following Monday, May 9.

While I was in Florida, I wrote Sweet-L, an associate, at Greenhaven Correctional Facility, to try to find out if Baby Sam and his people really did have a hit on me. Sweet-L and Baby Sam were exceptionally close, like brothers, so I knew that Sweet-L would know. Sweet-L assured me that Sam and his people didn't feel that I had anything to do with "A's" murder. He also said that this Puerto Rican guy, named Nelson, who was from the Hardy Boys, was killed by Baby Sam, believing that Nelson was responsible for "A's" death. *Sorry for poor Nelson. You never know, when you're in business, if you can be killed for the wrong reasons.* I continued visiting Sweet-L daily, until August 1988. During one visit with Sweet-L, I remember telling him that I did in fact give the order to hit "A" and told him the reason. But it didn't seem to matter to Sweet-L. I confided in him and if he wanted to tell, then he could've started World War III between Baby Sam and me, but he didn't.

April 6 88 - Staying Alive

In the middle of dealing with King Allah, on April 6, 1988 I drove my Volvo to the Fort Greene section of Brooklyn, when I ran into a childhood friend Calvin McCloud a.k.a. Allah Justice and his right-hand man KaSon. These guys were not associates of King Allah at the time. However, I was concerned because I did not have a weapon and months prior, I believed, Ka-son killed an associate of mine, and he knew I was looking for him. When I saw them, I was like dam, these mother fuckers got me. I didn't have my guns, I couldn't run, all I had was a neck full of jewelry and my bulletproof vest.

My friend's sister, China, who was with was me, but sitting in the driver seat drove off in my car, just moments before Allah Justice and Ka-Son and one of their solider approached me. For some reason, which I can't recall, my friend, Lox, who was also with me, had every opportunity to leave, decided to place her life on the line by staying and dealing with the possibility of dying next to me in a hail of bullets. As Allah Justice and Ka-Son approached me, reluctantly Allah Justice and I embraced, and he felt my bulletproof vest. He stated that I was right in being safe. Being a poker player, I played along with Allah Justice by standing my ground and fronting as if I was strapped. I proceeded to stand there with my hand close by my imaginary gun, while staring down Ka-Son. We were staring each other down. This little game went on for several minutes when Allah Justice finally intervened stating, "You guys have to squash this beef, (concerning the Ka-son killing Hollywood, an associate of mine)." He went onto say, that I was his people, and so was Ka-Son.

While I had Ka-Son's attention, I needed to go back into the past. I wanted and needed to know at this time did he murder, Christopher "Hollywood" Brothers my lieutenant's brother and my friend. Hollywood had been murdered in the latter part of January 1988 in the Bedford Stuyvesant Section of Brooklyn.

Ka-son and his people were from the Tompkin Houses in Brooklyn and the beef stemmed from Hollywood fucking Ka-Son's girl, Yolanda, while Ka-son was in jail during the summer of 1987. After I was acquitted on murder charges, Hollywood and I were together a lot and once I found out that he was sexually involved with Yolanda, I told him straight up to leave her alone, because she wasn't worth getting into a beef with Ka-Son. Ka-Son had plenty of girls, but he loved Yolanda and she meant the world to him. Hollywood was making fast money at the time and was buying her all sorts of things. Again, I told Hollywood that girl wasn't worth him losing his life over.

Ka-Son looked me dead in the eyes and responded as coldly as if he was me, "If you murdered someone would you tell me?" With his answer it only confirmed what I already knew. Yes, he was responsible for Hollywood's death. Ka-Son and I shook hands for the time being.

After shaking hands with Kason, Allah Justice said that he wanted to get down with me and be part of the M&M crew. I told him if he really wanted to get down with me and hit him with a large drug package on consignment, he should page me later. I didn't believe he wanted to get down with me; it was just another excuse to hit me. We made arrangements for him to meet me in Cypress Hills in order to get him started that evening with a large sum of crack or heroin or both. Our trio left; I knew then I just escaped with my life. I couldn't understand, it was three against one. Why when they had their best and only chance, they didn't kill me? It was not until years later that I found out why. When they spotted me, they knew they had me, but they were worrying about which one of them would be shot and killed first, by me, during the shootout, not knowing I wasn't strapped.

Lox stayed there the whole time; she didn't budge. I asked her, what was wrong with her and why didn't she go and protect herself she stated, "If they were going to kill you, then they were going to have to kill me as well." That was touching, but foolish. Ka-Son and Allah's crew had numerous of murders under their belt. They were known as "stick up kids" with a reputation that when they went somewhere to rob you, they would kill everyone, no witnesses, including the intended target, their families, cat, dogs, roaches and rats, anything that moved.

I thanked Lox for her sacrifice. Her sister China arrived back with my car and I headed to the Cypress headquarters where Allah Justice contacted me and agreed to meet me that night. *My childhood friend, Allah Justice would die that night, for several reasons. Reason one, when I was away, he was plotting to kill and rob a close family member of mine. Reason number two, his man Ka-Son was responsible for Hollywood's murder. Reason number three, I didn't like people who were just as dangerous as me that I couldn't trust.*

We would meet that night. Allah Justice was a slick and sneaky individual. He arrived to 1266 Sutter Street from the rear of the adjacent building, headed to the roof that connected to 1266 Sutter. I laid in the cut (discreet hiding place) for him as he knocked on my 4B apartment door, after several knocks he turned to enter the staircase when I pulled the trigger. The first bullet hit Allah Justice knocking him back. As I squeezed off the second shoot, that bullet hit him in the face; blood sprayed everywhere as he hit the floor and lay dead. After I shot and killed Allah Justice, I headed to the Marriott Hotel near the airport for an Alibi. While at the hotel the next morning I received some disturbing news, Allah Justice, this person who was just as dangerous as me, was still alive. He was carried out on a stretcher by EMS and he did say that Glaze tried to kill him. I am pissed, how in the hell does the founding father of M&M botch a hit. I was beside myself; I took pride in my work. I considered myself an expert, especially if I am that close and failed to deliver. Guess he was beyond lucky too!

It was war, and someone was going to win. I had everything moved from my Cypress Hills headquarters to a couple of my other locations in Queens. Would you believe I started receiving calls about the attempted hit on Allah Justice and the fact that he is just as dangerous as I was? Wow! Tell me something that I didn't know. The next few weeks were different; I was in attack mode and we were involved in several shoot outs throughout the metropolitan area.

Allah Justice Put a Hit on Me

After my April 6th Botch hit on Allah Justice, while still in the hospital, he summoned a large amount of the

Five Percenters from all over Brooklyn to his hospital bed and instructed them to locate and murder me, and anyone of my crew on sight. On that evening of April 8th, it was still daylight when several of my crew and I were walking through Cypress Hill headquarters coming from a shopping spree at Ralphie Sportswear. We were always on point, scanning the surrounding area, watching each and every one as soon as we got out of the car or leaving the apartment. *Criminal life was stressful, but you didn't go to your doctor asking for any Prozac.*

Another time, I can recall exiting Cypress headquarters, when I and a total of six of my guys were leaving the building. Three walked out and went down the front staircase, while the other three walked out of the back stair case. Everyone was heavily armed with guns drawn as we meet up on the first floor. We were surprised as two uniformed NYPD Housing cops were standing in the hallway. Time froze, as the officers saw us with our guns drawn. Then they said, "Good evening," and quickly exited the building. Make no mistake we left right after, realizing we were no match for New York Finest.

Suddenly, as we hit the streets a hail of bullets rang out as we took cover and started firing back in broad day light. Bullets were making their mark on the surrounding cars and buildings with the sound glass shattering. Miraculously no one was hit, including my crew, or my enemies, or innocent bystanders. At that moment the war hit a higher level. Allah Justice and anyone who was affiliated with him would have trouble sleeping. I purchased several motorcycles at $8,000 dollars apiece; the purchase of those bikes was to be used as means of getaway after killing anyone.

A short time passed and on the evening of April 17 I got a call from an associate telling me that one of the shooters, Keith Reedy a.k.a. Universal Justice, was spotted in area of Canarsie, Brooklyn. I paged my man Du and gave him the information. With that Beaver and Bumpy

Face, Rick Williams and Du caught up with Universal Justice at a Chinese restaurant. Upon entering the restaurant, they saw him with a young lady and with a baby in his arms. Du suggested that he, Universal Justice, give the girl the baby. Universal refused to do so, so Du shot him in the leg with his 9mm, which lead to Universal Justice finally giving the child to the mother. Once the child was out of his hands, Du, Beaver and Bumpy Face took aim and fired the 45 automatic and 9mms into Universal Justice causing his death. His body and head were hit with so many hollow point bullets that there was no face to recognize. The young lady went into shock as her baby starting crying. My guys headed back to Cypress as they entered into the apartment to inform me of a job well done.

Sometimes, Good Help is Hard to Find

After the botched hit on Allah Justice, and the killing of Universal Justice in the Chinese restaurant the Cypress headquarters was hot, police were everywhere. This was April of 1988, so I took off to the Poconos for a romantic weekend with my wife, who flew up to visit.

My romantic weekend lasted only 27 hours before I headed back to Brooklyn. My second in command, Herm, had made a fatal mistake. Because of the attempts on my people at the Cypress Hills projects, I decided to use a house in Queens as our new headquarters. It was to be used for supervising all our moves; including cooking up all of the cocaine to turn it into crack; bagging it up and have the drugs transported and the money dropped off. Well, Herm had taken about five kilos of crack and around $200,000 in cash, along with a vast number of capsules from the Cypress Hills apartment and was supposed to be going directly to the house in Queens. He was with two of our crew members, both of whom were heavily armed. The three of them left Cypress Hills in a cab and instead of going straight to the house in Queens and dropping off the drugs and money, they went grocery shopping in Brooklyn.

This knucklehead, Herm, got out of the cab with one of the crew members and left the other one in the cab with the drugs and money. Herm and my little man went into the supermarket and Herm grabbed a cart and started filling it with everything he figured we needed. As they were about to go to the counter to pay for everything, a black male wearing a security guard uniform approached them and said that Herm had stolen something. Herm whipped out several thousand dollars and told the security guard that he wasn't stealing anything but came there to buy. Unfortunately, the security guard still acted funny and tried to grab Herm. My little man, with his hand on his gun, told the security guard to back off. That made the security guard focus on my little man and he jumped and grabbed him. The gun went off two or three times, hitting the security guard, killing him, while putting a bullet in his own leg. Herm and my little man ran from the store to the cab which pulled out of the parking lot as the cops were pulling in. Some of the supermarket employees waved down the cops and told them that the shooter had got into a grey-colored cab that raced off. With that, the cops sped away, sirens blasting, looking for the cab.

Herm got word to me in the Poconos regarding what had happened at the supermarket. From what I understood, when I received the word, was that the police were on their trail, chasing them, and other police cars were going to block them off and they were about to be arrested. My head was spinning. Here I was about to lose two of my people for murder, drugs and weapons charges, to say nothing of the loss I was about to incur involving the drugs and some $200,000 in cash. I started shouting and screaming over the telephone that those dumb fucks couldn't do anything right without me being right there.

My wife and I were packed and about to walk out of the door and head back to New York City when another call came in. Good news; the cops never caught up with Herm and my other two men.

That should have meant, that my people were safe, and I didn't lose the money and drugs. Then came the bad news; the gunshot wound to my little man's leg was serious. He'd lost a lot of blood and the pain was unbearable. So, he was taken to the hospital -- the same one where the security had been pronounced dead. The hollow-point bullet had ripped through the main blood vessels and when he got to the hospital the doctor told him that if he hadn't been brought in when he did, then there was no doubt he would've died.

In New York, anyone admitted to the hospital to be treated for a gunshot wound was reported to the police. It's the law. So, my little man's incident was reported and at first it looked like nothing was going to happen. But early the next day witnesses from the supermarket came to the hospital with detectives and identified him as the one who murdered the security guard. He was placed under arrest and held under police guard while in the hospital. Funny thing is that not only was the security guard taken to the same hospital as my little man, but Allah Justice was there, too, recovering from the gunshot wounds he sustained from me.

Thereafter Brandon, my little man, was arrested and charged with that murder. I just lost a good member and about to get more heat and for the life of me how dumb could Herm be? I ripped Herm a new asshole. "You are going to Queens, why are you riding around in a cab with all of the money, drugs and guns and still in Brooklyn? You could have dropped everything off in Queens and then gone shopping. News flash, they do have supermarkets in Queens." I wouldn't let him answer, if he did, I'm sure I would have had smacked him up on the side of his head.

My lady and I arrived back home and from there I called Country to come and pick me up. We went to Harlem, Uptown Manhattan to S-N-S an afterhours place. The main reason for me being there was that I was trying to get ready for the war and contact with connections for guns and bulletproof vests.

Later that day Country came and got me, and we went to the house in Queens to check on my other people. Then Country, along with ten of my people and I, went to the Cypress Hills apartment and set up heavy security at that location. Anytime me or any of my people left or entered the building, all of us were well protected. In fact, anyone who entered or left the building was well protected. I refused to have any of my people, or any visitors for that matter, gunned down as a result of the war. It was like Fort Knox, I just always wanted to be prepared and for anything. I was the motivation and the inspiration for my crew. I taught them the way I needed for them to act; let them know that we were all like family, and I loved them like we were flesh and blood relatives.

I took care of my people and I can honestly say that during my entire reign, I never lost anyone, i.e. none of them were murdered and none of them went to jail with a life sentence, or even a very long sentence -- due to drugs or murder charges. Everyone who went to jail was immediately bailed out if they had a bail set, and each one received a good lawyer, and if someone did end up having to do some time in jail we took financial care of their family.

The only person who can be counted as a loss was my little man who got shot in the leg. The funny thing about that whole incident was that the security guard was really an ex-security guard. He had been fired a day or two before the incident and was back in the supermarket that day trying to get his job back, by making himself look good and acting like Herm was stealing.

I hired Murray Cutler to represent my little man and took care of his family. I received information: names, addresses, etc., regarding all the witnesses against my little man. There were four witnesses and I was going to have all of them killed to prevent my man from getting convicted. I passed the assignment to Herm, because I felt like the whole thing was his fault and it was his responsibility to make sure that my little man didn't get convicted. Herm said that it would be taken care of, but he didn't. My little man was only 17 years old and was convicted and received a sentence of 25 years to life. I hated that. A young kid's life wasted, all because of Herm's dumb ass. Damn near every day after that, either I, my people, or all of us together would go out searching for Allah Justice and Kason. One time we went through the Lafayette Garden Houses, because we'd received word that they had just opened a drug spot around there and they all would be there.

There were about three or four groups, three or four men in each group, and entering from different sides of the project. My directive was to kill them on sight, but as we got closer to the building and were about to make a move, I called it off when I noticed several undercover police officers getting ready to raid the drug spot. All we needed was to get into a shoot-out with a bunch of cops.

Sometime Wishing Makes it So

Shortly after the incident, Ka-Son and his girlfriend, Tawana, were shot and killed. It happened at the Tompkins Houses. Ka-Son and his girl was shot on a Sunday afternoon in May 1988. From my understanding, Ka-son just opened the door and let the killers into his apartment. I guess an argument broke out between Ka-Son and his assailants, and they ended up shooting him two or three times in the stomach and chest. Tawana was in the bedroom, undressed, it was likely they had just finished having sex. I understand the assailants were searching the apartment, for money, guns and jewelry. When they spotted Tawana she ran and made it to the door. Wrapped up in a sheet she ran down a couple of flights of stairs; unfortunately, she had an asthma attack. The assailants caught up with her and shot her several times, killing her. Ka-Son didn't die instantly. Rumor had it that he made several calls to some of his so-called friends and told them what had happened before he died.

Of course, word on the Street was that me, and my M&M crew were dressed in Army Fatigues, armed with our Uzis. We supposedly had the keys to his apartment as we busted into Ka-Son's bedroom. When Ka-Son was killed, there were contracts on both him and Allah Justice. Herm was going to pay for Ka-son's hit, and I was going to pay for Allah Justices. We were willing to buy anyone a 190 Mercedes Benz for each one. But we never paid anyone for the hit on Ka-Son, because no one ever came forward. Besides, one of Ka-Son and Allah Justice's partners had a $5,000 contract on Ka-Son at the time, too, and I honestly believe that it was one of Ka-son's own people who murdered him, over a robbery or something that he and the murderers were in on together.

I found out about Ka-Son's death, because I was trying to find out where he was so I could make a move on him myself. I called Ka-Son's girl, Yolanda, but her mother answered the telephone and said that she wasn't home. So, I asked if Ka-Son was there. She asked me who I was, and I told her that I was Allah Justice, Ka-son's friend. She said, "Are you sure that you're Allah Justice"? I responded with, "Yes, I'm Allah Justice, Ka-Son's best friend". So, she finally said, "Justice, haven't you heard that Ka-Son was murdered a little while ago"? Sounding disappointed, I said that it couldn't be true, but she said that it was, that Ka-Son and a girl named Tawana were murdered together. Once I realized that she was being sincere, I said, "That's good! That no good bastard is dead, and he got what he had coming for killing Hollywood." Then I hung up the telephone. Herm was right there with me, and we celebrated the news of Ka-son's death.

Firebombing of Fat Cat's Mama's Home

My lifeline seemed to be getting shorter every day. War in the drug trade was like the Hatfield–McCoy feud (1863–1891), two families from West Virginia, Kentucky (the war isn't over until the bloodline is ended).

The past kidnapping of Fat Cat's wife Mousey was still causing problems, although others believed differently.

Allah Justice, now out of the hospital, he and his people got together late one evening and threw a firebomb through Fat Cat's mother's house and shot up her car. The Firebombing only added insult to injury, to Fat Cat. It was only a month prior that in March that King Allah had one of his crew send a dead rat and three bullets to Mousey's Long Island home. On each bullet appeared one of the Fat Cat's kid's names: Yolanda, Lorenzo Jr., and the baby Lenard.

Some believed that King Allah had manipulated Allah Justice and the rest of the Five Percenters (their crew's name) into believing that I lived at Momma's house, which was a lie. The bombing occurred for several reasons. One was to kill me for supposedly killing Kason. The other was that King Allah was still putting pressure on Fat Cat to prevent his wife, Mousey, from testifying against him for her kidnapping back in May of 87.

Around 11:30 P.M., May 20, 1988, Allah Justice and his people circled the block several times to make sure the area wasn't hot, leaving two of his crew on the corner of 139th Street. The last time they made the rounds, one stayed on the corner with his gun drawn, and the other walked up the block to their car, a gray Chrysler. The car's motors were running, but their lights were out. Allah Justice got out and gave a sign to a man on the corner, meaning that if anyone were to show up, then they were to be killed. The one with Allah Justice was on point; if anyone were to come out: of any of the houses, especially Momma's house, he was to shoot and kill them. Then Allah Justice threw a cocktail bomb into Momma's house.

The fire from the cocktail bomb hit the living room curtains, sending them into flames, with the fire spreading quickly. I think Allah Justice then spotted someone trying to put out the fire, because he ordered his men to start shooting. Momma's house was immediately splattered with 9mm bullets. Allah Justice got back into his car and backed out of the block, as the gunman walked to the corner to take of any witnesses, but there wasn't.

Momma had fallen asleep while watching television, when the bombs crashed through the living room window waking her up. The fire spread quickly throughout the three-story house and once Momma realized she couldn't stop it. She first went to the back of the house to the master bedroom, and woke up her husband, Amos "Daddy Amos" Coleman, who was 75 years old at the time. Momma and Daddy Amos then went upstairs and woke up the grandchildren: Tamekia, who was 12; Wy-Nell, who was 10; and Turtle, who was 4. All of them were gathered from their bedrooms and Momma told Daddy Amos to take them out of the house to safety. Wy-Nell was the only one of the grandchildren who was badly burned. He stayed in the hospital and ended up having several skin grafts.

Momma proceeded upstairs, to the third level, and tried to get her daughter, Mary, out of the house. Mary was confined to a wheelchair, as a result of a stroke she'd suffered about six years earlier. Mary weighed about 250 pounds and there was no way Momma could help her down the stairs. So, Momma tried to push her to the window, knowing that was the only way she could save her daughter's life. She tried and tried, but Momma told me over and over again that she couldn't move her. Smoke and fire were everywhere. Momma was choking from smoke inhalation, and she was crying. She knew her daughter was going to die and there was nothing she could do to save her.

When she heard the fire truck's sirens, Momma ran downstairs and told the fire fighters that her daughter, who was in a wheelchair, was on the third floor. By the time they had reached Mary, she had died from smoke inhalation. When Momma found out that Mary had died, she started crying and became hysterical. By that time I had arrived at the scene Cookie, Fat Cat's niece, had called me and told me what had happened.

Country and I had just left Momma's house about 45 minutes prior to the bombing. That meant that if Allah Justice and his followers had come a little earlier, as we were exiting the house, then they could've killed me right there. I believe that after making an attempt at me, they probably wouldn't have thrown the bomb into Momma's house. If they would've caught me then it would've been just me and Country. Neither of us were strapped with guns nor were we wearing our bulletproof vests. There's no doubt we would've been ambushed and killed. I tried to console Momma and Cookie over the loss of Mary, who was Cookie's mother as well as Momma's daughter. Different news stations were there with cameras rolling and all the major New York City newspapers had reporters on the scene. I found myself grabbing and holding Momma back, as she was trying to run back into the house for Mary, even though she knew that Mary was dead. I waited there for hours, until daybreak. By then, we'd finally convinced Momma to go to Cookie's house to get some rest which was on the corner of the block.

I set up shop at Cookie's house and summoned several of my people to be there twenty-four hours a day, as a security measure. My people were always heavily armed and on point. They walked the area and looked for anything that seemed even minutely suspicious. Cookie's house was full of Cat's family members, and family friends, coming to pay their respects and extend their condolences.

Later that day Lynn and I went to visit Cat at Shawangunk Correctional Facility in Walkill, New York. Several hours after the fire I heard that some of Cat's family members felt that it was my fault the firebomb was thrown into Momma's house, causing Mary's death. To a degree, I was hurt by that and when I saw Cat in the visiting room I embraced him and told him that I was sorry for what had happened. Cat reassured me that it wasn't my fault.

Cat sent Lynn to the bathroom and we discussed the incident. After weighing all the facts, we concluded that, without a doubt, King Allah and Allah Justice, and their followers, were responsible for firebombing Mamma's house that killed Mary. Cat and I began making plans on how to deal with Allah Justice, King Allah, and all the others responsible for firebombing. All of them would have to pay.

During that whole week I spent my time at Cookie's house with Cat's family and going back and forth to visit Cat. I set up all the security arrangements for the wake and the funeral. Not wanting to underestimate those scum bag Five-Percenters, all of my people were on point, heavily armed, all around the funeral parlor. Without my people there wouldn't have been any security at Mary's wake and funeral. We were everywhere. My main objective was to prevent any attempt on Mousey's life, or any other member of Cat's family. I had my people with all the family members, including riding with them in the cars. However, we weren't the only ones in the area; detectives from the New York Police Department were also present, even though they tried harassing my people, but it didn't work.

One of my men was standing point and started sweating, because of the hot weather and the bulletproof vest he was wearing. He just turned to the detective who was trying to pressure him and said, "Don't you think it's kind of hot here?" My people knew that the worst thing that could've happened was that they got arrested for possession of a weapon. But nothing happened. Besides, if it had, then my people knew that they would have been bailed out immediately.

I didn't feel comfortable going to Mary's wake or funeral, as Mott, Cat's niece, and a few other family members, were still saying it was my fault that the firebombing took place resulting in Mary death. Somewhat feeling guilty, I finally decided to go to the wake and funeral. Mousey expressed she didn't feel like it was my fault. She had the feeling that her kidnappers were responsible for everything. Mousey was scared, because she'd not-so-long-before testified against two of the guys who were a part of the kidnapping -- both were convicted on all charges and sentenced to 25 years to life. If I remember correctly, the firebombing occurred only a day or two after those guys were sentenced although King Allah was not one of the two.

Cat and I knew that King Allah would try anything to make sure Mousey didn't take the stand against him in the upcoming trial. Believing that, I told Cat I didn't think it would be wise for Mousey to go to the funeral. He agreed. So, she was protected more than any other member of the family.

Retaliation for the Firebombing

During that week after the firebombing, some of my people and I found time to do some looking for the culprits but were unsuccessful. My opinion is that everyone involved with the firebombing left New York the same day, knowing I was out to gun them down on sight like the animals they were. First, the beef was between us and not the family. Mousey wasn't a part of the drug game and nobody in the house had anything to do with the business. If they wanted to involve family members, then there's no line drawn and no rules to be followed -- everything goes.

What I probably didn't realize (the irony) that we had done the same thing to Perry Bellamy's family. "Do onto others as you would have done unto you."

Putting aside that I was a hypocrite, during one of my visits with Cat I told him all of those responsible for the firebombing had left New York and that my people and I were going on a mission to find and kill all of them, as well any of their family members. I felt an example needed to be set; if innocent family members were brought into wars against us, then they would be subjecting their own families to total annihilation. Fat Cat was in. I informed Cat that as soon as it got dark, my people were going to go to several different housing projects, knock on the doors of certain apartments, then run in and kill everyone in that apartment. The intended targets were the family members of those responsible for the firebombing. Cat told me that he didn't care if the adults in the various apartments were murdered, but he didn't want any kids to die. I told him that we either did it my way or we didn't do it at all, while reminding him of Mary's death and that he almost lost all of his own family. Cat and I ended up getting into a big argument and he wouldn't back down. Cat stood firm; he didn't want any children to die. He didn't want a child's blood on his hands. I told Cat if that was the way he wanted it, then I quit. Then I took off my Roundtable Ring and tried to give it back to him, but he refused to take it. It was all a bluff on my part and it didn't work. I then told Cat that he was calling the shots and the decision was his to be made. *Fat Cat prevented additional guilt from following me through the rest of my life.* When I left the visit. I called my headquarters in Queens and had my order transmitted to the streets -- the hits were called off.

Cat put a price of $25,000 each on the head of King

Allah and his people who were responsible for the kidnapping and bombing. I visited several guys throughout the New York State Correctional System and put out the word, so the Welcoming Committee was waiting for their arrivals. A lot of guys in prison who are serving long sentences and had families to support would do just about anything to support them. There were others who had no families or friends or any source of income and would stab and kill a facility's warden for $25,000. I still believed that if certain circumstances hadn't occurred in August 1988, then King Allah and his whole crew would've been murdered for the money on their heads. There was no way in the world they could've survived, not even in protective custody, because I knew guys who would've signed into protective custody just to get to any one of them. *So, for those who are thinking about getting into the drug business, again, think twice, maybe three times.*

Obviously, it wasn't only the hoods targeting each other, it included mothers, fathers, brothers, sisters, babies - it involved everyone. So, right then and there, was when I decided to move my wife, Tamia, out of New York for her safety, as well as our unborn child. While Tamia was out of town, I visited her quite often. I would fly in and out of town, making sure she was alright, and giving her money for bills, etc. She spent most of her time with my family and they would drive her wherever she needed to go, but she wanted her own car. I told her if she gets her driver's license, then I would buy her any kind of car she wanted. She took the test once, failed and didn't try again. She would tell me that I didn't have a license and was always driving, and I informed her I drove, because I paid for all my cars. Averaging close to $40,000 a day, so to buy Tamia a brand-new car would have meant only a day's profit.

Protecting My Family

Prior to what would be known as Operation Horse Collar, which would be my downfall, I focused more on my wife and my unborn child. I had already moved my wife out of New York months prior to her giving birth. Initially we were looking for a house in Long Island but based upon Fat Cat's wife kidnapping and the firebombing that all changed.

The farther away from violence the better; I can honestly say my wife, Tamia, was happy about living in a brand-new home. I was flying in and out of Charleston at least three to five times each week. I always wanted my wife and son to be protected and I needed to step up my security. So, on a trip to New York, I purchased a brand new, bullet proofed, Nissan pathfinder. I had a family to protect and look after. Maybe this was the beginning of my increasing value for human life. *How many Christmas ghosts would come to possibly haunt me?*

Lieutenant Hit & Sty

In the drug business you had to rely on your associates. One of my lieutenants was Herman Brothers a.k.a. Hit. Everybody always thought he got the name because he was a killer, far from the truth. I gave Herman the nickname Hit because he reminded me of the boxer Tommy "The Hitman" Hearns. Hit lived in the next building at 1260 Sutter Avenue. He was a few years younger than me, which made him somewhat like a little big brother. Hit ran the lab workers, cooking up the coke into crack, cutting it and bagging it up. One day I showed up to one of our locations and he had a ledger with names and numbers detailing what and how much money that was due to be paid back to us. I screamed at this idiot "You dumb mother fucker, get rid of this ledger, this can be the key to our downfall"! I kept track of details in my head. My mind was like a computer; my memory like an elephant. Hit wasn't the smartest, but he served his purpose. Also, I knew he was loyal to me, even when his brother Hollywood was shot and murdered, and others rumored and suspected me as the killer.

My hit men included Juneau "Sty a.k.a. Du" Wilson may his soul RIP. Him and Shorty G, these "brothers" were fearless. If anyone of those dudes were at your door or sitting behind you in a car - lights out and you are out of there. I meet up with Sty when he was on the run at the time and was in hiding in a brownstone building in Manhattan. We bonded with one another and began talking about finding him a safe haven. I decided he would be better off if I sent him to a place I had in South Carolina. As time went on, I would send for Sty to come to New York to make hits. Sty stayed on the run from June of 1987 until his death in June of 1994. He was found pistol whipped, tortured and shot in the head by two of his associates named Lite and Scar, who he took under his wing. They also tortured his lady friend Star who was with him; stabbing and shooting her numerous times, but she played dead. By that time, Sty's body count from New York to South Carolina was probably twenty. According to Star; the surviving witness, Lite and Scar killed Sty over a gold Rolex watch taken from a drug dealer, during a home invasion that left a husband and wife dead six months prior.

Sty was my most loyal member. I can remember the last time that we spoke. He asked me, if he ever was going to see me again. I thought for sure, the answer would have been yes, not knowing that it would be the last time that I would be speaking with my little brother. It hurt like hell when I learned of his death. As strange as it seemed, I know I was changing; revenge was becoming too expensive in human terms. The change was gradual; both culprits were shot and killed. Lite was killed a few days after Sty near the Apollo theater and Scar and two others were killed a couple of years later after leaving a night club in Manhattan. Again, all eyes were on me - go figure.

Maybe I Was Starting to Get Soft

As for Shorty G, he had big balls that he tripped over. I learned that Shorty G had opened up shop in the Van

Siclen Houses. The sad and the unfortunate part , he was stealing one half to one kilo of crack at a time from me. He knew the penalty would be death if caught. One day my lead person from the lab told me that they cooked five to ten kilos at a time, and by the time he and the crack left point A until it arrived to point B we lost a half to one kilo of crack. I told him it was probably due to the potency of the cocaine, probably wasn't as pure as we thought. I made a mental note and it wasn't until one day I was approached by Tyrone, an associate complaining to me that every time he saw Shorty G, he always pulling out his gun threatening him. So of course I asked him, where were you seeing Shorty G? He said, "At your spot in Van Siclen Houses". First of all, I didn't have a drug spot there and just like that I realized Shorty G was responsible for stealing the missing drugs, which was every time he was picking up from the lab. It was all making sense, when these guys got paid; they were jerking their money off on clothes, jewelry and girls. Shorty G always had money when everyone else seemed to be broke; even after he spent money on shopping and everything else. Shorty G had extra funds, because he was stealing product and selling it as his own. Not knowing this cartoon character was buying me gifts, sweat suits, sneakers and jewelry with my own money. *And that was a crack of shit..* I was seeing blood. I needed to use him as an example. I could not wait to get a hold of Mr. Shorty G.

I caught up with Shorty G the very next day. He was at one of my places of residence in Laurelton, Queens, along with several other members of my crew. When we picked him up, there was my lieutenant Country, Rollo and myself. Rollo was on point and was ready to unload the clip into Shorty G's head on my command. As Shorty G entered the Jeep I had Country and Rollo search him, making sure he wasn't strapped with a pistol - he wasn't. As he got into the back seat of my brand new, decked out, red, fully loaded Cherokee Limited, I really didn't want to get blood on my seats. I paid forty to forty-five thousand dollars for it. Rollo and Shorty G sat in the back; the whole time Rollo is awaiting the signal. As I started quizzing Shorty G about him stealing drugs and operating his own drug spot in the Van Siclen Houses; of course, he initially denied it as we drove off. I made several stops and each and every time I entered back into the jeep, I confronted him about his betrayal and he continued to deny it. He just sat quietly before entering Brooklyn as I made one more stop at Fat Cat niece, Cookie's home. Ever since the firebomb that killed Cookie's mother back on May 20th, 1988, I had been providing twenty-four hour, round the clock protection for Cat's family with other heavily armed crew members, wearing bullet proof vests.

After checking on Cookie, I got back in the jeep and was about to head to Brooklyn. Shorty G knew I didn't like going to Brooklyn in the daylight hours. He knew, if his stubbornness forced me to go and meet up with Tyrone to find out that he had a spot in Van Siclen Houses to prove that he had been stealing my drugs, I was going to let Rollo empty every bullet from his clip into his head, and leave his dead body in Brooklyn. He finally came clean and started crying. Surprising myself, I forgave him and sentenced him to security duty at Cookie's House and told him he would not be getting paid for months while working his tab off. On the real tip, despite Shorty G's crossing the line by stealing from me, knowing the repercussion, I had to admit for some reason I admired him and because of that, it saved his life or I was definitely getting soft; I just didn't want to admit it.

In retrospect, there was another situation that made me question myself. I confronted some stick-up kids in Coney Island that were scheming on robbing one of my drug spots. The issue was resolved; the so-called stick up kids didn't know that the spot was mine and they begged for forgiveness. I spared their lives and they assured me that nothing will ever happen to my spot or workers

Fight Night Tyson vs. Spinks

All work and no pleasure didn't work. It was Fight Night, June 27, 1988 Iron Mike Tyson vs. Michael Spinks at Trump Plaza, Atlantic City. I made reservation for a white Mercedes Benz stretch limo to pick me and a couple of guys up from my house in Queens. We were all dressed in white silk suits, $2,000 each. My associates had their shoes, shirt and ties to match. I was dressed all white from head to toe wearing my white gator shoes, cost $1,300, white shirt and tie for $600 dollars.

As our limo arrived in front of Trump Plaza, the main entrance was packed with a crowd of fans to greet the celebrities including: Michael Jordan, Doug Williams of the Washington Redskin, Hector Camacho, Meldrick Taylor , and Jesse Jackson who was then running for President of the United States along with his Secret Service team. Anybody that was somebody was at that fight. As we exited the limo the crowd was trying to figure out who we were. They start calling us New Editions. We had $1500 front row seats. Michael Jordan and Doug Williams were sitting behind us. I ran into Cat's Boy Chuck who had placed a bet of 30,000 dollars on Spinks. Fat Cat and I were putting up $15,000 dollars apiece, betting on our Brooklyn Home Boy, Iron Mike. Within ninety-one seconds the fight was over; Iron Mike knocked out Michael Spinks. I wouldn't believe it if someone told me but being that close and witnessing it with my own eyes - Michael hitting the mat.

After the fight we hung out in Trump Plaza partying and mingling with folks. Back then I didn't drink or get high. My high was money and fucking as many different women that would have me. Call it my shallow period, although it lasted awhile. As the night went on, I almost got into an altercation with former junior welterweight boxing champion Meldrick Taylor. He was signing autographs, partying, mingling with crowd, flirting and talking to a bunch of different women; when I saw this exotic looking young lady dressed up, standing elegantly to the side. I couldn't tell her nationality, who cared, she was drop dead gorgeous. She seemed to be very interested in the man she stood next to. However, not thinking, just acting, I went over and interrupted them. It was one awesome, serendipitous moments and I convinced her to leave with me. My next move was to get a room; we went to the lobbies front desk, no luck, fight night and everything was sold out. I was pissed, horny and wanted her so bad that she dared me to meet her in the lady's bathroom. Now that was tricky, it was crowded, and women were moving in and out of the ladies' room. After thinking about it, and as soon as I watched six or seven women walk out of the bathroom drunk, I entered. She was at the end stall waiting. As I entered the stall and locked the door we started kissing, touching and feeling each other. I removed her panties and started finger fucking. Every time we heard someone enter we tried not to make any noise, so she started sucking on my dick as I ran my hands thru her jet black silky hair. I wanted her body, turning her around and we started fucking doggy style. Her pussy was so wet and hot, keep in mind we are both in the stall, my white pants, jacket and shirt are off and I'm standing there with my white socks on, fucking away. My adrenaline is running, I am on a high thinking we might get busted at any moment.

I finally bust one as our hearts are beating uncontrollably. She went out first, as I got dressed and exit the ladies room. We met up at the bar, ordered drinks, and I'm already trying to get Natalia, sexy name - right, to move to New York, when he, "Meldrick Taylor," comes up to us popping shit like, "What are you doing with my girl"? First of all, I didn't know she was with him, she didn't say a word. Funny looking back, we got into a heated conversation. Boxing champion or not, he did not have a clue who he was fucking with. He did not know that his whole career and life could have ended that night, over a piece of ass. Security arrived and my guys pulled me away. As I think about it, Natalia used me to give him a taste of his own medicine. *She could have used me anytime.*

Back to Shorty G and the Real Culprit

Was getting soft causing me pain? Back to business, on Tuesday June, 28, 1988, after arriving back from Atlantic City and settling in, I received a call that my stash house in Laurelton Queens was robbed. Country picked me up in a brand new 1988 Lincoln Town Car. We drove over there to get all of the facts. It was not a break in, it was an inside job. My total loss was $260,000 in cash, 13kilos of cocaine and 1 kilo of heroin and over 30 guns including; tech 9s, Uzis, 9mms, a 45 and ammunition. This move had Shorty G's name written all over it. I had Country drive me to Brooklyn and its broad day light at this time; didn't like doing that, made me too exposed. This time when I catch Shorty G, I am going to kill him with my bare hands. We went to Van Siclen Houses in East New York where he had the spot and where his aunt lived, he wasn't there. We drove to Lafayette Garden Houses in the Bedford Stuyvesant section of Brooklyn where his girlfriend resided - no Shorty G. I then went to downtown Brooklyn, anywhere he could possibly be - no Shorty G.

I finally went to Louis H. Pink Houses, his mother's place of residence. As Country and I got there, some of my crew were waiting: Sty, Beaver, Rollo and a few others. We went into Shorty G's mother's building, knocked on her door and his sister let us in. I am very respectful when it came to mothers and addressed her, "Ma'am, your son took some things from my place that I want back. All I am looking for is what he took, if everything is returned nothing will happen to anybody." His mother starts going off. You need to do what, you need to do....?" She didn't give a dam about anything, keep in mind this exchange must have went on for 5 minutes. Even her daughter tried to calm her down and talk sense to her, but Shorty G's mom wasn't having it. All I know I lost it, my eyes started bulging out of my eye sockets and my guys start pulling out their guns and pulling down the shade in the apartment, because they knew I was going to say kill everyone in the apartment. It was almost comical; this tiny woman was staring me down. To my surprise I gave the order to leave. I didn't know what it was, but I didn't feel right about this hit, so we left.

I had Country drive me straight to the Airport and I took a flight to my mother's newly built home in South Carolina, to cool off. I later received a call that night and my man on the other end of the phone told me he heard that I was all over Brooklyn looking to find and murder Shorty G and he made mention of the almost hit on Shorty G's family. He said, "Once I heard you went to the airport and hopped on a plane that was one of the smartest moves you made. And don't worry about Shorty-G I will take care of him for you."

A couple nights later I received another call that they had pinpointed Shorty-G and fired upon him several times in front of the 88th Precinct in Brooklyn and they believe he was hit. I paged Shorty G and his Girlfriend called me back. I ask her to put him on the phone and she tells me he's been hit. I tell her, I don't give a fuck and if she didn't want a problem with me, she better put him on the phone. She gave him the phone and first thing out of his mouth was, "I didn't rob the stash house"!

Okay! I ask, "How did you get all of the Jewelry you been wearing?"

His response, "I took it from Big Daddy Kane."

"Well, why didn't you meet me In Coney Island and why did you abandon your post at Cookie's house?"

"I thought once I got to Coney Island, you were going to kill me from stealing the crack from the lab."

I hung up with Shorty G and contacted my people that just shot at Shorty-G and asked them, did he shoot back at you? The answer was no. My question to myself then was why would somebody who just robbed my stash house for the money, drugs, and guns knowing I am looking for him, not have a gun on him to shoot back? At that moment I realized that Shorty G didn't rob me. That's how you learn, that sometimes you have to pause, think, and follow your instinct. I could have murdered Shorty G's family for nothing. However, I found out who robbed my stash house. This guy, Simp, was found sitting in a rental with a single gunshot wound to the head and his throat slit. Again, I was one of the usual suspects.

1984 - 1994 Rappers verses Gangsters

On a lighter note; the first rappers that ever came around Cypress Hill Houses were the Fat Boys. Especially, Prince Markie Dee, who always wore large amounts of jewelry. Keith Watkins, a local DJ from Cypress PJ's whom a lot of the rappers liked hanging out with. I saved Markie D on several occasions from being robbed. To the best of my recollection it was1984-1985 when the rap group the Fat Boys, originally from East New York, became famous from their record sales and their roles in several movies like, *Krush Groove*. The Fat Boys were a funny bunch of guys, but they were not your average street guys, so on several occasions they were stuck up at gun point and robbed of their belongings.

You also had the likes of Big Daddy Kane from Bedford Stuyvesant. He was a rapper who later became an actor. He was about 6'3", but to me he was more of a girly man, than a wannabe tough guy. Good old, Shorty G, stuck up Big Daddy Kane for all his Jewelry in the summer of 1988. But I guess the mere fact that he saw Big Daddy Kane fronting as if he had enough balls to be laced out with all of that jewelry was enough for Shorty G to victimize him. Again, Kane is 6'3" and Shorty G is approximately 5'6", but don't let the size fool you, Shorty G knew how to let his gun talk for him. He was one person you didn't want to be your enemy. During 1986, Eric B and Ra-Kim used to hang out in the Fort Greene section of Brooklyn with the Five Percenters. My little man Kevin Martin a.k.a. was the real "50 Cent." The rapper Curtis Jackson stole the name from my little man. 50 Cent also stuck up Eric B for his jewelry, but I don't think he messed with Ra-Kim because the Five Percenters were protecting him.

It always amazed me how Hip-Hop Rappers or young celebrities imitated the life of criminals, in other words the life as a thug. As a person from the street my objective was always to make fast dollars. As I got older it evolved into making a ton of fast dollars, hit the millionaire status. In the process as you're traveling down that road of darkness with that FTW attitude (Fuck the World) and DGAF (Don't Give A Fuck) attitude it illustrated who I once was and who I had grown to become. But during the process of making both your name and your mark on the street by becoming a ruthless cold hearted person and as you get older you realized it was best to stay under the radar by being low key and staying off the law enforcement's hot list.

In 1994 at the Quad Studio where Tupac Shakur was shot and robbed of his jewelry initially the word was my old friend, Walter "King Tut", Johnson was the culprit. As time went on this cat name Dexter, presently serving a life sentence, claimed Jimmy Henchman Rosemond paid him to rob Tupac. At this point, you really don't know who to believe. The result, he was robbed of his jewelry and no repercussion. You cannot come to the hood pretending to be something you're not and assume you're not getting robbed.

The same situation came up with Curtis Jackson a.k.a. 50 Cent, who again duplicated the name 50 Cent from Kelvin Martin. To add further insult to injury when he made the movie, "Get Rich or Die Trying" Curtis Jackson stole 95% of the story from my life, my crew, and my associates. From the hit on the cop, the battle with the

Columbians, the only true part in that movie is when little Darrell "Homicide" Baum shot 50 Cent nine times which was a hit ordered for a high-ranking drug lord. First of all, the drug lord should have known better to pay a stick-up kid to commit murder. Stick up kids rob people, they don't usually kill them. For years rap artist have and continue to idolize those that actually live that life and seek to introduce it as their own -- good luck with that.

Knowing When to Quit

Back in the beginning of April 1988, a rival organization wanted to take over the area. They felt if I wasn't the area protector, the path would be clear for taking. Therefore, I was offered $50,000 cash and $70,000 per month to retire and step away from the drug trade. I would no longer have to get my hands dirty and the $70,000 monthly was guaranteed. I turned down the proposition -- and it ended up costing me daily, not only in money, but also in the time I would in spend in jail. However, on the other hand the organization that was making the offer would eventually fold, so nothing gained, nothing lost. However, an Apocalypse was approaching.

Monday June 26, 1988 Atlantic City Nj. Iron Mike Tyson vs. Micheal Spinks at Trump Casino. Fat Cat's girlfriend Lynn, Brian and Lynn's sister.

Fat Cat

From left to right: Herman Brothers, David Mcalary (shooter of Myeshia and NYPD Rookie, Edward Byrnes) and Glaze.

Walter Johnson a.k.a. King Tut

Pappy Mason

Brian and Half Brother, Country

Juneau "Sty" Wilson #1 Trigger Man for M&M

Kevin Doyo a.k.a. King Allah

Fat Cat, Corley and Supreme

Brian Gibbs and "LD" Lannie Dillard

Brian "Glaze" Gibbs

Glaze, Amare, Drac and Sid

Sid, Tiny and Glaze

David McClary and Todd Scott

Shooting of Rookie Office Edward Bryne

Edward Bryne Rookie Cop

Chapter Seven - The Apocalypse
The Killing of Edward Byrne, Rookie Cop

The execution style killing of young rookie Police Officer, Edward Bryne, enraged the whole country, and brought about Operation Horse Collar, and changed my world as I knew it.

Around 3:30 A.M. on February 26, 1988 a rookie cop Edward Byrne was on duty, assigned to keep an eye on the house of a witness; local Guyanese immigrant, named Arjune, on 107th Avenue and Inwood Street in South Jamaica, Queens. Arjune had repeatedly called the police to report illegal activities on his street. Pappy Mason ordered his home firebombed on two separate occasions. This is my personal knowledge of the murder of Police Officer Edward Byrne. Pappy was highly upset when he was remanded back to jail after losing a case in February 1988, and bitter about his girlfriend, Vanessa, betraying him. So, after returning to Brooklyn House of Detention, and a couple of days before the actual crime took place, he told Cat that he was going to have a police officer murdered. Cat, dismissing his rambling, told Pappy to get away from him with that dumb shit, and didn't take Pappy seriously.

The New York Police Department only fueled the situation by some of the officers making statements to all the major newspapers and other news reporters that, "Nobody takes orders from a lifer or anyone else in jail." The newspaper articles and television broadcasts continued and matters just got worse. Pappy took the article personally, and loved proving people wrong, especially those who opposed him.

Marshal, Pappy's associate in crime, came to visit him at Brooklyn House, at which time Pappy told him that he wanted a police officer murdered. However, he didn't stipulate a specific officer, only that he wanted an officer killed. At the end of the visit, Pappy gave Marshal his gold and diamond Roundtable Ring, and told him to round up the guys and make sure the job got done. The Roundtable Ring impressed Marshal, believing in the prestige it represented and only a chosen few wore the ring. Pappy also told Marshal to get Dave McClary and Todd Scott for the job. Todd was a member of the Be-bos and Dave was more or less on his own. Pappy was impressed with Dave on the account that I relied on him to handle the Myeshia's hit and that he got it done.

After his visit with Pappy, Marshal returned to Queens and ran into Todd at the Forty Houses Projects. He informed him in what Pappy wanted done, which scared him to death. Todd didn't want to murder a cop and Marshal knew it.

Later Marshal and Todd met Dave McClary at the Fiesta's Restaurant, on 116th Street and Sutphin Boulevard. Marshal then told Dave what Pappy wanted done. Dave hesitated for a minute but felt that he owed Pap for all he had done for him in the past and he was in.

Over the next day or so the three of them -- Marshal, Todd, and Dave -- discussed a plan to hit a police officer. They talked about which cop was going to be killed and where the hit was going to take place. Dave said that for the past couple of months or so, he noticed an officer sitting in a police car on 107th Avenue and Inwood Street. Marshal and Todd said that they'd noticed it, too, and then asked Dave why an officer had been posted to that spot. Dave said he thought the cop had been assigned to prevent drug sales in the area, because the neighbors had been constantly complaining. It sounded logical and nobody from the Be-Bo's, Cat's crew, or anybody in that area who participated in the drug game knew that Arjune's family was receiving protection, against further assaults on his home and family.

After a day or two of preparation, it was around 2:45 A.M., when Scott drove a yellow two-door Chrysler, with Alabama license plates, into South Jamaica, Queens and picked up Todd. About 5 minutes later they picked up Dave, in front of Fiesta's Restaurant.

Scott parked about one block away from 107th Avenue and Inwood Street, where the police officer was sitting in his parked patrol car. Todd and Dave got out and walked towards the parked vehicle. They spotted another police car and Dave ducked down behind a nearby car, until it passed, while Todd kept walking. A few minutes elapsed before Todd approached the police car. He walked to the passenger's side and knocked on the window awakening Police Officer Edward Byrne from a light sleep.

Todd told Officer Byrne that he was lost and needed directions. Byrne signaled Todd to walk around to the driver's side of the car. At that moment, Dave came from the blind side of the car, wielding a .357 magnum handgun and firing hollow point bullets at Officer Byrne. The first shot was the killing blow, but Dave hit him with all five shots. The hollow point bullets ripped into Byrne's head and face, then exploded. The scene was blood-soaked and littered with brain tissue and glass.

Dave was so caught up in what was happening that when he first started shooting, he almost shot Todd, who was able to get out of the way and ran to the driver's side of the police car. He was jumping up and down in the street excited, then bent over and looked into the car, with his head and chest partly over the driver's side door where the window once was. Todd was slightly inside of the car, shouting and yelling that the cop had blue eyes. Dave grabbed Todd and started pulling him away from the car, telling him to, "Let's get the hell out of here"!

Dave and Todd trotted towards their getaway car, got in and then told Scott to drive off. Todd was really happy, because he knew that Pappy would be proud that the job was taken care of and his wish had been granted.

Later that Friday morning, between 9:00 A.M. and 10:00 A.M., I was on the telephone with the Spanish owner of this bodega on Supthin Boulevard and 109th Avenue where Bug-Out and I were partners. The bodega store was one of our main drug spots. In the back of the store there was a steel door and behind the steel door was where our workers received money and sold drugs.

The owner of the store must have beeped me about 15 times, back to back, putting in his telephone number and code 911. So, when I finally called him, he was totally hysterical and blabbing. He kept repeating, over and over, that 20 cops were all over the place and that they were trying to knock down the steel door. My response to him was not to worry about it. I told him that the cops were going to leave soon, because that's how cops were. They would come around and distract business for 30 minutes or an hour, then disappear. However, the store owner continued beeping me even after hanging up the second time. Over the radio I heard that a New York City Police Officer had been shot and killed execution style, as he sat on a post, guarding a witness housed at 107th Avenue and Inwood Street.

Hearing that, I was stunned and totally baffled. I considered that area to be ours and nothing went on in our areas that we weren't fully aware of, especially a major move like that one. So, I automatically knew that Cat and all of the crews who were down with Cat weren't down with the hit on a police officer.

The reason I felt that our crew or Pappy's crew had nothing to do with the hit on the rookie cop was because anything Cat wanted done, he first brought it to my attention. Even if someone else was about to make a major move, Cat brought it to my attention for me to be aware of what was going on. Since nothing about hitting the cop was brought to my attention, I automatically felt that none of our people were involved.

I suddenly understood why the cops were trying to knock down the steel door at our Spanish Bodega. I went into the living room and turned on the television, trying to get more news and information about the cop's murder.

Bug-Out called me and said that South Jamaica Queens was hot all over with cops, including New York City Police Department, F.B.I., D.E.A. agents, and the newly founded Tactical Narcotic Task Force of the New York Police Department (T.N.T. for short).

The law enforcement agencies were raiding all known drug spots in South Jamaica Queens. They were arresting drug dealers and seizing large amounts of cocaine, heroin, marijuana, crack, and huge sums of cash and large numbers of handguns and semi-automatic weapons. This was the first time I knew of the feds and New York City were really combining forces and working together as a team. They were putting a lot of effort into finding the person, or persons, responsible for Officer Byrne's murder which initiated the war on drugs. The raiding and seizures continued. They were kicking down houses and apartment doors, and seizing everything: houses, condos and co-ops, jewelry, money, an all sorts of vehicles. You name it and it was being confiscated and everyone who was arrested was told in no uncertain terms that everything was brought on all because of Officer Byrne being murdered, execution style.

Pappy called me shortly after Bug-Out that Friday morning. He was on a three-way line with Cat's girl, Lynn, so all three of us were talking. Pappy told me that Cat was moved shortly after 4:30 that morning. (Both were in Brooklyn House of Detention at the time.) Pap said that several correctional officers, all wearing bullet-proof vests, jackets and helmets, came to the floor, opened Cat's cell, woke him up and instructed him to strip off all of his clothing. They searched him, and then told him to get dressed, because he was being moved right away.

After Cat got dressed, they packed his property and took him out of the building, refusing to tell him where they were taking him. Cat told Pappy to take care and to get in contact with his people to find out what was what.

Lynn told me that she called all over New York City, as well as several New York State Correctional Facilities, trying to find what had happened to Cat, but was unable to find out anything. Everybody was worried. Lynn, Cat's wife, and I were together waiting for Cat's call so we could go to see him. As I spoke to Pappy, I told him that I was glad he was back in jail because if he was still on the street, then the Police would've automatically sworn that he killed that cop. Pap said, "Yeah, you're right." He went on to say that this is a time we all really need to stick together as a family. Pap ended it by saying, "One Love."

I told Lynn that I was there for whatever assistance she, Cat or the family needed. She knew I would give my all. I've got to say that during the conversation that Friday morning, February 26, 1988, Pappy seemed like his normal self and didn't give any indication that he was involved with the hit on the police officer. The way he talked and behaved convinced me an outsider was responsible.

After I hung up the telephone from talking to Pappy and Lynn, my phone started ringing again, and it kept ringing and my beeper kept beeping. Everyone wanted to know what I knew about the officer being murdered.

All I knew at the time was what I heard on the radio or television. Guys called me from all the different jails in New York City and all throughout the state, wanting to know what was going on. Damned near all the drug dealers

I knew were calling me and asking me what was going on in Queens and about the police officer's murder. My answer was always the same, I didn't know anything.

I kept calling Cat's mother and nieces, damned near every hour, to see if they'd heard from Cat. But the answer was always, "No." I stayed in the apartment and around Brooklyn most of the day.

Between 9:00 P.M. and 10:00 P.M. that night, Country drove me to South Jamaica, Queens to, Viola's house, Cat's sister. Bo-Bo was sitting beside Viola, and Dave was there too. All of us sat in the living room and talked about the rookie cop's murder and how hot it was around there. Nobody was making any money; state and federal law enforcement agents were all over the place. We were trying to figure what the motive was and where the hit came from. I said right then and there that whoever killed the cop only did it to make our areas hot. If I found out who was responsible for the officer's murder, I would personally kill them for the trouble they caused. We all stayed at Viola's house and talked about everything for about another 20 minutes and step outside to get some fresh air.

While Country, Bo-Bo, Dave and I were outside, Dave pulled me to one side and the first thing that came out of his mouth was that he had killed the cop. I looked directly into his eyes and he repeated himself. I knew then that he really did it. Dave went on to say that Pappy gave the order! When I spoke with Pap earlier that day, I really believed that he didn't have anything to do with it. Now, Dave was telling me the whole story, exactly why and how and who was involved with the actual shooting.

After Dave told me everything, I knew right then and there that Cat didn't have anything to do with Byrne's assassination. All I kept saying to Dave was that it was a dumbass move. Dave responded by saying that he was only following orders.

223

Country and I got into the car, left and met-up with
Bug-Out several blocks from 150th Street and 107th
Avenue. We parked about three blocks away and walked
the rest of the way, cops were everywhere.

Bug-Out and I were walking all through our areas, a
ten-block radius, and checking on the damages that had
been done to the spots in an apartment building and some
other locations.

The bodega was closed and to our surprise a spot we
had around Liberty Avenue was doing excellent. That spot
usually generated anywhere from $5,000 to $10,000 a day,
jumped up to $20,000 in less than 24 hours and $39,000 is
less than 36 hours. That spot was moving strong as all the
other drug spots within the area had been closed down.

The feds and cops weren't aware of the Liberty
Avenue spot, and every drug user who couldn't buy drugs at
his or her regular location was running to Liberty Avenue
to buy their goodies. Unfortunately, before the 40th hour
had rolled around, the cops and feds had also closed down
the Liberty Avenue spot.

Once Liberty Avenue was shut down, that was it.
Bug-Out and my partnership died; all the drug spots had
been put out of business because Queens was too hot. There
was no way the heat that was being applied was going to be
let up by the Cops and the Feds. So, that's when I really
started concentrating on my Brooklyn spots.
Everything was going well there, especially with my Coney
Island spot in the Gravesend Houses, ever since I put in the
big capsules of crack, which sold for $5. I also had this spot
at the Fort Green Houses that remained active.

Byrne's murder created a nationwide moral outrage.
Ronald Reagan personally called the Byrne family to offer
condolences, while George H.W. Bush carried Byrne's
badge using it on his campaign for President in 1988. Both

police and government officials, fearful of such atrocities unchecked, would lead to attacks on law-enforcement officers such as those common in Colombia and other Latin American countries. A dramatic response was initiated, known as **Operation Horse Collar.**

Eventually convicted of the actual killing were two of Byrne's killers, Phillip Copeland and David McClary. Ironically David McClary after serving four years of his sentence in solitary confinement, he again enraged the NYPD as written in the New York Times, by Paul Zielbauer, on February 28, 1999.

Article Regarding Killing of Rookie Cop

Adding to the crescendo of outrage and disappointment among many New York City police officers, state and city officials yesterday condemned a $660,000 Federal jury award to a man convicted of killing a rookie officer in Queens 11 years ago.

The inmate, David McClary, 33, who is serving a 25 years-to-life sentence for the 1988 slaying of Officer Edward Byrne in Jamaica, Queens, spent four years in solitary confinement, from November 1989 to March 1994. On Tuesday, a jury in Rochester found Mr. McClary had suffered mental distress during the time that prison officials kept him locked in a tiny cell and that his civil rights had been violated.

In Albany, Jim Flateau, a spokesman for the Department of Correctional Services who responded to calls to Gov. George E. Pataki, denounced the jury's decision. "Certainly, we do not believe that a cop killer should be getting $660,000 of the taxpayers' dollars," said Mr. Flateau.

The condemnation has not been unanimous, however. Tom Terrizzi, the associate director of Prisoners Legal Services of New York, which helped Mr. McClary file his case, has defended the verdict as fair recompense for the debilitating psychological effects of Mr. McClary's forced isolation.

At the time of the shooting, crack cocaine was ravaging New York City's poorer neighborhoods like those Officer Byrne patrolled at night. As a result, thousands of criminals flowed into state and Federal prisons, said Mr. Flateau. And that forced corrections officials to place Mr. McClary in what officials call "administrative segregation," or solitary confinement, to protect him from other prisoners, Mr. Flateau said.

"Our first concern was that he might not be too popular with the prisoners," he said. "Our second concern was that someone might want to take him out -- kill him -- believing they thought it might have put them in good stead for taking out a cop killer."

If they chose, Officer Byrne's relatives could seek to deny Mr. McClary the $660,000 award through a wrongful death or personal injury suit in civil court, legal experts said. Though the statute of limitations on the state's wrongful-death statutes is eight years, family members could bring a case based on laws that prevent convicts from unjust enrichment related to their crimes, said Conrad Johnson, a law professor Columbia University School of Law.

As word of the decision to award Mr. McClary $660,000 in damages spread, police officials expressed bewilderment.

End of Article of the Killing of the Rookie Cop

I can't tell you if he ever got any money, but his attorney probably did. Forgetting what was said. He was put there because he killed a cop. He deserved what he got. You don't assassinate cops.

T-N-T, The Rookie's Cop Murder

After the rookie officer, Edward Byrne's, was murdered on February 26, 1988, New York City formed the drug task force, called T-N-T. Along with the federal government, the war on drugs began. Big drug raids and confiscated vast amounts of cocaine. They busted several drug spots and arrested lots of drug dealers. The Byrne murder affected the whole world and in the United States alone drug seizures increased by tons and tons, making it difficult for us to buy lots of kilos at once. I honestly believe that if Pappy hadn't ordered the hit on Police Officer Edward Byrne, the Queens District Attorney's Office wouldn't have turned to the federal government for help. Because of that murder the Queens County District Attorney's Office and the feds started working hand-in-hand to shut down the selling and buying of drugs in Queens.

Byrnes murder brought about a drought during March and April of 1988. I remember trying to buy as many kilos as possible and all I could come up with were three kilos, from three separate sources. Just before Byrne's murder the price of cocaine was down to around $13,000 to $17,000 a kilo, but after the murder and increased seizures, it went up. One day I paid $25,000 for a kilo, then the next day it would be $26,000, and the day after that it would be $27,000. I remember visiting Cat, in Attica, and telling him how hard it was to find and buy cocaine, and how fast the price was rising. Cat said he hoped cocaine it would reach $50,000 again, high prices would force a lot of people out of the drug trade, by being unable to afford to buy it at that price

After the feds completed their investigation against us, and teamed up with the New York Police Department, the raid code named "Operation Horse-Collar" took place. It was pre-dawn on Thursday, August 11, 1988, when Operation Horse-Collar took place, and several people involved with Fat Cat's organization were arrested. The feds and Queens County continued to work together through the end of December 1988.

Pappy's Upbringing

Pappy was brought up during the time when he considered all police officers enemy. Like the song Fuck the Police by NWA he witnessed as a little boy watching several riots between police officers (mostly white) and African Americans. Many times, he saw police officers using their blackjacks to beat down African American men and women, placing them into paddy wagons all covered with blood, while their children yelled and screamed for their parents. Pappy witnessed how the police officers (again, mostly -- white), treated black people, who were doing nothing more than standing up for what they believed in and seeking to find a better way of life. It was that imagine of police brutality that Pappy learned to hate police officers, and I personally believe that's the reason Pappy hated all law enforcement.

The Murder of Clifton Rice

Days after Edward Byrnes execution, I was arrested on suspicion for killing a Clifton Rice and for questioning relating to the murder of Edward Byrne. The facts were that as Edward Byrne was being murdered in South Jamaica, Queens, Clifton Rice was being murdered at the same exact time in Cypress Hills, Brooklyn. However, his death didn't receive the same publicity as that of the Edward Byrne. The word on the street was that Clifton was involved in robbing one of my associates.

On a Sunday afternoon Tamia, Herm, and Country came to visit me. My main concern was emphasizing the importance of them getting with our sources to find out exactly who the district attorney had as witnesses against me, regarding the killing of Clifton Rice. I wanted their names, addresses, dates of birth, where they worked -- everything. I told them that once they found out who the person or persons who would be testifying against me, to get my people, the hit squad, to kill the person or persons before they got the opportunity to testify against me at a grand jury hearing. They kept assuring me the matter would be taken care of. Then we talked about business. I might have been getting a little soft, but I had no intentions of going back to jail. I still had a murderer's mentality.

During that time is when I was really making my mark in the drug trade and became classified as being one of the many drug kingpins in New York City. I went to court the next day. I took a prison bus with several other inmates to Brooklyn Criminal Court, and stayed locked up in the bullpens all day, and without having my name called. After 5:00 P.M. the transportation officers arrived and started taking the guys who were finished with court back to Rikers Island. They still hadn't called me. I was pissed off, since I thought I was going to be in those bullpens all night. But, to my surprise, around 6:00 several court officers called out four other guys and me.

From Wikipedia, the free encyclopedia: A **drug lord**, **drug baron**, **kingpin**, or **narcotic trafficker** is a person who controls a sizable network of persons involved in the illegal drug trade. Such figures are often difficult to bring to justice, as they might never be directly in possession of something illegal but are insulated from the actual trade in drugs by several layers of underlings. The prosecution of drug lords is therefore usually the result of carefully planned infiltrations of their networks, often using informants from within the organization.

The court officers let us out of the bullpens and escorted us up to the processing room. I was exceptionally happy when they told me that I was being released. They fingerprinted me, and I had to answer some questions to prove my identity, then they let me go.

I was beyond lucky I guess, as they didn't have enough to hold me on Clifton's murder and I had no knowledge of Byrnes assassination, yet I was under the impression I would be brought in front of the Grand Jury for the murder of Clifton Rice.

When I got downstairs, one of my girlfriends was waiting for me, with her daughter. I kissed and hugged them both and asked where Herm and Country were. She said they had left about three hours earlier, after learning that I was going to be released. Murray Cutler was my lawyer at the time, and she briefed me on what he had told her. Then we flagged down a cab and went to my headquarters.

When we arrived, I greeted my people, and then went straight to the bedroom with her. We made love for an hour, before I got up, showered, and got dressed. The very next morning I was on a plane, headed upstate NY to visit Fat Cat in the Attica Correctional Facility. Cat and I talked about Pappy's dumb ass move, by having that policeman murdered. I asked Cat if he wanted me to pay for Dave's lawyer and he told me no- way; he didn't have anything to do with Officer Bryne's murder. Cat said that it was Pappy's move, so let Pappy pay for Dave's lawyer. Besides, Cat felt that if either of us paid for Dave's lawyer, then it would be like we sanctioned the hit on the cop -- when we didn't.

After the visit with Cat I returned to Brooklyn and went to visit my wife and then my mother. When I got to her house, we hugged and kissed, and she told me that she knew I had been in jail. So, call me a Momma's Boy. While I was in jail my mother was concerned of where I was. So, I admitted to my mother that I was in jail. But I also told her that they had made a mistake, charging me with murder, and once they realized I didn't do it they had to let me go. I loved my mother too much to tell her any details of what I was into regardless of what it was. I would lie to her to keep her from knowing the truth. I knew the truth would hurt her and I never intentionally wanted to do anything to hurt my mother. *I didn't learn this until I became a father, that parents take our actions personally.*

I should've realized that all the crime and criminal activities I was participating in was the opposite of my upbringing. The sad part is I was never really a criminal minded individual. I hate myself for losing grip on reality and going astray. Now, I'm dealing with reality. I realize now that by my past stupidity and foolishness I hurt the people who loved me the most. I let myself become a product of my environment; the streets and people who made that fast money. Whereas, now I can see with my very own eyes, that the hustle life and the people affiliated don't love anyone or anything, but the money.

The truth, which I can tell you now is, I killed Clifton Rice, truly not proud, but this is a "tell all book" and that's what they tell me the readers want. They say the truth will set you free and hopefully God will forgive me for my sins. Well, here goes; it was extremely foggy that early morning when Clifton paid his debt. Even as I sit back and think about it now, I was very reckless, egotistical and careless. Where the execution took place, there were eight buildings with windows everywhere. Despite it was in the early morning hours, there's no telling who was looking out of their windows seeing everything. My state of mind was always security first, not allowing anyone to sneak up on me. I had just returned from Queens where I had hooked up with Bug-Out. He handed me $40,000 in cash, my cut from a day's work. Bug-Out and I were generating 1.2 to 1.8 million in cash every 30 to 45 days for Fat Cat. After leaving Bug-Out, I headed home to Brooklyn at about three in the morning.

As I was entering the projects, I was on point, scanning the area for possible enemies, those who wanted to annihilate me; or the stick-up kids who were always a threat looking for an easy target. At that moment I spotted someone from a distance walking in my direction. As he approached, I recognized him. It was Clifton Rice, a twenty-two-year-old young black male from the neighboring area. He was walking from Euclid Avenue train station toward Cypress Hills PJs. We recognized one another, and we slapped hands. As he walked off, I remembered about the robbery of one of my associates, which caused me to get upset and want to take revenge for them. Cliff continued walking into the dark toward his building, trying not to look back. When he got near the 1240 building pathway, I ran up behind him and shouted to him the reason why he was about to die. He sought to defend his position, while talking, I grabbed and pulled out my handgun and that was it. All I saw was blood as my happy trigger finger cut loose with both 9mm automatics in my left and right hand. Hollow point bullets ripped thru Cliff's head and body as he fell to his death on the concrete pathway which we both traveled thru so many times. Before his body hit the ground, I had disappeared into the dark of the night, heading to my headquarters at 1266 Sutter.

My Reputation Grew with The A-Team

While all that was going down, I was alleged to be the new leader of the original A-Team. I Brian "Glaze" Gibbs was never the leader nor was I a member of the A Team. Most of the A-Team members and I were associates. I was only the founder and leader of the M&M crew. Being that I was the most well-known amongst the A-Team, all the outsiders labeled me as the leader.

Not bragging, just the fact, cause taking someone's life is never anything to brag about. So, you can put things into prospective, during 1985-1986, my name came up in numerous murders and I was on NYPD's watch list. From my understanding after my acquittal on June 22, 1987, for Sybil's murder, and based upon my reputation I was on the chart of the NYPD's list of notorious criminals. That information was shared with all the area police precincts. My name kept coming up in several of unsolved murders. Based upon my reputation that I built on the street and spending time in and out of jail, I was label as a menace and a vicious blood thirsty killer. *I had no real desire to kill or had a taste for blood, it was just a byproduct of the business, call it collateral damage, the irony.*

From 1987 up until November 1988 the Police Departments of the Five Boroughs truly believed that I was responsible for any and every murder that occurred in New York City that they couldn't solve. When Officer Edward Byrne was murdered the Queen's and Brooklyn's police departments combined a task force and immediately as they started their investigation, they placed my mugshot at the top of the board as his killer.

Chapter Eight - The Collar Tightens

Wire Taps - Operation Horse Collar

Again, after the hit on Rookie NYPD Officer Edward Byrnes, enough was enough; the Federal Government got involved and initiated Operation Horse Collar. The main reason, they truly believed we had no respect for Law enforcement and authority - really. I hate to be sarcastic, but yes, we didn't have much respect for the law, we were criminals. First the hit on a Parole Officer, Brian Rooney and now the killing of a 22 year old rookie cop, who would never get married or have a family of his own, because some ruthless individuals who couldn't think on their own, and that some orders that are given are best ignored. As part of the Operation Horse Collar authorization for wire taps on several phones were granted by New York Eastern District Judge, Raymond Dearie. By the time everything was completed, there were over 1100 hours of tapes from picking up and dropping off drugs, to bagging and transaction, and to possible hits in the making. Those wire taps were the beginning of the end.

With pressure increasing I continued to stay away from Brooklyn avoiding a warrant for my arrest as part of Operation Horse Collar. I was initially wanted to testify before the Grand Jury against those I associated with and or had knowledge of. *The operation was detailed in the article, "Fewer Turf Battles, More Drug Arrests," written by Steven A. Holmes and published January 21, 1990.*

Excerpts from the Article:

In six years as an assistant United States attorney, prosecuting hundreds of defendants, Mr. Ray went to trial dozens of times. One of his biggest cases was "Operation Horse Collar," a 2 1/2-year wiretap investigation in which

48 people were charged with narcotics trafficking in the Bronx and Westchester County.

QUIETLY, virtually unnoticed by most New Yorkers, a three-year effort by Federal and local law enforcement officials had made some notable gains against some of the city's most notorious narcotics traffickers. Government officials say that 150 dealers, including some major traffickers who controlled drug distribution in parts of Manhattan and Queens, have been locked up since 1986 in an operation that has become a model for Federal and municipal cooperation.

But even the success of the effort of Operation Horse Collar points up the intractability of the drug problem. Federal and local authorities acknowledge that drug sales, especially cocaine, showed no significant decline in those areas where the arrested kingpins had operated.

"As far as a decrease in the amount of heroin and coke coming into these areas, you're not going to see that," said Jules Bonavolonta, who heads the organized crime and narcotics division of the New York office of the Federal Bureau of Investigation. "That involves the problems of interdiction and reducing demand," he said. "We all tended to act like independent contractors," said Sterling Johnson Jr., New York City's special narcotics prosecutor. "And when we got together, we would end up fighting like cats and dogs." Mr. Johnson attended the strategy session, along with representatives of the F.B.I., the Federal Drug Enforcement Administration, the United States Attorney offices in Manhattan and Brooklyn and the city's Police Department.

In contrast to past practice when different agencies often conducted separate and sometimes overlapping investigations, Federal and local law-enforcement officials began sharing informants and witnesses, money for undercover drug purchases and wiretaps. One Federal and one local officer were assigned to each case.

The aim was to get the top leader of various drug distribution gangs and as many lieutenants as possible, and to seize their assets. "Once they're in jail, the people out on the street couldn't care less about them if they don't have any money," said Mr. Bonavolonta.

In the last three years the operation was credited with the arrest and conviction of key figures, like Frank Lucas. Also Leslie Atkinson, who while serving a prison term arranged the smuggling of heroin into the United States in body bags containing dead American soldiers from Vietnam as part of an operation to import heroin from Thailand. (This operation was included in the film, *American Gangsters*, starring Denzel Washington playing the part of Frank Lucas.) Others arrested include James Smith, considered one of the top heroin dealers in Queens; Kenneth McGriff, whose gang controlled the cocaine trade in much of southeast Queens, and Thomas Mickens, who was described by Government officials as the cocaine king of the neighborhoods near Kennedy International Airport.

The operation also helped snare Lorenzo (Fat Cat) Nichols, another Queens' trafficker, and Howard (Pappy) Mason, who was convicted in December of ordering the killing of a police officer, Edward Byrne, who was shot to death while guarding the home of a witness in a drug case.

But if the effort has won some battles, victory in the war on the crack trade remains elusive. A reason, law enforcement officers say, is the decentralized nature of the city's cocaine distribution system, a tangled web of independent gangs each controlling a slice of the city. To get to the top of each disparate organization involves the long and often dangerous process of infiltration.

The authorities say they do not even know the total number of distribution networks in the city. And, as a recent spate of shootings in Queens has indicated, new groups are already vying to see who will replace those that have been broken up. So, while those involved in the operation liked to boast of its success, they acknowledge that they are much closer to the beginning of their job than the end.

End of Article, but the story.

Bad Drug Buy, Country and Moochie

With Fat Cat's incarceration and the heat still on getting product for the street meant spreading our wings. My half-brother Country, the sensible one, always thinking and coming up with different ways and ideas to making money.

As I said, after the NYP Eddie Byrne's hit we saw the price of kilos of cocaine shoot up from $18,000 per kilo to $40,000. So, Country went to Los Angeles, California in attempt to purchase some kilos at $12,500 each. He tried to convince me to put $125,000 up and he would bring back 10 kilos. I wasn't feeling warm and fuzzy on having $125,000 of my money going 3000 miles away to California with no guarantees. He flew to Cali and meet with Moochie, our old-time friend and benefactor from Brooklyn. Moochie at the time traveled back and forth to L.A. doing business. He'd been in the game forever and he was always seeking to broker deals.

A week later, still in L.A. and no deal, I told him to come home. Unaware as he entered LAX airport, he was profiled by the Drug Enforcement Agency, detained, question and my fifty thousand dollars was confiscated. They released him after several hours. When he arrived back to NY, I recall going off on his ass and letting him know that the loss was his to pay. I shouldn't have busted his balls; it was only a little more than a days' pay.

My Mini Me was Born

Operation Horse Collar was currently in full force. I was back in New York when my pregnant wife, Tamia, was admitted to the hospital. After packing from my Grand Central Parkway co-op, I flew to Charleston.

I was in and out of the hospital that whole weekend, visiting Tamia. I was right there in the delivery room when she gave birth to my son. It was shortly after midnight, Monday, August 1, 1988. He weighed 7 pounds and 13 ounces. When the doctor spanked him on his butt and he started crying, it made me cry, too. I can honestly say that was the best and happiest moment of my life, to have received a baby boy -- my pride and joy. He was born with my family trait, the nose. The birth of my son changed my whole outlook on and about life. I guess I started putting my defenses down and began being the best father I could possibly be. I love my wife and my son – my mini me.

In the days to come, I would feel like I'd betrayed him by not being there to give him the fatherly love he deserved. I would miss him daily. I just wish I had the chance to do my life over again - my life would've been totally different. Unlike Frank Sinatra, I would have more than a few regrets. My aunt came to help Tamia with the baby. Tamia pleaded with me to stay with her and our new baby, but I told her that I was only going to be gone for a few days.

As I flew back to New York, more or less to quit the drug game and turn it over to my crew, all I thought about was just sitting back and watching my son grow up. When I arrived back in New York, everything was crazy. Someone, either Fat Cat's sister; Viola, his niece; Mott, or Joseph "Bo-Bo" Rogers had cut a large package of heroin that was for me. They cut the package of dope, so many times, in order to cover up the theft of what they'd taken. I was out of town when Country and Herm picked up the package and didn't discover why the heroin wasn't selling until I got back and examined the package. Bo-Bo was up to his old shit.

I hooked up with everyone at a place in Queens. Fat Cat's girl, Lynn, was having a party for her sister, Quick. Quick was supposed to be Kenneth "Supreme" McGriff's girl at the time. The next thing I noticed was a lot of people screaming. I was slapping the shit out of Bo-Bo and I turned back to see several of my men with their guns cocked back in Bo-Bo's face. My men told me that when I slapped Bo-Bo and turned around he reached to his waistband for a gun, and that's when they pulled out their guns and were going to finish him off. I told Bo-Bo that if it hadn't been for the love and respect I had for Cat, he and his niece, Mott would've died that night. I told him that when I went to see Fat Cat, and if I had gotten the okay, he would have definitely been murdered.

After that situation I had a limo take me to Shawangunk Correctional Facility. I went to see Cat, to give him back the Round Table Ring. I was tired of the bullshit I was going through and didn't want him and me to have bad blood between us. I knew I would've ended up killing a lot of people he grew up with and cared about. However, he talked me out of it and in the short run, in or out, the outcome was going to change.

Fed Raid On Headquarters

Now, back in Charlotte with my family, my serenity ended when I was awakened bright and early on a Thursday morning. Operation Horse collar was closing in on me. I was in bed with my wife and my 10-day old son who was sleeping in his bassinet. The phone rang with urgency as I answered the call both sluggish and tired. It was one of my guys, his voice on the line sounded almost like a morning news flash, "The Feds, FBI, DEA, US Marshalls, and the fucking NYPD," - *except for the fucking* - he continued, "they have the whole Cypress Hill Houses blocked off. The area is surrounded with hundreds of law enforcement personnel, stopping and checking ID's of everyone entering and exiting 1266 and 1260 Sutter."

The caller went on to tell me that they had a Fugitive Warrant for my arrest. The word on the street was that when they raided my apartment 4B, beside drugs, money and guns they were informed about several dead bodies. At times the headquarters would've at least a million dollars in cash, 30 to 40 kilos of cocaine and 1 to 2 kilos of pure heroin, and a hundred semi-automatics; Uzis tech 9s, and handguns. *I was now awake.* That was supposed to be the time of my life, with my son. I laid there for another moment, thinking how I thought I was smarter than my predecessors. I am Glaze; this was not supposed to be happening to me, not now. I hit the shower, trying to sort things out - I wanted to scream. My mind was racing, my life had seemed like it was changing for the better, but now I was officially a fugitive. My wife unaware of the situation came in bathroom to remind me that my son had a doctor's appointment and I needed to hurry.

As my Cypress headquarters was being raided, simultaneously Fat Cat and Pappy were being transferred from the state prison to the Brooklyn Federal Court. Cat's mother and stepfather were being arrested in Bessemer Alabama. Cat's wife was being arrested in Virginia Beach VA., his sisters, nieces and other associates were being apprehended in Queens and Long Island. Pappy's mother, uncle, girlfriends and crew were also arrested. Operation Horse Collars was moving at full speed. That day they arrested over 40 people, except me.

I drove my wife and son to the hospital for his appointment. As we arrived at the hospital, I assumed every white gentleman that I saw was a possible Federal Agent. It safe to say, my nerves were shot, and I was more than a little paranoid.

That evening I went to a pay phone and called some members of my crew. I can recall one of them who watched eyewitness news on channel 7, tell me about the footage of how the Feds had Cypress Hills Houses surrounded. Sty was telling everyone if I had been there when the Feds showed up, I would have ordered them to shoot it out. No way! We were no match for the Feds. I'd seen enough gangster movies to know that doesn't end well. I told Sty, "If I was there, I would've been praying that we all had on white boxer shorts on, in order to take them off and wave them out the windows to surrender. *Like Clint Eastwood said, "A man needs to know his limitations." Or was it that I had a family and life was becoming more precious?*

Looking Back - All That Money

Prior to Operation Horse Collar and with Fat Cat's mentoring and blessing, running the M&M Crew was financially awesome. Making easy and fast money was one hell of a sensation. The more money I made, the more money I found myself giving away. Those who knew me and were in my good graces knew if they needed something, they could consider it done. My late Aunt would always tell everyone. "If Brian had it, everyone would have it, because he wasn't a cheap skate."

Here today, gone tomorrow. I did and didn`t have time to enjoy the money. I was always speeding, going a million miles per hour, traveling back and forth from New York, South Carolina and Virginia. I had a brand-new townhome that I purchased in Virginia Beach that I seldom stayed in, which I also had to put it in someone else name. My friend and crew member, Juneau Wilson was staying there during a time that he was on the run. However, for getaway weekends, I enjoyed my brand-new condo on lovely Virginia Beach.

I maintained two co-ops, one in Kew Gardens on Union Turnpike. I really enjoyed that place; doorman, security, my own parking spaces, 2 bedrooms and 2 baths.

It's funny as I sit back and think about the folks who resided in that building, including the door man, the security guard, and how they all assumed that I was a college student living in the building; thinking my parents were probably either doctors or lawyers. Not knowing this young 23-year-old owned the place.

The second co-op was off the Grand Central Parkway which I lived in most of the time. It was in the same neighborhood as the late Geraldine Ferraro, who ran for vice President with Walter Mondale. I had these upscale homes, but they were all in other people's names. That was the worst thing about being a criminal, you have to turn bad money into clean money and if you can't prove how you're making a livelihood it can make it impossible to show income, get credit and place anything in your name: property, cars - nada.

Reminiscing about when I was making over $1,000,000 a month for myself, selling heroin and crack cocaine. Imagine being in your early twenties making that type of money and having a personal limousine driver taking you to wherever. I was definitely living on a different galaxy, but I was still down to earth and kept things in perspective, even though I was always on the go, flying in and out of town, three out of five days per week. Unfortunately, it was hard to even think about giving it up. My life was unbelievable; I was making love to so many different girls at that time I felt like I was a porn star. I was no Wilt Chamberlain, but I was getting more butt, then an ashtray. Fucking and having oral sex in my limo. Sometimes I was having sex with three to four different women within twenty-four hours. Either I had a very healthy sexual appetite, or I was a sex addict. I figured if I wasn't living the life I could be murdered at any giving time or put into prison so I made it my business to get as much pussy as possible. I was addicted to pussy. Even when I did my ten-year federal sentence, if a female friend came up to visit me and if the opportunity presented itself when the right C.O. (correction officer) was working, my friend and I would find a spot to discretely fuck, so they came prepared with condoms.

I was ghetto rich. Now maybe you think you're in the wrong business? Well, I was thinking like every other fool, like it was going to last forever. I was doing weekly trips and my trusted associate Juneau Sty Wilson, "Du" traveled from New York to South Carolina with $50,000 to $100,000 in cash to be put away for a rainy day. During that time I was lucky enough to have my mother's dream house built on her own land, from the ground up. It was a beautiful two-story home with six bedrooms, four bathrooms, a two-car garage and no mortgage. I wanted to add a swimming pool, a tennis court and a basketball court in the back of the house, but mom declined saying, that would be an over kill.

Being "Fly" changed my childhood. I had a hell of a wardrobe, from designer suits and footwear to match, including jeans shorts, etc, For my urban wears, I would shop at S&A on Ralph and Broadway in Bushwick and Simon's in Brownsville, Brooklyn. One day I went in with some of my crew and $7,000, but the total purchases were twelve grand. Simon told me not to worry about it, that I could pay him the difference anytime. I sent back the five thousand that same day. As time went on some of my crew tried to buy on credit with Simon but were told flat out that the offer was only good for Glaze. I enjoyed shopping as much as woman and appreciated the finer stores at Gucci, Bloomingdale, A.J. Lester's, and Leightons, where two to three thousand-dollar suits fitted perfectly which made you feel good. The most I ever spent on shoes was two to three thousand dollars. Women could spend more. I wasn't a jeans and sneaker type of guy, always dressed up, especially when flying in first class: a fine conservative suit, with my little brief case and Presidential Gold Rolex. I don't know how much envy was going on, but I'm sure some of the other passengers were wondering what line of work I was into.

Giving Back to The Street

There was a time that I knew I wasn't going to change anytime soon. Seeing the young kids on my streets, subconsciously, my conscience wanted to give back to the street. Making easy fast money was one hell of a sensation. The more money I made, I found myself giving it away to those who knew me and in my good graces. They knew if they needed something, they could consider it done. For years my mother would not accept anything from me because she knew my money was illegal and she didn't want me going astray. I guess once she realized that I wasn't going to change any time soon, she finally decided, it was time to learn how to receive since she had been giving all her life. At least the money I made always went back into the economy. In that way it was I justified.

Some would say I always had a big heart. *I'd probably throw a little guilt into the mix.* Anyone that I knew that couldn't pay their rent in the neighborhood I would pay it and give them money for groceries. I helped underprivileged families out during back to school days, to purchase new clothing and school supplies for their kids. It always made me feel good. I wasn't changing, but I knew there was hope for some before they turned into me. But then there were the junkies, they were lost and would probably never be found, but their kids needed help. I tried to do my part. Christmas was still my favorite time of the year. Giving money to "drug free parents" to do their Christmas shopping was simple. For the parent's with addictions, I would take care of their kids directly. What was the most important; I always lent a helping hand to my people that were incarcerated from visiting them in jail, to bailing them out, to hiring attorneys for their trials and appeals. I always made sure my people and their families were well taken care of financially. Everybody! Even drug dealers incarcerated get lonely. From 1985 to November 1988 whether I was on the street or locked up I was still calling shots, paying others to go see my associates who didn't have people to come visit them and drop off money and food packages. What a guy?

Chapter Nine Arrested on Fugitive Warrant

On August 11, 1988, ninety-nine days after being a fugitive, stemming from Operation Horse Collar, two hundred Federal Law Enforcement did a massive raid in Metropolitan New York, New Jersey, Virginia and Alabama.

I knew the day of my arrest would come while I was on the run. I literally sought to have plastic surgery done on my face and fingerprints. The doctor that I had lined up in New York was afraid due to the publicity of the case. I believe, he was afraid that I would have to murder him after the procedure to protect my identity. I ran into the same problem in Los Angeles. Sometimes you can have all of the money in the world but having a notorious reputation can work both for and against you, and it was working against me.

On November 10, 1988, the day of judgment, I woke up that morning not knowing that the US Marshal's fugitive squad located me and my days as a free man would be crashing down on me. I always flew first class, in and out of South Carolina, with an open ticket. Unlike a regular return ticket, an open-ended airline ticket sends you to a destination on a specific date, with a flexible return date -- usually within one year of your departure date; although the ticket may be more expensive than a set return or one-way ticket. I was planning on leaving the day before, and I decided to stay one more day to hang-out with my wife and son.

That morning I got up shaved, showered, dressed and drove to Macky's, the town's local barber shop. Before heading home, I picked up my mom at the beauty parlor, in my new Cherokee Limited - I liked that vehicle. Driving home, I glanced into in my rearview mirror and suddenly saw my future, realizing I was being tailed. Not realizing I let off on the gas which seemed to signal the US Marshal that I was aware of their presence. Once they knew I made them, they backed off to only to allow another team to pick me up. I wasn't doing anything wrong, so I proceeded to drop off my Mother, picked up my five-year-old stepson and three-year-old niece, then headed to McDonalds. I spotted several more unmarked cars now following me. As I pulled into McDonald's parking lot, I removed my stepson and niece out of their safety seats. Heading into the restaurant, deep down inside, I was a little scared knowing that I was going to jail that day and there was a good chance I would be facing a Federal death penalty or possible multiple life imprisonments. As the kids and I entered the restaurant all hell broke loose. US Marshal and Federal law enforcement were rushing me with their guns drawn. My stepson ran out of restaurant as they placed three different sets of handcuffs on me. I was shouting at the Marshall to get him, I didn`t want him to get hit by incoming traffic in the parking lot. *I could swear the McDonald's clown eyes snapped wide open.* I was taken to Charleston county jail, no bail and as far as they were concerned; I was indeed a menace to society. I needed one hell of a lawyer and based upon everything that I heard Barry Krell, was The Perry Mason of South Carolina, and I needed a miracle.

The Federal Judge in Charleston South Carolina hit his gravel to conclude my two-day bail hearing. I hired the best lawyer money could buy at the time; although, I must admit the government had too many charges against me. There was a total of five US Attorneys verses Brian "Glaze" Gibbs. Barry Krell was the best of the best and he put together one hell of a defense, which included some family members from the church with strong community ties. He portrayed me as a wonderful, young family man, a real nice person with a big heart, as pure as gold, and I was not the ruthless person that the government was portraying me to be.

With that said, I was looking around in the Court room to see the person my lawyer was talking about. I can recall the judge's words as if it was yesterday. *"Mr. Gibbs, based upon the testimony that was giving on both sides I have to deny you bail. For a young man who admits in his own words that you are unemployed, yet you are able to fly from city to city, 1st class and with open airline tickets. Mr. Gibbs, I am a Federal Judge and I cannot afford that luxury. When I travel, I have to book and make reservations months in advance to receive a good price. Anyone who is able to fly from city to city first class on open tickets is someone who has unlimited cash flow and money is not something that you value."* I believe the judge was doing everything he could, without bursting out laughing and calling me a drug dealer.

Deal or No Deal - No T.V. Show - Part One

My lawyer came to visit me after the ruling on my bail. I thanked him for a great job despite the fact we lost. He then told me, "Look I can get you out right now, but only if you agree to cooperate with the Government." Apparently, the late flamboyant, Assistant US Attorney, Charlie Rose had made an offer to get me to flip (give state evidence). Charles Rose worked right under Eastern District of New York, (EDNY) US ATTORNEY Andrew J Maloney. Rose prosecuted plenty of wise guys, including Vincent "The Chin" Gigante for organized crime and for plotting to kill John Gotti.

I responded as politely as possible to, "Get the fuck out of my face with that bullshit. You are fucking crazy, MY MOTHER FUCKING NAME IS GLAZE, DEATH BEFORE DISHONOR. DON`T TALK THE TALK, IF YOU CAN`T WALK THE WALK." Would you believe after I literally cursed him out, he said listen, "I really don't give a dam about a lot of the clients I represent, but I have a good feeling about you. I don`t know whether you are innocent or guilty, the odds are stacked against you, and if you don't make a deal you will die in jail." Once again, I thanked Mr. Barry Krell and dismissed his services.

About one month later I was extradited back to New York City and sent to MCC with the rest of my codefendants.

We were spread out from the fifth to the ninth floor, even a female co-defendant was on the opposite side on the fifth floor. When I arrived, it was as if I was a celebrity. Here it is, I am fighting for my life and I get a hero's welcome. We were all meeting daily for attorney conference visits with co-defendants. We listened to over 1100 hours of wiretap recordings – *un-fucking believable*. My New York lawyer was Murray Cutler, the father of Bruce Culter who was John Gotti's attorney at the time.

He gave me a heart to heart speech similar to what Mr. Barry Krell had presented in Charleston, South Carolina. He told me we been through a lot together, "But this situation right here, the odds are stacked against you. I don't want to see you die in jail."

As time went on and I went back and forth to Federal and State courts, I was being indicted on murder charges. Then out of nowhere our cases were severance. Whereas initially I was considered under Fat Cat and Pappy on the case, but by severance the case I became the #1 guy, the king pin and charged of, 21 USC 848 (Continuing criminal enterprise. Any person who engages in a continuing criminal enterprise shall be sentenced to a term of imprisonment which may not be less than 20 years, and which may be up to life imprisonment) and 21 USC 841 (DISTRIBUTION OF A CONTROLLED SUBSTANCE,

Realizing the situation, I sat down and talked to Fat Cat, I said, "You know we are all going to get life and we need to allow all of the women, including your mother, sister, wife and girlfriends to go free, so we have to allow them to make a deal and give ourselves up (Fat Cat, Pappy and me)." All in order so the women could go home or at least get as little time as possible. I remember Fat Cat looking at me and saying, "Glaze why don't you go to trial first and let's see what they have against you and then we'll go to trial."

Stunned! "Nigger, you are crazy. You're not going to use me as a human *guinea pig*." From that moment our relationship was never the same and I can honestly say that was my wake up call.

To Snitch or Not to Snitch

Awaiting trial, as faith would have it, I was on the fifth floor with several of my co- defendants, and I got into a slight argument, no fights just words. Just like that, out of nowhere, due to my reputation the unit was in lock down and I was removed from the unit and transferred to Seven North. Hard to believe, but I cannot make these things up, they placed me in a cell with Andy Mack. Andy and I were in the Brooklyn House of Detention two years prior when one of my associates was shot and dam near murdered and I tortured Andy's ass for information, now two years later I am cell mates with Andy. With our relationship established Andy was telling me how he always felt I was good people, "But Glaze you are in a lot of trouble this time, this is not like the State, the Feds don`t play games." As the day went on Andy would constantly throw different scenarios my way and trust me when I tell you none of the options looked good. One evening as we were looking out of the window, I could see the floor on the lower level and a TVs inside some of their cells. *So, I asked Andy who were those guys, trustees?* And how in the hell were they allowed to have TVs in their cells? Andy went on to explain. "Those are snitches, cooperative witnesses, and from my understanding they get everything they want." A seed was planted.

Trustees are chosen for having better attitudes and a willingness to work. Trustees are used in minor indoor services such as cleaning, maintenance (sweeping, mopping, trash removal), foodservice (prep, cooking and serving) and laundry room. They are under the direct supervision of an officer. The main advantage of being a trustee is more freedom within the jail (you aren't locked in a cell all day) and usually have a larger and better selection of food. In some courts additional goodtime can be applied for any inmate who has trustee status. (Source, Knightrider 5 years with the Sheriff's Department and 21 years as a Correction Officer in a max prison.)

Andy also said he heard, "Down in the witnesses' unit they would also be fucking and their wife's or girlfriends are allowed in their cells." Call me gullible but being able to be in the positions to have sex with your lady during visiting hours, while doing time was really huge.

After a month of talking with Andy and weighing the pros and cons, I placed several calls to the street calling my crew to give them the heads up; that I, Brian "Glaze" Gibbs, was seriously leaning towards cooperating with the FEDS. I personally couldn't believe it that after half of my life of being a wannabe gangster, the irony of me contemplating snitching -- cooperating. Knowingly I would have murdered or ordered the murder for anyone that was snitching. And possibly kill the family members of a snitch, or plot to murder the snitch at their family member's funeral. Now here it is, I'm going against the grain. I was crossing over and joining the enemy. Why? Because I realized that I really didn't have it in me, after all of this time - I was fronting. I wasn't this big bad tough guy, murderer from Brooklyn. The definition of fronting is when one is acting other than their self, as my childhood friend Jeffery Flare Hylton called it "wannabes". We were all wannabes on the big stage of the Metropolitan, New York. From every gender, nationality, and age bracket we all appeared to fall in love with the glitz, glitter, and lights that the fast life offered. That was: fast money from hustling, robbing, stealing, selling drugs, doing any and everything to make a fast buck without punching a clock. It is sad, street hustlers looked at the working-class as suckers, afraid to take chances and wished to work for the man.

As I reflect back upon my life now, I regret all of my past transgressions; wishing I was the sucker with the 9 to 5 job. By now I would have been in a position to retire, from being a correction officer, a cop, sanitation, or a housing employee, or so many other careers, but no I was that lost sheep that went astray. I was like a million and one others picking up a brick and throwing it at the prison wall for nothing. Not realizing the Street Life was a temporary high, and once that high wears off you must go back out and commit another crime. You might look at it like an addiction, a psychological addiction. That's not to say, it's an excuse, just a fact.

Most Likely Suspect - Looking Back

What's really screwy about the whole thing is that damn near every unsolved murder in Brooklyn, New York, during the time was attributed to me! That is to say, the various homicide detectives considered me as a suspect. The whole thing sounds ridiculous and it is! But it's also the truth.

I did fare a little better in Queens, though; only the 103rd and 113th Precincts felt I was in some way responsible or otherwise connected to a variety of unsolved murders in their zones. Whatever, the number, there would've been more had Cat not constantly changed his mind. Cat told me to kill his niece, Mott, Denise McKoy, Bo-Bo, Early, Bimmie, and two of James Corely's former bodyguards, Crush and Nice. I guess Cat cancelled the hit on Mott, because she was his niece. He cancelled the hit on Bimmie, because of his relationship with Supreme. He cancelled the hit on Early, because he realized that he and his brother, True, were just being men when they were fucking Mott and his girl, Denise. It wasn't like they raped them. Denise's hit was stopped, because she disappeared for a while. Bo-Bo's hit was stopped, because Pappy told Cat to let Bo-Bo live. Plus, Bo-Bo also disappeared for a long period of time. The hit on Nice and Crush wasn't called off. I believe, to this day, that they were saved by the federal government when Operation Horse Collar went into force and Cat and Pappy were removed from New York State custody and taken into federal custody.

So, when I was on the run Crush and Nice were the last things on my mind. If Cat hadn't changed his mind, and the federal government hadn't come into the picture, I would've been responsible for eight additional murders in Queens. All of them would've been on Cat's orders and that means that I would've had an additional 10 murders and two attempted murders in Queens. That's not counting another 10-15 murders Cat wanted me to do once I was extradited from Talledega, Alabama, to the New York M.C.C., in December 1988. As soon as I arrived, Cat handed me a list with between 10 and 15 names on it and told me that they were all witnesses in our federal case and that they had to be killed in order for us to beat the case. Even though I was in maximum security custody at a federal institution, Cat knew that I could've easily had the people on the list hit without any problem, but I didn't.

Reality Sets In - Being a Better Man

Sitting in my cell, trying to decide my next step, I reviewed how I felt. The game was over, and the show had stopped. Taking matters into our own hands had to stop. We had to start accepting responsibility for our wrongdoings, and deal with the punishment that we all surely knew was going to be handed down.

We were so accustomed to believing and feeling that killing people to get what we wanted, or to stop them from doing things that we didn't want them to do was the solution to our problems. But, as I now sum it up, I've come to realize that murdering someone never solved any of our problems; we just made them worse. Had things not gone the way they did, Cat changing his mind and all, I would've been responsible for upwards of 30 more murders in Queens. I'm glad it didn't come to that.

Regrets were mounting. Unfortunately, I wasn't using my best judgment during my marriage, and once I was acquitted I spent more time in the streets with my crew and a vast amount of other women. Nothing to be proud of, but I did. Sorry Mrs. Brian Gibbs. She was very supportive and still supports my efforts -- thank you.

Anyway, I was a horrible husband who didn't have a clue. Again, I do have a few regrets. I was also like so many other street guys, a hypocrite who wasn't loyal or faithful. It's funny and I wasn't alone with the thought that as soon as you get locked up then all of a sudden you want your lady to be that loyal, faithful, and supportive girlfriend or wife. No applications for saint hood at the time. Suddenly you become very insecure in your relationship, wanting to keep tabs, inquiring on your girlfriend or wife. You find yourself being jealous and asking questions. What have you been doing? Where have you been, and why didn't you answer the phone when I called? Don't let her miss a visit. If she misses a visit, man there was really hell to pay. Despite being in jail, I still paid the household bills and took care of responsibilities. I had it all wrong. You can't improve until you're honest with yourself.

I realized that a relationship consists of spending quality time with your wife and doing things that couples who are in love share. When I was supposed to be at home at a reasonable time, having dinner with my wife, helping her raise our child, attending church, or family functions, and taking the family on vacations; I was too busy visiting Fat Cat, Pappy and several others in jail. I was flying or taking limousine services all over New York State visiting my criminal minded colleagues. I was too busy focusing on the day to day operations, seeking to establish my brand, and putting my stakes in the ground of the polluted Big Apple. Those actions caused me to lose my title of being husband and father of the year. Anyone can get married and have kids, but it takes a real man to truly be both husband and father.

Not to make light of my actions, but I understand to many in the non-criminal world, I resemble those known as work alcoholics, therefore finding themselves failing in their marital and family duties. I'm not one to judge or give advice, but there it is.

I've been asked how many opportunities and breaks one can get and continue to expect to receive when you keep continually doing the same dam things repeatedly. I've been in and out of jail since the age of sixteen and have I missed so many Thanksgivings, birthdays and Christmases that I have become numb being away from my wife, son and family.

Chapter Ten - The Art of the Deal
Deal or No Deal - Charlie Rose - Part Two

The day came upon me. Andy got me the telephone number to Eastern District New York US Attorney's Office. I placed the call and made mention to the person on the other end that my name is Brian "Glaze" Gibbs, and I would like to set up a meeting with Charlie Rose regarding a possible deal. Within a matter of seconds, I was on the phone with Charlie Rose. The very next day I was escorted from the MCC (Metropolitan Correctional Center) facility along with numerous of other inmates to 225 Cadmen Plaza, Brooklyn Federal Court. Upon our arrival we were all un-shackled and placed in a holding cell waiting to be escorted to court. My name was called, and I was taken to the AUSA (Assistant United States Attorney's) office, where I meet the flamboyant attorney Charlie Rose wearing one of his thousand-dollar suits as if he had just walked off the cover of GQ magazine. Rose was highly intelligent and knew his shit. My first meeting with Rose and his team of FBI agents, to say it went well, would be pushing it. It was like a game of chess, with both opponents trying to figure each other's next move. Initially I was sitting in the office with Rose, FBI agents Richard Martinez and Dave Higgins. They seemed to be in shock, or maybe my own paranoia; I had crossed the line to the other team. Richard was average height, kind of a stocky built, real nice guy, and outgoing. Higgins was slender about 6ft. 4in. tall and very outgoing. He also had more street smarts than a lot of those who grew up within them. He had excellent people skills and acted as if he was a brother. With that approach it made him an instant success with me; good cop, bad cop, he was the good cop.

At the time the State of New York held me under indictment for Supreme Bey Allah's murder and Clifton Rice's murder. I knew there was plenty more murders to follow, not to mention the king pin charge which carried a minimum 10 years with a maximum of life. Being that I was contemplating in making a deal I decided to shoot for the stars. I told Charlie Rose's team that I wanted immediate release and I didn't want to do one more day of jail time. Surprise, Charlie Rose got up and walked out of the office. I in return got up and attempted to walk out of the office when David Higgins got up in front of me and pushed me back down into the chair. As I replayed that incident back and forth repeatedly in my head I had to laugh. I can recall Higgins exact words, "Glaze, be smart don't throw your life away. *You have a chance; you are here in this office for a reason.* Take a couple days and think about this. Just like that the meeting was over. I was escorted back to the holding cell and eventually taken back to MCC with plenty to think about.

As I arrived back to MCC, New York and went back to my housing unit, Andy was the first one to greet me, wanting to know how the meeting went. I took my time and explained it to him step by step what had happened. At that time Andy reached under his mattress and pull out his plea agreement with the United States Government. He was testifying against Delroy Uzi Edwards. Andy went on to explain, that he couldn't believe that I actually went to the US Attorney office, considering my reputation, and based upon what was at stake and how dangerous and crazy I once was, he never thought in a million years that I would be looking to make a deal. He went on to say, that he made his deal quite some time ago and he wasn't going to tell me anything because of the time I tied him up and tortured him in Brooklyn and knowing what I would do to snitches. So, once I went finally down to the US Attorney Office, he knew he was now safe. Andy then went more into depth about how the deal process and everything worked. He showed me his agreement, despite he was part of a large drug organization, involved in murders and attempted murders etc. I knew my situation was more complicated, but I listened.

257

A Drug Dealer Gets a Sentence of 7 Life Terms

By LEONARD BUDER

Published: December 2, 1989

A 30-year-old drug dealer who ran one of the largest and most violent drug rings in Brooklyn and was responsible for 6 murders, 17 assaults, a kidnapping, a maiming and other crimes, was sentenced yesterday to seven consecutive life terms in Federal prison.

As the defendant, Delroy (Uzi) Edwards, stood in Federal District Court with his hands clasped and his head slightly bowed, Judge Raymond J. Dearie said he wished the sentencing could have been on a Brooklyn street, so young people could "see what this fast-lane life style has to offer."

Mr. Edwards, a Jamaican who lives in Brooklyn, was the first dealer to sell crack, the smokable cocaine derivative, in the Bedford-Stuyvesant area, in 1985, law enforcement authorities have said. They said he received his nickname because he sometimes concealed an Uzi submachine gun under a trench coat.

The End of the article

Prison life can be lonely, and you have a tendency to reach out. Delroy was a perfect example. The following is a partial letter reaching out for anyone to correspond with, Maybe you?

My name is Delroy Edwards. I'm currently being held at the notorious United States highest federal super-max isolation facility in Colorado, USA called ADX.

A place described by representative of the United States as a clean version of hell. This means total isolation; and, generally, 24-hour a day in a tiny single person cell the size of two queen-sized mattresses.

258

Most convicts held here at the ADX are not allowed visits or phone calls. Some have no T.V. or radio. Some never lay eyes on each other. Some go years without talking to any other person or years without fresh air or sunlight. And for many, this is death row. A place where most, like myself, are, literally condemned to death. I've held at the ADX since 1995. And, of course, I am sick, literally, of prison and of being alone.

After decades without visits and crushing loneliness in both two United States most notorious super-max federal facilities: U.S. Marion and the ADX Florence, the true loneliness of prison hasset upon me.

So, in the midst of this pain, my sincere hope is to find a pen-pal. My hobbies: Being as though I was born and raised in a coastal/seaside neighborhood I've always been an outdoor adventurous person. I enjoyed pristine beaches, crystalline waters, boats, the ocean and seafood. In prison I read a lot, write, study, and have successfully participated in multiple educational courses and earned multiple certificates of achievement.

If you recognized my plight or if you're just curious, please give me a chance and treat yourself to a friend. I am absolutely confident in saying that I would be honored and humbled if I am the object of your choice for a friend. I will make tremendous efforts to connect with you and my responses will provide additional insight.

Thank you kindly for your time and understanding, and thank you for considering writing.

Respect!

Mr. Delroy Edwards #25109-053

ADX - Florence PO Box 8500
Florence, CO 81226

Deal or No Deal - Charlie Rose - Part Three

A week after my first meeting with Charlie Rose a second meeting was arranged. In attendance was: Rose, and Assistant United State Attorney Leslie R. Caldwell, FBI agents: Rick Martinez and Dave Higgins. They got straight to the point.

Question 1- What was my involvement with Rookie NYPD Edward Bryne's murder? (From the beginning of the hit on Edward Bryne every NYPD Brass and officers in the borough of Queens and Brooklyn targeted me as their # 1 Suspect. They felt I was crazy enough and had the balls to execute a cop.

Everyone was baffled that my name was never mentioned which lead law enforcement to believe that those guys were so afraid of "Glaze" the killer, the mad man, the lunatic, that they would give up Fat Cat and Pappy before they would utter my name. Imagine what that did for my ego? My answer to the Feds was true, "I didn't have anything to do with the hit on Bryne."

Question 2- What was my involvement with Parole Officer, Brian Rooney's Murder? I answered by saying the Brian Rooney hit was before my time and there wasn't anything that I could add to the Brian Rooney file.

As time went on, they had so many guys in jail with life sentences that were all coming forward to get on the band wagon seeking to cut deals. For example, Michael Smith aka Little Piez was convicted for murder and sentence to 25 years to life during his bid. He came back down several times seeking to cut a deal. He helped both State and FEDS to build a case against Darryl Tyler aka Little Dee, but eventually he didn't testify against Dee due to the fact that the Federal Government couldn't do anything to commute his sentence, but that didn't stop him from trying. He also told them that Jug Head confessed to him that he killed Fat Cat's parole officer. When the Feds came to me with what Piez said, I told them that was bullshit. Jug Head was a boss, Piez was only Little Dee's flunky. Why would a boss tell a flunky, "By the way I killed Fat Cat's parole officer," it didn't happen. Several years later the FEDS finally busted open and solved the murder of Brian Rooney when Pappy right hand man Jeffery Rafael Ruffin aka Ruff was arrested. He made a deal and spilled the beans and implicated the Lucas brothers; Lamont and Randy as the trigger man and he gave information on each and every one who planned and took part in Rooney's murder.

A week after my first meeting with Charlie Rose a second meeting was arranged. In attendance was: Rose, and Assistant United State Attorney Leslie R. Caldwell, FBI agents: Rick Martinez and Dave Higgins. They got straight to the point.

Question 1- What was my involvement with Rookie NYPD Edward Bryne's murder? (From the beginning of the hit on Edward Bryne every NYPD Brass and officers in the borough of Queens and Brooklyn targeted me as their # 1 Suspect. They felt I was crazy enough and had the balls to execute a cop.

Everyone was baffled that my name was never mentioned which lead law enforcement to believe that those guys were so afraid of "Glaze" the killer, the mad man, the lunatic, that they would give up Fat Cat and Pappy before they would utter my name. Imagine what that did for my ego? My answer to the Feds was true, "I didn't have anything to do with the hit on Bryne."

Question 2- What was my involvement with Parole Officer, Brian Rooney's Murder? I answered by saying the Brian Rooney hit was before my time and there wasn't anything that I could add to the Brian Rooney file.

Question 3- What was my direct involvement in The Nichols organization? I was in charge of security any problems pertaining to anyone that was down with us. I and my crew handled the problems. I was involved with the large purchases of cocaine or heroin. Anytime a large sum of money was being transport I was there. When it came to disciplinary actions or a hit, I was there to take care of it or ensure it got done. Cat was smart he wanted layers. He would prefer for me to not get my hands dirty. He always wanted to use other folks for the hit so if they ever turned, they would turn on me not him. Because he gave the order to me and I gave it to someone else, he was protected. We discussed other numerous murders per Fat Cat.

At this point I still had no idea what my cooperation was going to buy.

Deal or No Deal - Call to the Street - Part Four

During my time in MCC, N.Y. I placed a call to the streets, to my people, my crew. I informed them of my thoughts, my thought process, and the fact that I was leaning toward making a deal. In addition, I made calls to several individual from different organizations who were allies. Strange and unique as it may seem, I basically placed all my cards on the table and presented all of my options. One of which was, if I didn't cooperate with the Feds, I would be spending the rest of days of my life in prison, meaning I would die in jail, The response that I received was unanimous, none of them wanted me to spend the rest of life in prison. As it turned out, my people knew ahead of time before it became news, public knowledge on April 13, 1989.

Will Sing for the Feds

The NY Daily News had a picture of Pappy Mason and me and the headline of the story read, "Henchman Will Sing for the Feds." I was receiving all types of feedback: half and half both positive and negative – no surprise. One in particular was, "You must not love your mother!" This was obviously a sensitive topic. What I believe everyone, at the time, failed to realize was that I was Fat Cat's Muscle (me and my crew) M&M, Money and Murder. Who in the world was Cat going to use to put a hit on me? Was he going to get Me on Me? If anything would have happened to my mother or anyone in my family, the way I was back then with my mentality, his whole bloodline would have been eliminated. Back then I had some real blood thirsty loyal supporters. It took some years for me to stop reaching out to them. WHY? Despite I cooperated I could use the phone to call from federal prison, however the phone conversations were all monitored. My guys would get on the phone as if I was still out, by telling me another one bit the dust. I constantly had to remind them that I was in jail, on a monitored line. Most of my guys were handpicked, either we grew up together in Brooklyn or we did a bid together (jail time).

It was strange that there were so many undercover snitches that didn't receive the publicity that I did. I never once took the stand at a trail, nor at a grand jury to testify on or against anyone. Yes, I was debriefed, and I did render information on everything that I was part of indirectly and directly.

It doesn't take long for everyone to start looking to make a deal. Guys that I knew, for a fact, that cooperate with the Eastern District of New York United State Attorney Office was James Gibbs aka Kool Aid. He drove from South Carolina to New York to sit down and cooperate against Darryl Tyler. I can recall him calling me, crying that he didn't know what to do, but yet and still he wasn't in hand cuffs nor was he under arrest. He drove over 900 miles to snitch and would you believe he didn't even get reimbursed for gas. But he was always bragging and talking about that he is a real Don.

There was Jeffery Rafael Ruffin aka Ruff, Ruff was the whistle blower who solved parole officer Brian Rooney murder. When Ruff was charged federally, he made a deal and gave up everyone involve from the Lucas brothers to Fat Cat. The word on the street was they had to slap Ruff to shut up as he was giving up too much info.

The parade continued with Victor Breland of the Baby Sam Edmondson crew who initially agreed to cooperate against Baby Sam, Kyle, Amar and everyone. He sat down and wrote out a list of over 10 murders and was writing more when Johnny Ray's name came up. Vic told them he would give up everyone except Johnny Ray Robinson. He was told Johnny Ray would have to be part of the deal, Victor took the plea agreement off the table and ate every page of the agreement: NO DEAL! Vic was later convicted and sentence to multiple life sentence with everyone else of Baby Sam's Crew.

Pappy Mason and The Junk Bond King

Operation Horse Collar was collecting on its efforts. Pappy went to trial during October-November 1989, and was convicted in December 1989, in Brooklyn Federal Court, on all counts; including the murder of rookie cop, Edward Brynes, and continuous criminal enterprise. Since then, he'd lost his mind. He didn't shower and from what I understand he'd gone seven months without a shower or bath. When he goes to the toilet, he wipes himself with his hands, and stories told say that he has actually eaten sandwiches made of fecal matter in front of various psychiatrists in the mental ward at the Federal Bureau of Prisons facility at Springfield, Missouri. He didn't use the telephone, write anyone, or get visits from family members. I believe Pappy caused himself to go crazy, because he let his mother get convicted for working for him and sentenced to 10 years in prison, knowing he could've prevented it simply by pleading guilty.

The fact that Pappy's mentor, Fat Cat, had also decided to sell his soul to the Devil by making a deal with the United States Attorney and telling that Pappy gave the order to kill the policeman, as well as other illegal activities, is what really destroyed Pappy. Pappy loved Cat to the point of even dying for him. Cat introduced Pappy to the drug game, laying down the laws of the game and teaching him everything he knew. But Cat believed that Pappy's stupidity destroyed the whole organization, including getting several of his family members sent to jail.

The media broke the story that Fat Cat turned rat in the fall of 1989. Cat had made a deal with the federal government and agreed to testify against Pappy -- and anyone else they needed. Pappy knew that is was his fault that Cat was cooperating with the feds, and he knew it was his fault that his own mother might die in prison. Add to that the fact that he'd been convicted and was facing life in prison; losing touch with reality and going a little insane wasn't a difficult thing for him to do.

He even went to the psychiatric ward at Kings County Hospital. The government had doctors who were saying that Pappy was incompetent, not only then but during his trial.

Pappy returned to the M.C.C. during my stay there for my sentencing. It was Sunday, February 23, 1992. He was returning from the Medical Center at Springfield. I was on the tier for my hour of recreation when I saw Pappy. I looked up and saw somebody climbing the stairs. The person was wearing an orange jumpsuit, had long dreads, and was escorted by correctional officers. I didn't say anything, but when the officers came back down the stairs, during their rounds, I asked if they'd brought Pappy Mason back. The officer said they had. Pappy was just upstairs from me. I wanted to talk to Pappy, but I said that I'd catch him during recreation.

Pappy was in court all day on Monday, February 24, 1992. The next day, Tuesday, I was sleeping, but thought I heard him talking. It sounded like he was asking someone to send him some potato chips. When I got up I asked Bruce -- that's Bruce Black, co-defendant of the "Junk bond king" Michael Milkens -- about what I'd heard and he said that Pappy did ask him for some potato chips and he sent him a bag. Bruce also told me that Pappy seemed to be back to normal. Later that day Bruce asked an officer if Pappy had been taken back to the hospital ward at Springfield, and the officer said that Pappy did leave.

I believe it was the next day, Wednesday, when I was using the telephone when Jeffrey "Ruff" Ruffin passed by and made a smart comment. I was talking to one of my aunts about my mother when I noticed an inmate and an officer passing by on the main floor. The inmate doubled back, looked down where I was, then made a slick comment, but nothing registered to me. Then, it dawned on me that it was Ruff. I didn't recognize him, because he'd cut his dreads. Leslie Caldwell did tell me that Ruff was cooperating with them and being debriefed about Parole Officer Brian Rooney's murder, as well as a lot of other criminal activity.

When I got off the telephone I went into the shower. While I was showering I heard Ruff's voice. I came out of the shower butt-naked and shouted his name. Ruff was heading up the stairs with the officers but stopped and called me a snitch -- among other things. So, I shouted back at him, saying, "Ruff, don't front on me, you punk motherfucker, bitch ass nigger! You know who I am and what I'm capable of doing!" Then I said, "Better yet, you punk motherfucker, you're doing the exact same thing I'm doing! You're telling, too"! Ruff just dropped his head and the officer escorted him back to his cell. I went back and finished my shower.

On Friday evening I was in my cell, looking out of the food slot, when I saw Ruff coming back from somewhere -- probably court or a debriefing. When Ruff got back to his cell, he and Pappy got into a lengthy conversation. They were shouting back and forth to each other, asking about each other and their families. Ruff told Pappy about his legal affairs and Pappy told him that hearings were being held to determine whether or not he was sane. I was amazed at the conversation, because I honestly believed that Pappy had in fact lost his marbles and had reached the point of no return.

I never thought he was faking it. But after listening to that conversation there was no doubt in my mind, that if Pappy did lose grip with reality, he was now definitely back to normal. He sounded like the old Pappy, talking like the man I've known, with authority and possessing a dominant leadership. I knew that despite his present situation and predicament, he was still perfectly in control. Unfortunately, what Pappy didn't know at the time and probably didn't find out for another six months or a year, was that his so-called brother, Ruff, had signed a plea agreement and had been cooperating with the federal government since his arrest in July or August of 1991.

Ruff told Leslie Caldwell about Pappy's present state of mind: that he wasn't insane. He was sane as ever, because of their conversation. Ruff told Ms. Caldwell that because he wanted to receive the best departure letter he could from her. A departure letter is presented to the judge hearing a defendant's case; the better the letter, the lesser the prison sentence.

Caldwell was pleased to learn of the information, because she, along with the Brooklyn Federal Court System, wanted to get Pappy's psychiatric hearings over with, so the court could make its determination of Pappy's mental status. If Pappy was found sane, then he would be subjected to receive several consecutive life sentences for his Kingpin status, CCE drug conviction, and for giving the order to have the rookie police officer, Edward Bryne, murdered, execution style.

I was able to psyche out my conscience by thinking that if Pappy hadn't given the order for those four jackasses to murder that rookie police officer, then none of us would've been indicted by the federal government. So, with that mental note, it was a little bit easier to take the stand against my once, longtime associate.

I've realized that there are a lot of things in life that a person does that he really doesn't want to do. But at times, you've got to be able to put your principles and morals to one side and do what is best for yourself; because, in the end, what it all boils down to is self-preservation.

Anxious and unbeknown to me at the time, my sentence date would arrive on Thursday, February 27, 1992. I still had no idea what my deal with the Feds would save me in prison time, yet I prayed until my sentencing was over. Even murderers believe God hears their prayers - really.

Memories of Mom

One of my main and most important reasons for making and signing a plea agreement with the government was that I didn't want to receive life imprisonment and have my mother die on me while I was in jail. I anticipated my mother would live a healthy and peaceful life for at least another twenty years, maybe more. I figured that by receiving as little time as possible, I could return to society and be able to be there for my mother when she needed me most.

On February 9, 1992, at approximately 10:00 P.M. Eastern Time, I was trying to call home, but the line was busy. I kept trying and finally did get through. My aunt, Pauline, answered the telephone and when she recognized my voice, she told me to hold on. My sister, Tia, then picked up the telephone and I'll never forget what I heard. She said, "Keith, I know you don't want to hear what I'm about to tell you."

I was in administrative detention in a federal witness protection facility in the upper Midwest when I made the call, and I just dropped the receiver and put my head face down into the bed. My son had just been operated on a few days earlier and I thought something had happened to him.

Then I thought that may be something had happened to my brother, because he still lived in New York City, however, I had just talked to him the night before. I picked up the telephone and the words I heard were the ones I feared most. My sister said, "Keith, Mommy is gone."

I just threw myself to the grey concrete floor, crying uncontrollably, and banging every part of my body. This lasted for about ten minutes before I managed to gather myself and try to find out what had happened. When I picked up the telephone again my brother was on the line. He tried to console me the best he could, telling me that my mother didn't suffer when she died. But I still couldn't control my emotions and constantly kept breaking down and crying. Here it was, the person who had been there for me through everything, had given me my life, the person who I loved with all of my heart, and suddenly she was gone. I just found it too hard to believe. My brother, KoolAid, explained to me what happened. I kept breaking down like a little baby.

My mother, sister, and Aunt Pauline had just returned home from Sunday church services and after dinner all of them were sitting around the table and talking. The subject of death came up and everybody was talking about what colors they wanted to be buried in, my aunt first, and then my sister. My mother said that she wanted to be buried in blue and only a few seconds later she started complaining of a sharp pain in her head. My mother told them she felt like her head was about to burst open, like she was going to die. She then grabbed one of her eyes and fell out of the chair. Aunt Pauline and Sandra ran to her and one of them called for an ambulance. My cousins, Tasha and Junnie, who is a police officer, both came over and gave my mother C.P.R. The ambulance came and my mother was taken to the hospital. But from what I understood, my mother had already passed away before the ambulance reached the hospital.

I just couldn't understand why; I didn't want to believe it. It was like the whole thing was a nightmare and that I would awaken shortly.

The detention officer came to my cell and told me that my time on the telephone was over and I had to hang up. I told my brother that I'd try to call back at the next available opportunity. It was almost midnight New York time when I got the telephone again.

During the time that passed between the telephone calls, I was like a walking zombie. I didn't really have any sense of time, but now I know it was about an hour and 40 minutes before I got to use the telephone again.

While I waited to get back on the telephone, I just cried and cried and cried while walked back and forth in my cell. Several times I found myself standing on top of the bed or looking out of the window in a state of shock and total confusion. That was the one time in my life that I didn't know my hand from my elbow. It was like I was talking to my mother, asking her over and over again, "Mom, what am I going to do without you? How am I going to survive, function and carry on without you?" I kept looking at her picture and crying and I kept repeating to myself, over and over, that this wasn't really true and that it was a nightmare and that when I woke up everything was going to be alright.

My head was spinning around, and I remember grabbing a burgundy leather-covered Bible; it was a New King James Version that my mother had given to me back in April of 1989. I had some pictures of my mother and son together, taken back in March of 1989, and I remember putting them in the front of the Bible. I bent down on my knees and prayed.

I prayed hard and asked God to give me strength. I asked God to please allow my mother to know that I really loved her and that I will always love her. I asked God to give all of us strength and be with all of us: me, my brother, my sister, all of my family, and friends of the family. I asked God to allow my mother's soul to rest in peace and asked God to let all my family and friends know that my mother is in heaven. If ever there was a time when I needed my prayers to be answered, it was then.

I called back home around midnight New York time, and spoke with my brother again. I couldn't keep from breaking down and crying. All I remember my brother saying was: "Let it out." The more I cried, the more I realized that things remained the same. I knew that my life had changed and that things would never be the same. Never in my life had I experienced such sorrow as I felt then. I didn't want to believe it. That was one time that I, Brian Gibbs, just didn't want to deal with reality. What I really wanted most was to be able to trade places with my mother. I would've preferred to have died, instead of my mother. I've felt like that for as long as I can remember. I always remember praying to God to let something happen to me and let me die in place of my mother, son, sister, brother, nephew, or niece. That's how much I love them.

After my mother passed away, I often asked: "How can you love and hate life at the same time?"

I loved life and all the wonderful things that life had to offer; all of the good times and experiences in dealing with living, including all of the beautiful people who had come into my life and made it worth living. Then the people you love leave this earth, without a sign or warning and there's nothing you can do to bring them back. There is absolutely nothing in this world you can do to cope with the death of someone who means so much to you. There's no cure, no remedies, no answers -- there's just no easy way to deal with it. I contemplated suicide. My reasoning was that I wanted to be right there with my mother, forever. I didn't ever want to live without her. To lose someone who means

271

as much as my mother meant to me and my family hurt so bad. That's why I love and hate life at the same time; because the pain is so unbearable and difficult to deal with on a daily basis. I once believed the saying: "Time heals all wounds." Well, I know for a fact that because of the loss of my mother, my life will never be the same. My life has changed forever and all the time in the world could never heal my wounds.

The only thing I honestly believe in my heart that would heal my wounds, is the day I leave this earth and meet with my mother again. To be able to hug her and kiss her and tell her how much I really missed her and beg her not to ever leave me again.

I don't know how I got through that night. The officer came for the telephone when the shift changed. After I hung up the telephone it was like I was there, but I wasn't. It was like I was in another world. Before I hung up, my brother and I agreed to go on a liquid fast from then until the time my mother was buried.

That whole night I stayed up and sucked on ice cubes. I sat in front of the open slot in my cell door and talked to the officer who was working the midnight to 8:00 A.M. shift. The officer tried to console me, and we talked until 6:00 A.M. the next morning, which was when I was allowed to use the telephone again.

When I got the telephone, I called several family members and friends. I believe I was the last one to know about my mother's death, out of my closest family members. I also called some close family friends and told them of my great loss. They all sympathized with me and my family, but none of them really knew what to say except that they were sorry for our loss, and that everything was going to be alright.

I also spoke with my father. He tried to console me the best he could, but I guess it was difficult for him, too. He was at a loss for words; his mother was still alive and I felt unless a person has actually experienced losing their mother, then it's difficult for them to reassure someone who has.

The night of my mother's passing I briefly spoke to my mother's sister, Helen, who attempt to console me, saying she would be my mother. I snapped at her and told her that no one would ever be able to take my mother's place. I know that she really didn't mean anything by it. So, the next morning I called Aunt Helen back and apologized to her. I knew her intentions were good, and she was genuine, and I didn't want her to be offended by what I'd said. I told her that I knew she was suffering as well; knowing my mother was her sister long before she was my mother. Out of my mother's four sisters I always saw my Aunt Helen as the strongest, never witnessing any sign of weakness in her. But she took my mother's passing really hard as well.

I then got in contact with my cousin, Rosa. She and my mother were very close. It was more like my mother was her mother, too, instead of her aunt and was extremely upset. I was on the telephone with her and my sister, as we were all trying to comfort each other. I told Rosa that my mother hadn't been retired a full two months and then this happened. I said, "She didn't even get a chance to enjoy her retirement and her new home." Rosa said that my mother used to always tell her that she could either retire at 52 or wait until she reached 65; but since 65 wasn't promised, she decided to go ahead and retire. Rosa said, "You know your mother enjoyed herself, because she was always traveling." That was definitely true.

Sorry Mom, Happy Sixteenth Birthday

Nobody could say anything to make it easier. After my mother passed away, I faulted myself for her death. I felt that I'd put my mother through a lot by constantly getting into trouble. My mother had always told me that it seemed like the day of my 16th birthday, December 1, 1979, that I completely changed and really became committed to the street.

I remember my 16th birthday party. After school that day my mother baked my favorite cake, German Chocolate. Finishing dinner my aunt and her kids, and some friends and other cousins from the projects came to sing Happy Birthday to me and eat some ice cream and cake. Unfortunately, I recall making all kinds of sarcastic remarks and irking my mother's nerves.

My mother kept warning me about my behavior, but I paid her no mind. I constantly disregarded her warning and boy did my mother make me pay! She jumped on me and started slapping my face. I was trying to get away, but she kept grabbing my clothes and pulling me back to her. I must have been slapped at least 20 times. All I remember is that I was crying, and I believe my lip was busted. But all and all, I believe that I brought that punishment on myself. I think the remark that brought it on was: "Everyone is here eating my cake and ice cream, where's my birthday gifts?" And when I said it, I really was being sarcastic. After the incident that night I was more embarrassed than anything else, since everybody was present when my mother slapped me. She kept saying. "What's your problem? Do you think you're grown? Have you been sniffing your funky underwear? Do you think you're 61 years old, instead of 16?"

I think the problem was that I felt that someone owed me something and that I was supposed to get everything and anything I wanted. I know my mother loved me and the rest of her children. However, I know she didn't like the fact that I was in and out of trouble from my participation in all the negativity and nonsense in the street. But despite my mother's feelings about what I did on the street, I was already burglarizing, committing robberies, and other minor illegal activities to make money; although, back then I didn't have a criminal record.

When I was arrested 25 days after my 16th birthday, with Clyde Gibbs -- no relation -- I can still hear the hurt in my mother's voice when she answered the telephone when I told her that I had been arrested for robbery. I'm truly sorry for everything that I've put my mother through.

Every time I had to go to court, my mother was there for me. She made sure that I was properly dressed and on time. She even took time off from work to be in court with me. I hate myself for that! I put my mother through an awful lot of stress, pain and suffering. My mother worried about me a lot, especially while I was out in the streets. It seemed like I was her lost child and always into something. All she wanted was for me to get my life together and she didn't want me to die a violent death in the streets. I never intended to hurt my mother and I'm sorry that I went astray. Unfortunately, some kids don't realize how their actions affect their parents, especially mothers.

After my mother's death, my eyes opened up to a lot of things. I realized the extent of the trial and tribulations I subjected my family to, and friends. *And especially to the family members of the victims I was responsible for killing. I'm truly sorry for all of it.* I'm sorry for killing Sybil. I can only imagine the pain, the suffering and heartache that I put Sybil's children and family through, and how they tried to cope with the death of a loved one. I wish I could turn back the hands of time and bring back all of my victims, because I'm only a human being who didn't have the right to say who lived or who died. *I realize now the judgments for their demise were ironically the same things I come to eventually repeat*. Over the years I've constantly asked God for forgiveness and the victims and their families and the loved ones, for destroying their lives.

On Sunday, March 1, 1992, while in the hole in a witness protection unit in the Midwest, I was talking to Mrs. B., who told me that I only had to ask God once to forgive me for all of my sins and all of my involvement in criminal activities. Mrs. B. told me that God forgave me the very first time I asked for forgiveness, but I didn't forgive myself. However, on Thursday, March 6, 1992, between 2:00 P.M. and 3:00 P.M., I was in my cell with Chaplin Bob and I accepted the Son of God, the Lord Jesus Christ, as my Savior. I confessed all of my sins, and from that day forward I've lived a positive and righteous life, according to God's words. When my time comes to leave this earth, I hope and pray I'll indeed rest in peace with our Father in Heaven and my mother. I know that's what my mother wanted me to do and that's what I'm going to do. To live my life here on earth the way God sees fit for Brian Keith Gibbs. Sad, that it took the loss of someone so dear to me and meant so much to me, for me to get my life in order and my soul's salvation right. It really hurts, because I know I could've and should've got my life together without losing her. I wanted to make it all up to her and prove to her that I've changed, and that I'm going to live a clean-cut, decent, honest, positive, and righteous life, and be successful in a free society. *The- should've, could've, would've blues.*

It was March 8, 1992, when I first wrote this, I was still burdened and crying, trying to cope and deal with the loss of my mother. I read the Bible on a daily basis and that was extremely comforting. I prayed throughout most of the day which helped me a great deal. I can still remember my mother always telling me that she wasn't always going to be there for me and I always replied by saying, "Mom, don't tell me that, you know that I can't deal with the loss of you and that I'll go crazy." My mother always replied by saying,

God would give me strength and carry me on. She said that when her mother, my grandmother, passed away, she thought that she wasn't going to be able to go on with life, but that God gave her strength and she was able to take it one day at a time and carry on. But all of that is easier said than done. At the time I still couldn't, and more or less didn't want to believe that my mother was no longer with me. That I couldn't pick up the telephone and talk with her and that I couldn't see or hug or kiss her and tell her over and over again how much I really love her. No more birthday greetings, no more Christmas cards, and no more special occasions with my mother and German chocolate cake.

I've accepted the Lord Jesus Christ as my personal savior. I read the Bible daily and attend services every Sunday, and constantly prayed. I've always wanted to change, and I've always prayed, but the turning point was my mother's death. If it wasn't for God carrying me on, then I don't know how I would've been able to continue living without her. Since the day I was born, my mother always told me that whatever I do in life to make sure that I put God first and to love no one more than I love God. She would always tell me to ask God for strength and guidance through troubled times, and that when I read the Bible to ask God to bless the word that I was reading and allow me to understand those words and be able to live by his words.

My mother's death made me feel like I just didn't care anymore. I was like a zombie, living in the twilight zone. I didn't know which direction I was headed but my mother's constants words prepared me for that moment once it came. God definitely took control of me and gave me strength. On the 9th day of each month I go on a 24 hour fast and pray in commemoration of my mother. I also do that on her birthday, Mother's Day, and the week of her death every year. I'll continue doing that for as long as I live.

My mother was always there for me, through the good and bad experiences. I remember once, when I was about 13 or 14yrs old, I broke my left hand while playing basketball in the Cypress Hills Houses. My hand was all swollen and the pain was unbearable. My mother came home from a hard day's work and took me straight to Saint Mary's Hospital. While we were waiting to have the X-rays taken, my mother had gotten a box of fresh donuts from the bakery and we ate them together while we waited. The Xrays confirmed that my hand was broken, and I was admitted to the hospital for several days. I hated it and was in pain a lot of the time. But my mother was there, telling me that everything was going to be alright.

Regardless of what I was up against or what I did, if my mother told me that everything was going to be alright, then I knew it would be alright and that's how it was.

My late mother witnessed me getting upset and exploding and heard me made mention that I was going to eliminate someone. My Mother would say, "That's your problem, is that you think you can kill other people's children and get away with it. You have to remember you have a child of your own now." That woman always knew what to say to put me in check.

Deal or No Deal - Meeting Pappy - Part Five

After my next meeting it was still like a chess game, both sides still trying to feel each other out and develop some form of trust between, myself, a career criminal, versus the Federal Government. A very awkward situation to say the least but it was something that I had to decide and commit myself to; there would be no turning back.

Before my next meeting with Rose and Caldwell I went upstairs for a co-defendant meeting with Pappy on the 9th floor. At that time Pappy wasn't allowed to go anywhere but court. I can recall Pap coming into the attorney conference room and we embraced one another.

He went on calling me, my brother Glazie Azie. A little small talk was exchanged when I told him that I, Brian "Glaze" Gibbs, had struck a deal to cooperate with the enemy and if he felt I was wrong he could take the razor blade out of his dread locks and cut me across my throat. One of the most dangerous, vicious, and craziest person I knew looked me in my eyes and said, "I can't do that to you, you are my brother and I love you."

He went on to ask, what is everyone going to say and think? Pap continued by saying everywhere he went from a N.Y. State Prison to Prison how everyone from The Lugo brothers, Ivan Johnson, KO Smitty and many other legends that were incarcerated who spoke highly of me, what are they going to say? I can remember telling Pap in reality it doesn't matter what anyone's says or thinks. Those who love and care about you will continue to love you; those who didn't care about you they still are not going to give a dam about you. **The biggest problem in life is that people worry about what other people think or feel about us and we give them too much control over our life. I wanted my life back and wanted to be in control of my own destiny.** I no longer chose to be a follower by participating and doing what the majority does. I officially decided to go against the grain; becoming someone I despised, if that's what it takes to be free of this image and game, so be it. Pap and I hugged and stated we loved each other and best wishes. At that time Fat Cat had stopped all forms of communication with Pap. Again, he blamed Pap for Operation Horse Collar. Although Fat Cat and Pap were on the outs, they were both on 9 south, maximum security, Cat totally ignored Pap as if he didn't exist.

Nicky Barnes - The Legend

As a kid growing up I heard so much about the Man, The Myth, The Legend Mr. Leroy Nicky Barnes one of the biggest heroin dealers in the 60's and 70's. From the street to state prisons the stories of Nicky were non-stop, "Mr.

Untouchable." During the early 80's Nicky decided to cooperate with the Federal Government giving up information on his organization and the Mafia. He was eventually placed in the witness protection unit.

The first time I meet Mr. Barnes was in the summer of 1989 when I entered the witness protection program; we hit it off quite well. Nicky was a private person and only dealt with a chosen few and I happen to be one of them. He would just get on me about why I was putting very little effort into the classes and was still receiving a 2.5 GPA. But that wasn't good enough; I should be striving for a 4.0 according to Mr. Barnes. Nicky was highly intelligent, earned his degree and spoke several languages. He was in tip top shape and watched what he ate. However, he could cook his own meals. Nicky worked the mess hall breakfast shift and I refused to get up for breakfast, during the time pancakes or French toast was served. Nicky would bring a plate to my cell and drop it off with one of his many statements. "You still have what you ate last night on your tongue is the reason why you couldn't get up for breakfast."

Deal or No Deal - Meeting Fat Cat - Part Six

My next meeting was with Fat Cat and a couple of my co-defendants. When I told them my intention to cooperate, Cat's exact words were "How could you hurt me like that?" At that time one of our other co-defendants, happened to be my half-brother Country. He stated, if anybody can hurt me, he can by cooperating against me. That hurt me. Reason being, if he had anything to say to me he was to do it in private - just him and me. At that time I felt he chose to side with Fat Cat and ironically I was in the process of putting up the money to bail Country out. But after that meeting and his action, fuck him, let Fat Cat bail him out.

That was the sign that our organization which was one of the most powerful organizations on the East Coast had accepted defeat. We were no longer a force to be reckoned with and that helped me to realize that my decision was "RIGHT FOR ME." It was the end of the Round Table.

As time went on, we had co-defendants fighting. A couple of my co-defendants including Pap got into a big melee on the ninth floor that made the news back then, when a couple of them ended up getting stabbed. The whole time Cat was in the cut, it was his doing (cut meaning not getting his hands dirty), his plan, but and still his hands didn't get dirty. He didn't confront Pap; he used the others to do it for him.

Cat developed a strong relationship with Greg Scarfa Jr. They spent their idle time gambling, from betting on basketball and football games, both pro and college. Scarfa was the jailhouse bookie giving spreads.

His father was a known affiliate of a crime family as stated in Wikipedia, the free encyclopedia **Gregory Scarpa, Sr.** (May 8, 1928 – June 4, 1994) also known as "The Grim Reaper" and "The Mad Hatter" was a capo for the Colombo crime family and an informant for the FBI. During the 1970s and 80s, Scarpa was the chief enforcer for Colombo boss Carmine Persico. Scarpa was responsible for at least three murders in 1991. Scarpa was born to first generation immigrants from the impoverished village of Lorenzaga of Motta di Livenza near Venice, Italy. Scarpa was the brother of Colombo mobster Salvatore Scarpa, who may have introduced Scarpa to the Colombo family.

A career criminal, Scarpa eventually became a capo regime in the Colombo crime family, as well as the proprietor of the Wimpy Boys Social Club. Scarpa was involved in illegal gambling, loan sharking, extortion, hijacking, counterfeit credit cards, assault, stock and bond thefts, narcotics and murder. Many of the highest-ranking members of the Colombo crime family today were members of Scarpa's crew. In March 1962, Scarpa was arrested outside for armed robbery. To avoid prosecution, Scarpa agreed to work as an undercover informant for the Federal Bureau of Investigation, beginning a 30-year relationship with the agency. By point 99% of the time, the bigger you are the harder you will fall.

The Sand Castle Crumbles

But before Fat Cat decided to cooperate with the feds, he got together with Bo-Bo at the M.C.C. New York and made a deal with him.

During April 1989, Cat told Bo-Bo that we all knew that Pappy was the one who got us all jammed up on the federal case, because of the order to kill a cop. Cat went on to tell Bo-Bo, "You know, the Feds aren't playing. They don't discriminate, and they aren't sparing anyone." He told Bo-Bo, "You see what they did to Peter Monsanto's' mother." Monsanto's' mother, who was in her late fifties or early sixties, was convicted on drug charges, right along with her two sons and their co-defendants, and was sentenced to 10 years. Pappy's mother, Claudia Mason, was also convicted on drug charges. Her bail was revoked, and she was remanded back to jail at the M.C.C. New York as she awaited sentencing.

When Fat Cat knew his trial date was nearing and there were still others left on his indictment, which included Cat's mother, Louise Coleman; Lynn; and Bo-Bo and he knew they would be last to go to trial with him.

So, Cat told Bo-Bo that it would be wise for all of them to make a deal with the feds and plead guilty; because, if they didn't, then the feds were going to smash their worlds. Cat said, "With Glaze already cooperating with them we really don't have much of a chance, because if anybody can hurt me, Glaze can, and it's no telling what he's told them or what he's going to tell them. But just as long as he didn't give me up for any murders, I don't mind. He can tell them about all the drug transactions. I don't care, because they know that I'm a drug dealer. "So, Cat and Bo-Bo made a pact to cooperate with the government, but steadfastly deny that either had any involvement in the Brian Rooney's murder. They agreed not to tell the feds anything they didn't already know, and that's exactly what they did. They didn't volunteer any new information, only confirming what the feds already knew. But Federal Prosecutor Leslie Caldwell and F.B.I. Agent Richard Martinez caught both Fat Cat and Bo-Bo in numerous lies. Fat Cat and Bo-Bo finally jammed up each other and ended up implicating one another in different murders.

Cat asked Leslie Caldwell to polygraph him on his involvement in or knowledge of the Rooney murder, insisting that he was innocent. Cat took three polygraph tests regarding the Rooney murder and badly failed all of them. But despite that, Cat still insisted that he didn't have anything to do with his parole officer's murder.

Before it became public knowledge that Cat had made a deal with the federal government, he sent word to Jug Head, Supreme, Prince, and several other close associates, that the feds had him by the balls and he was going to cooperate with them, but that he was only going to be giving up information on "Glaze and Pappy." Cat told his close associates that he decided to make a deal with the feds, because he wanted to get his mother and Lynn off the hook.

Fat Cat - Bad Deal

The 40-year sentence Cat received on February 7, 1992, was handed down under the new Federal Sentencing Guidelines, which means that he would have to serve 85% of his sentence -- 34 years and 8 months -- the new guidelines also abolished federal parole.

Cat cooperated with the government and I honestly feel that he got fucked, despite the fact that he bullshitted them, and they knew it. Cat only told the feds what he wanted to tell them; they'd ask him questions about the big drug dealers he was cool with and Cat would out and out lie, telling the feds that he didn't know those guys.

The feds knew Cat was lying to them; they showed him pictures of himself with the guys they were asking about. In some of the pictures everybody, including Cat, was wearing diamond-faced gold Rolex watches and expensive clothes, and standing around several Mercedes Benz convertibles. But Cat continued to lie and say that he'd just met those guys -- like at a Broadway play or musical concert. He told on Pappy, me, and anyone he didn't like at the time or felt that had fucked him in some way.

Fat Cat turned Rat - The Wire Taps

Cat's cooperation became public knowledge during the last week of September 1989. The front-page of every New York newspaper had something to say about it, and one even printed: "Fat-Cat turned Rat."

Fat Cat's mother, Louise Coleman, and Lynn, Karolyn Tyson entered guilty pleas in Brooklyn Federal Court the same week that Cat pled guilty and signed the agreement with the government. Cat's mother and Lynn were sentence separately, on different days, in December 1989. Cat's mother received five years' probation and a fine. Lynn also received probation, which was to start after she'd completed a 90-day jail term, and a fine.

When Lynn went to jail that was the straw that broke the camel's back, it ended the relationship between her and Cat. Everyone in our case was given the 1100 hours of wiretap tapes to listen to in reference to our case, so all the defendants and their lawyers could prepare for trial. This included Lynn.

Besides all of the illegal activities, there was a lot of gossip, and just plain bullshit on the tapes. Lynn heard several conversations between Cat and his wife, Mousey, as well as his girlfriend, Michelle, and other girls. She heard Cat telling Mousey, Michelle, and the others, that she, Lynn, didn't mean anything to him and that she was just one of his top workers who took care of a lot of his business which included storing cocaine and heroin and making sure that the people who were supposed to get the drugs in fact got them.

I believe what hurt Lynn the most was hearing Cat refer to her as a *bitch* to the other girls and knowing that Cat had said the same thing to her about them. Lynn finally realized that her shining prince charming was tarnished. Lynn really loved Cat and I believe he loved her more than his wife. But when a man is trying to hold on to more than one woman, he has a tendency to put his foot in his mouth, and that's exactly what Cat did.

If Cat had fully cooperated with the feds and given them everything he knew, then I honestly believe that Assistant United States Attorney Leslie Caldwell would've recommended that Judge Korman sentence him to only 20 to 25 years and to run concurrent with his sentence for his involvement in the Rooney murder. If things would've gone that route, then he would've been eligible for release from prison a lot sooner. But Cat being Cat, he was what you'd call a "hostile witness." Plus, he was one of the biggest drug dealers in the history of New York City and he was responsible for the death of his parole officer. An although everyone in law enforcement knew that Cat had nothing to do with Officer Byrne's murder, they all believed he played a major role in bringing about Byrne's murder by helping create the monster who did give the order to hit a cop; that monster being Pappy. So, Cat had too much against himself and in fact did himself an injustice by not fully cooperating with the feds. Fat cat was eligible for parole in 2010 in New York but denied. His federal sentence expires in 2026.

Passing Time - Prison Gourmet Dining

In spite of my present situation, looking back, my stay in Witness Security custody was sweet; sweet; sweet excluding some exceptions. The reason being I didn't want for anything. I had anywhere from $1,000 to $1,500 dollars placed in my account every other month while my family, including my wife and son were being financially and personally protected. Even though, I was incarcerated, I received visits once a month and I was still having sex in the Witness Protection Visiting Room.

Once a month inmate who could afford it was able to purchase just about anything they wanted from the outside. Hard to believe, I used to make sure my visitors were well feed. One of my buddies "St. Louis" his older brother LB was a chef by trade and he would prepare some awesome meals for my visitors that you could only get at a five-star restaurant. Thank you, L.B. Only a chosen few received visit on a regular basis. If you were lucky, and wanted to have sex it was done discretely, with no one being disrespected or offended. However, we would talk ahead of time to negotiate time slots for use of the key locations in the visiting area where we wouldn't be observed. Most of the time the correction officers or counselors would leave the area, giving us the OK. Other times they would stay in a certain location and wouldn't budge. The microwave oven area was always open for game, and in some cases the few other inmates and their visitors knew that area was temporarily off limits.

Deal or No Deal - Leslie Caldwell - Part Seven

Since I had begun to cooperate, I still had no idea what my deal for any freedom would be. I truly put my life in God and my mother's influence. I meet with the Feds several more times, before I was officially moved from MCC population to Otisville FCI population, before I signed an official document with Leslie Caldwell agreeing to become a SNITCH, A GOVERNMENT WITNESS. *Being locked down in Otisville Segregation Unit and going thru the process to get into the Witness Security Unit, I was given a polygraph test. The test was to ensure I was being honest, and also ensure I was not agreeing to cooperate just to get into one of several of the Witness Security Unit's to try to kill another witness.* The process in order to be approved was long and tedious. I was locked down for approximately two months for twenty-four hours a day. The only time I was allowed out was for a shower every other day.

The day came when I left Otisville FCI Segregation Unit and was transported to one of several other witness protection units. When I arrived it was indeed something totally different. The writing was on the wall, due to my reputation and the publicity from the case I didn't last long - two months - before I was kicked out of that unit, for fighting and putting a couple of individuals in their place. It took me a while to realize that life and the way you dealt with adversity and problems were different from Rikers Island or a N.Y. State Prison.

Passing Time - Sex and The Convict

It took three years before I was finally sentenced on February 1992. I had to learn how to make good use of my time, especially during visiting hours.

I was receiving daily visit however; your wife or girlfriend weren't allowed to come to your cell or in it. However, during visiting hours the officers would leave and when they left, it was on and cracking. If I was alone, I would get butt naked as if I was free and start fucking as if this was the last time I might be having sex. If there were other inmates and visitors we would have already discussed what spots we wanted or which were taken. We were all discreet. The concept was to have your lady wear a skirt or dress and take her panties off and just sit on your dick and just rock it. The truth of the matter, it was very rare when I received a visit that I didn't have sex. Back then any of the young ladies that I was dealing with, knew if they were coming to see me and the opportunity presented itself, come prepared to fuck.

Unfortunately, Federals wanted to kick me out of the local areas and wanted to transfer me to a Unit in Siberia, like a million miles away from New York. Man, I was on the phone talking to everyone in the United States Attorney's Office expressing my concerns about moving. I told Charlie Rose and Leslie Caldwell how I didn't want to be transferred to Pluto. Long story short, I was moved to Siberia despite; I was kicking and screaming and crying like a baby. I must admit I did majority of my bid there and that was the best time I did. I didn't get visits daily, but they were monthly visits for three days at a time and sex was included.

Passing Time with Ceramics

It felt like that everywhere I went jealousy and trouble followed. Supposedly 90% of the inmates in the witness security program were major drug dealers, mobsters and whatever. Some had money, but most didn't. Fortunately, I had it at the time.

I was always on the phone, which you had to pay for. To make the situation less tolerable I had all the newest Air Jordan sneakers, as well as Jordan and Fila Sweat Suits.

At the time I was also a little over the top; wearing gold jewelry and trust me when I say the majority hated it

To pass the time away, making ceramics saved me. However, when I went to the ceramic's room, it went into lockdown. The white guys controlled the ceramics room and would charge outrageous prices to the other inmates to make something. So, I eased into the program and purchased about 100 different ceramic molds, a ton of mud, and paint. The molds would range from $20 to $200.00 and you could even buy gold paint. By the time I left I had spent thousands of dollars on materials. Almost anyone who wanted top shelf materials had to come to me. That didn't help me be anymore loved. I would wash and hang my sweat suits in the laundry room and these cowards would cut up several of my new suits. The only way I could get back at them was to order another ten new suits.

Because of my reputation I spent over two years in and out of twenty-four-hour lockdowns all because they were afraid of me. After a while I learned to stay away and keep my mouth shut - all I was doing was losing and it was getting old. I finally realized it was a combination of my east coast mentality and strong personality that when someone was lying, I would call them out on it. I became one of the most hated. Frankly, I really didn't care until I kept ending up in the hole for months at a time since they feared what they thought I might do.

Passing Time - Developing Work Habits

It had been almost three years and I still didn't know what my outcome would be. After reaching $40,000 a day on the street, would you believe they wanted me to get a job in jail and sign up with UNICOR where you made gloves and receive anywhere from $0.23 to $1.18 per hour.

Salary was based on your grade and job assignment. I was rich for general purposes. I had money and I wasn't working for no dam UNICOR, save it for the broke guys. Years elapsed when a girlfriend of mine, I will call her Knot, a name given to her by Rip, her late brother. She told me that I needed to develop "working habits" to know how it felt to get up like a normal human being and punch a clock, each day. It took some convincing on her part, but eventually I went and signed up for UNICOR. The shop foreman and the unit manager were in awe.

I could not imagine that I might eventually get out and must punch a clock like every other respectable citizen. Yet, I knew I had to change based upon all the suffering and pain I caused others and myself during my past years. From the loss of my beloved mother and to add insult to injury I couldn't pay my last respects to the woman I loved more than life itself. Because of my reckless behavior, I had become law enforcement public enemy and it was costing me when it mattered most. I had nobody to blame, but Brian "Glaze" Gibbs.

Passing Time - Poor Me

On Thursday, February 20, 1992, two U.S. Marshals escorted me back to New York. A third marshal was waiting for us when we arrived at LaGuardia Airport. I was driven from LaGuardia to Marshal Headquarters, in lower Manhattan, and then escorted to the M.C.C. Already in the Federal Witness Protection Program, I thought the staff at the M.C.C. would naturally place me in the witness unit, but to my surprise, they didn't. They made me change out of my Fila sweat suit and I wasn't allowed to keep anything except my Bible and the picture of my mother and son. I didn't protest, because I knew I was going to be sentenced the next day and probably be flown out of New York the day after that, back to my designated facility in the Midwest.

So, the whole M.C.C. building was locked down and a lieutenant and several correctional officers escorted me to 9-South, M-Tier, and I was placed in administrative detention. The lieutenant handed me the lock up order, which stated that I was on total separation from all other inmates. The cell was dirty, roach-infested, and freezing cold. All I had to try to keep warm were two paper-thin sheets and a worn out, itchy wool blanket. That place was hell in disguise.

I got the inmate who was out on the tier to roll the collect telephone time to me, so I could call F.B.I. Headquarters. I got them to call Agent Richard Martinez at his home and we talked through the F.B.I. operator. Mr. Martinez was supposed to make sure that I was placed in the witness unit when I returned to the M.C.C. and be able to get a visit. I explained my conditions to Mr. Martinez and he told me that my sentencing had been postponed from the next day, Friday, February 21, 1992, until the following Thursday, February 27, 1992. I blanked out for a few seconds, but when I collected my thoughts I became hysterical. That was about the third or fourth time my sentencing had been postponed and I just couldn't believe it, nor could I see how I was going to be able to live under those horrible conditions for another week. I just couldn't visualize it. Martinez kept trying to reassure me that he was going to get me to the witness unit and that I would be able to see my family.

After talking to Agent Martinez, I decided to call my sister. By then it was 10:30 P.M. I told my sister what happened with my sentencing being postponed and having to stay in that hell hole? I finally just broke down and started crying, sobbing over the telephone. I asked her, "How much can I take"? I was still coping with my mother's death and now I was suddenly tossed into Satan's den. My sister kept trying to encourage me, but I just kept repeating myself. Asking how much could I take? *Yes, even tough guys break down. How well do you think you would do?*

Eleven o'clock came fast and my time on the telephone ended. My sister said for me to remain strong and that she loved me and that all the obstacles were tests and we had to remain strong for one another. I told her that I loved her, too, and then hung up.

That was another time in my life when I contemplated suicide. But instead, I just jumped into the bed and covered myself with the rags they'd given me, holding my Bible and finally crying myself to sleep.

When I got up the next morning, I called Assistant United States Attorney Leslie R. Caldwell, F.B.I. Agent Martinez, and my Lawyer, J. Marks. I wanted them to pull some strings and get me on the witness floor and try to get me a visit with my family. My lawyer called Ms. Caldwell and her and Agent Martinez kept telling me they were working on it. I talked to Ms. Caldwell about why my sentencing had been postponed, too. She explained that her letter to the judge wasn't quite ready and when the judge did receive the letter, he was going to need time to read and examine it thoroughly. That letter could have a profound effect on the judge and my sentence.

I didn't want to hear all of that. All I wanted was to hurry up and get sentenced, so I could get out of that dungeon and back to the facility in the Midwest. I tried to get rescheduled for the following Monday, February 24, 1992, but the judge was going to be tied up all day in a psychiatric hearing.

My Sentencing - Joe Ponzi & Ms. Caldwell

The moment of truth, I awoke around 9:00 A.M. It was freezing cold in that M.C.C. detention cell. About 11:30 A.M., I was allowed out of the cell so I could shower and get ready to go before the judge. I also called several family members to see if they were coming to the courthouse for my sentencing. I called the Chief Investigator for the Brooklyn District Attorney's Office, Joseph Ponzi, too. I asked Ponzi what he thought I'd get, and he said that from what he gathered I'd receive a single digit number, somewhere between seven and nine years. My lawyer, Jonathan Marks, said he felt like I'd get somewhere between six and eight years.

I was talking to Ponzi on the phone when one officer and a lieutenant came to take me downstairs, so I could get dressed for court. I told Ponzi I had to go, and he told me to call him when I got back and let him know what happened. After hanging up the telephone, I went into my cell and picked up the Bible my mother had given me.

I was escorted from 9-South to the third floor receiving and discharging area. There, I changed from the orange jumpsuit I was wearing to a two-piece Gucci suit and lizard dress shoes. Once I was ready, I grabbed my Bible and was handcuffed and was escorted by U.S. Marshals through the heavy security doors, up the staircase that lead to the Southern District Federal Courthouse. Once inside the courthouse, we were buzzed into Marshal Headquarters and I was led to the sleeping quarter's area.

The sleeping quarter's area was like an efficiency apartment, with a full-sized bed, dresser and mirror, color television and clock radio, miniature refrigerator, closets, and a bathroom with a shower. Obviously, a major upgrade from Satan's den - thank you, Jesus.

I was placed in the sleeping quarter's area around 1:30 P.M., and I prayed during most of the time I was there. Finally, around 2:50 P.M., three U.S. Marshals came, handcuffed me, and took me to the garage. From there they drove me through lower Manhattan, across the Brooklyn Bridge and into Brooklyn Heights, to the East Brooklyn Federal Courthouse. We parked in the courthouse's garage, where a Marshal from Judge Edward Korman's court was waiting for us.

I was taken into the building and by elevator we reached the back of Judge Korman's courtroom on the fourth floor, where I was placed in a small holding cell. Around 3:10 P.M., Special Agent Richard Martinez came and sat in the holding cell with me. We talked for a while and he told me that I didn't have to speak on my own behalf to the judge, but to do so would be in my best interest. I told him the same thing I'd told my lawyer on several earlier occasions: I wanted to freely express myself, with an open heart, to Judge Korman, but I didn't want to start talking and end up stumbling over my words, sounding and looking dumbfounded. That was my biggest fear of all. I told Mr. Martinez that I knew exactly what I wanted to say: I just wanted to tell Judge Korman what was in my heart and on my mind.

I remember tears running down my face and Mr. Martinez passing me a clean handkerchief. He left and in less than a minute later returned with my three-year-old son in his hand. Mr. Martinez asked the Marshal to remove the handcuffs and take them out of my son's sight – I definitely didn't want him seeing me with those handcuffs on. I grabbed and picked up my son and hugged him tight and kissed him. I missed him so much. Exactly nine months had passed since I'd seen him. I remember sitting him down on my lap and talking to him. I also took out the picture of him and my mother and gave it to him. He said that it was "Grandmom," then kissed the picture. I started crying all over again.

My son was my mother's heart. She really loved him. Thinking about her death and that she's no longer was with us just tore me apart.

My mother spent a lot of time with my son. They traveled to a lot of different places. My son wasn't only my mother's grandson, but it was like he was her son, too. She used to always tell me how my son favored her father. I never met my grandfather -- he passed away before I was born -- but I've heard a lot of wonderful things about him, including that he was a good father. My mother always tried to spend as much time as possible with him. My wife and I had divorced since my incarceration and because my mother could provide much more for my son, she tried to help as much as possible in my absence.

Agent Martinez took my son into the courtroom with his mother, some of my family members and friends. Shortly after that, Leslie Caldwell came to the holding cell and we talked. She complemented me on how nice I looked in my suit and I thanked her. She asked me if I had received a copy of the SK departure letter she'd written to Judge Korman on my behalf. I told her I hadn't, but that my lawyer had informed me of it. She then left and shortly returned with a copy for me.

The letter she had written was nine pages long and explained the eight-count indictment. It also explained that the kingpin status charge against me had been dropped, which would have guaranteed me a life sentence. My lawyer and I spoke while I read the letter. He told me to take my time when expressing myself to the judge.

I walked out of the holding cell a few steps and into the courtroom when I saw my family and friends. I had the Bible my mother gave me in my hands the whole time.

I was told to stand next to my lawyer. My lawyer was in the middle, Ms. Caldwell was on the left side and I was on the right. We were facing Judge Korman and my family and friends were sitting on the right side. Agent Martinez was seated on the left, behind Ms. Caldwell. To my surprise -- and approval -- there was no media. *All the reporters were across the hall, covering the John Gotti trial. I was glad, because I didn't want any media attention.*

It was about 3:35 P.M., when my lawyer, Jonathan Marks, started talking to the judge. Mr. Marks expressed to the judge that I have a new outlook on life and its value. He told the judge everything I've been doing to better myself since my incarceration began -- attending classes and receiving college credits, developing working habits by maintaining a position in the prison factory, and maintaining close family ties. He spoke to the extent of my cooperation with authorities but added that he knew the crimes were heinous and that I must be punished. Then he said that I was pursuing my education towards a degree which would enable me to become a counselor -- to young and old alike. He continued by saying, he knew I had changed and believed if I was given the chance, then I would be able to return to society as a productive, law abiding citizen. Mr. Marks further said he felt I should receive a sentence that would require me to serve another three or four years before being released. Judge Korman replied by saying that he didn't ask him for any suggestions.

Before my lawyer addressed the court, Judge Korman said that if I had only drug charges, then he would have given me time served. He repeated that three or four times throughout my sentencing. He said that because of the nine-page letter Ms. Caldwell had written, he wanted to let me walk away right then. However, if it had not been for the five murders and two attempted murders, he would've let me go. After my lawyer finished speaking, Judge Korman asked me if I wished to address the court. I said that I did.

As I recall, I greeted the judge and courtroom staff, and let him know that I was indeed nervous, because my liberty and fate was in his hands. I took my time and expressed myself as sincerely as possible. I knew that my freedom and life were on the line, and I didn't want to stumble over my words.

I remember saying that I had no one to blame but myself. Neither Fat Cat nor anyone else made me do the crimes I committed. I said that each day I ask God for forgiveness and for the victims and their family members to forgive me for destroying their lives and causing them all the pain and suffering. I told the judge that at times I would just sit back and cry, asking myself who was I to say who lived or died. There is only one that can make that decision, and that is: God. I'm not God.

I expressed myself exactly how I felt and I was sincere. After I had finished, Judge Korman asked Ms. Caldwell if she had anything to say. She said that when I first walked into her office back in February 1989, she thought I was an animal, but now she knows that I'm a decent human being.

Throughout the whole proceeding I thought Judge Korman was going to hit me with the "Coney Island Hammer," because he kept emphasizing the murders and how awful the crimes were.

After Ms. Caldwell had finished, Judge Korman paused, looked at me, banged his gavel and said that he hereby sentenced me to 120 months to be served under federal custody and 10 years supervised release (similar to parole). Once I realized exactly what he had just said, I let out a quick smile, but for only a split second. My lawyer told the Judge that he should make sure that I receive the goodtime behavior while I was awaiting sentencing. Judge Korman ordered, on the record, that I was to receive all of the goodtime dating back from November 10, 1988. I turned to my family and friends and let them all know that I was alright with my sentencing.

The words: Beyond Lucky, echoed in my head.

I was then led back to the holding cell and as I entered the cell, I told the Marshal that I was supposed to get a short visit with my family and friends. But the Marshal said that it wasn't going to happen.

Mr. Marks came to the holding cell to see how well I took the sentence. We embraced, and I told him that I could live with it. I asked him to tell my family and friends that I was alright.

The first thing I remembered doing was praising and thanking God for the 10 years that I had just received. I made out extremely well and I consider myself to be blessed and lucky.

Unfortunately, there were some who wanted to have my sentencing overturned.

March 2, Article - "Lets' Be Courteous"

After I was sentenced from the information gathered from Operation Horse Collar. On March 2, 1992, I accepted to be interviewed by a Mike McAlary of the Daily News and he wrote the following article about me. Not that flattering, but that's the way it was. You're entitled to hear all sides of the story. This is what he wrote.

Beginning of Article

Brian Gibbs, a neighborhood killer turned federal informant, he appeared well in the federal courtroom in Brooklyn late last week. Already ancient by city homicide standards, Gibbs, 28, faced life without parole. The Judge Edward R. Korman, banged his gavel several times, and just like that, Gibbs saw a huge opening. He gets ten years.

"I'm a changed man," Gibbs recently told me, I'm in here reading books and what not. I got 600 hundred pages of my book written.

Brian Gibbs - the nickname is Glaze - admitted killing five people over a five-month period ending with his arrest in March 1988. No one talks about how many people the drug enforcer may really have killed, if only because the total looks like a calculus problem.

"How many did you really kill?" I have asked Gibbs.

NYPD says "70 something" he replies. "I'm admitting to five. You know what I'm saying." Brian Gibbs is the most infamous resident in the bloodied history of Cypress Hills Houses in East New York. In the mid 1980's, there were two basic career paths for a young man growing up there. Both careers involved use of a gun. Young men of shooting age either signed on with armed services or "The A Team," which was the name Gibbs gave his gang. It was about this same time last year that I met a young man from the Cypress Hills Houses in a Kuwait foxhole.

"Free Kuwait," the solider said. "What about the Cypress Hills Houses?"

"I'm, fighting Saddam Hussein, not Brian Gibbs," the soldier replied. "My mother still lives in the Cypress Hills Houses."

I was feeling for his own mother who still lives in East New York that prompted Brian Gibbs to placing calls to me last year (this was prior to his sentencing) when the federal witness protection program was under discussion by the federal government hearing committee. "You wrote that I killed 20 people," Gibbs said. "My mother reads that stuff. You know what I'm saying?"

Here is the way I understand it. Mrs. Gibbs gets mad, apparently, if say her son killed 20 people. Five is an acceptable total to the East New York mother. And you wonder why an East New York student thinks it is all right to kill two on his way to homeroom?

Brian Gibbs is a first-generation crack gangster. He is the prototype. A former student at Thomas Jefferson HS, Gibbs was carrying a pistol into the school long before it was fashionable. He was one of the first kids to grow up in East New York learning the Three R's - reading, 'riting and revolvers. On the phone, Gibbs sounds well-mannered and thoughtful. Drugs were a business, he says. Murder was accepted byproduct. In December, Gibbs sent me a birthday card. I felt chilled, quite frankly, upon receiving it.

"Be good," Brian Gibbs urged.

Gibbs is a protégé of "Fat Cat" Nichols, the imprisoned drug lord who ruled most of the $100 million crack trade in southeastern Queens during the 1980s. Gibbs worked in the gangs' employment office. If the gang member was determined to be working for both Fat Cat and the government, Gibbs fired them. Or, more precisely, Gibbs fired upon them.

"Was it any harder shooting woman than a man?" I asked him in December.

"It's hard shootin' anyone," Gibbs replied.

Gibbs was still on the streets in 1988 when drug dealers executed a New York police officer, Edward Byrne, Gibbs believed the assassination was bad for business. His first response was to scream, "I'm going to ice the stupid bastard who did this." His position hardened upon learning that the execution had been ordered by his partner, Pappy Mason. Eventually convicted of the actual killing were two of Byrne's killers, Phillip Copeland and David McClary. - Gibbs agreed to become a federal informant.

"When you hear "FBI" you think of Ephraim Zimbalist Jr... Gibbs explained, "You don't mess with them."

"The Cat never had to tell about killing anybody," Gibbs has expressed to me. If I'm going to call you, I'm not going to talk about it. I know what Cat needs done or did for him. You know what I'm saying?"

"I think so."

"I mean if you, Mike McAlary needed someone whacked, I don't have to come and ask for your permission, I just do it for you."

"But what if you kill somebody he didn't want killed?"

"We don't talk about that either," Gibbs said.

Another, more glamorous federal informant, Salvatore "Sammy the Bull" Gravano, is expected to take the stand in Brooklyn federal court this week. Gravano will sit in a fourth-floor courtroom just across the hallway where Gibbs sat last week.

"I don't understand why it is when a black gangster kills, no one cares. I mean, that's good for me, but still.... You know what I'm saying?"

It has long been my opinion that Cypress Houses shortened a David Dinkins speech on guns last year with a midday firefight. And the next time Dinkins braved a visit to the area, the mayors' address to Thomas Jefferson high had to be reworked to make mention of the morning's double murder.

Having seen our mayor duck bullets on one visit to East New York and step over teen-age bodies one after another, the neighborhood should have attention now.

The gangsters who have shortened the life of this city grew up around steaming vats of crack, not linguini. John Gotti is Italian, and because of that, he gets all the attention. As the Gambinos are not equal opportunity employers, black kids cannot grow up to be John Gotti. They can grow up to be Brian Gibbs. It is identification with Gibbs, and not Gotti, that puts a gun in the East New York homeroom.

We do not, as of yet, know Gravano's federally agreed-upon homicide total. I hear 20. The Bull's mother might protest anything higher than five. Gravano will testify, apparently, that he killed on verbal orders from John Gotti. That makes Gotti - a 1950's graduate of East New York - much dumber than anyone currently working Pennsylvania Avenue with a pistol.

"If you ask me (Gibbs), the Italians are unprofessional, "They talk too much."

(End of Article)

In another interview, Mike McAlary wrote the story that John Gotti once attended Thomas Jefferson, and that Brian Glaze Gibbs once attended Thomas Jefferson, John

Gotti grew up in ENY Brooklyn, Brian Glaze Gibbs grew up in ENY Brooklyn, Most black kids cannot grow up to be like John Gotti but they can grow up to be Brian Glaze Gibbs.

Another item I learned was John Gotti's attorney was Bruce Cutler, my lawyer was the late Murray Cutler, Bruce's father.

Deal or No Deal - Frustrated Public - Part Eight

The Game was over. In the very beginning when I first made a deal with the Federal Government I met with Charlie Rose, Leslie Caldwell and with their team on numerous occasions. As I made mention earlier it was a feel out process on both sides.

But as the meeting went on and they were able to verify the truthfulness of the information that I was rendering, a deal was struck. However, by that time Charlie Rose was no longer part of the team and the ball was now in the hands of Leslie R Caldwell who was then the number one Assistant United States Attorney on our case. Any moves, deals or shots called went thru her.

Despite I admitted direct involvement in several murders, conspiracy to murders and attempted murders the Federal Government did not charge me with any violent acts. Leslie Caldwell even agreed to knock down the King Pin charge 21USC 848. This statute makes it a federal crime to commit or conspire to commit a continuing series of felony violations of the Comprehensive Drug Abuse Prevention and Control Act of 1970 when such acts are taken in concert with 5 or more other persons. For conviction under this statute, the offender must have been an organizer, manager, or supervisor of the continuing operation and have obtained substantial income or resources from the drug violations.

Shortly after my deal had gone public the NY Daily News ran a story on April 13, 1989. "HENCHMAN WILL SING FOR THE FEDS" Ironically, they showed a picture of me with glasses on and a separate photo of Howard Pappy Mason. That article caused a major uproar between The United State Government of the Eastern District of New York and the State of New York Kings and Queens County.

Leslie Caldwell and her office received so many phone calls and visits from representatives of both Kings and Queens County Homicide Division. Their issue, Brian "Glaze" Gibbs literally got away with numerous murders. I was back in the Witness Security Unit way out there in Siberia. Via a conference call my lawyer and Leslie explained to me what the hell was going on. Both Brooklyn and Queens' county task force felt within a eighteen months span from 1987 until my arrest in November 1988 I was responsible indirectly and directly for a total of seventy eight murders.

I was going back and forth with Leslie Caldwell telling her that those crazy bastards in both Kings County and Queens were trying to clean their books and give me all their unsolved murders. I knew I was no angel; I did a lot of ruthless and evil things in my life that I was responsible for. However, this was a nerve wrecking movement and all I remembered was Kings and Queens county saying was if anyone including my co-defendants or whoever came around in those days, weeks, months and years to implicate me to any of those murders, they will take me to trial on each and every one. To me that was scary, because I know what I did and what I didn't do and what they can prove and could not prove. Call it a hunch they had a hard-on for me and trust me when I say they would have gotten me for some murders that I didn't do. And those were the hardest one's to fight because you really did not know much about them, so how in the hell can you defend yourself against lies.

The solution, I was taken back down to Brooklyn Federal Court where they wanted to charge me with a superseding indictment of racketeering, two drug charges remaining, and five counts of murder and two counts of attempted murder were added. Several hours after that hearing I meet with representative from Kings County and Queens County New York's Finest: Joseph A Ponzi, Frank Shield, Richard Brew and several more that I can`t recall.

The topics of conversation focused on how many murders did I, Brian "Glaze" Gibbs really commit? 78, 50, 20? They weren't buying FIVE murders.

During those meetings we spent hours going back and forth. There was a double homicide that occurred in Brooklyn during June of 1987, I believe June 17. They described how I walked up to these two gentlemen late at night and shot them both in the head multiple times in the Fort Greene section of Brooklyn. When that question was posed to me, I turn to Richard Brew from the 75th. Prescient, I asked him, "Mr. Brew when did I turn myself in for the Sybil Mims murder?" He looked in his note and said, "Monday May 5th, 1986." I then asked Detective Brew, "Was I out on bail?" He answered no. I asked one more question. "Detective Brew what day was I acquitted on the Sybil Mims murder and released?" Once again, he looked at his note and said, Monday June 22, 1987. So, I turned back to that gentleman and ask him, "Did the warden of Rikers Island allow me to be released so that I could murder those two gentlemen on the night of June 17, and return back to Rikers Island?" *It went on like that for hours. It got to the point when they asked, don`t tell us about the murders you and others know you were involved in. Tell us about the murders only you and the victims knew about. I got up and said, "What fun that would be". The meeting was officially over.*

When it got closer to my release date, I was afraid. Why? Because whereas before if I had a problem or situation, I would handle the matter the way I saw fit, by grabbing my guns and eliminating the problem. Now I would have to be like every law-abiding citizen and pick up the phone and call the cops and to me that was a scary feeling.

Out of Prison as a New Person

It was Monday July 28, 1997; I did not sleep much the night before. I was very excited the moment of truth after serving eight years, eight months, and seventeen days of a ten-year sentence, given to me by the Federal Government, for my involvement in Operation Horse Collar (United State vs. Lorenzo "Fat Cat" Nichols, Howard "Pappy" Mason, Brian "Glaze" Gibbs and approximately twenty others)

I know I was "Beyond Lucky", since I was facing life imprisonment for 21 USC 848 and numerous murder charges my lawyer and I made a deal with the government to get me this deal that allow me to walkout of Otisville FCI on this day. That morning when the correction officer open up the cell that I was no longer going to occupy, I showered, got dress in black slacks, black short-sleeve silk mock neck, a black and white checkered sport jacket and a black pair of slip on Johnston and Murphy shoes -- all from the Men's Wear House. Walking out of there at thirty-three years old in the best shape of my life, muscle everywhere, with a six pack; I was physically fit, I felt I had muscles in my teeth. I felt like I just walked off the cover of GQ magazine. LOL!

My next destination was unknown to me. I was one of the few who were given a new name, new social security number, and a new identity. Brian "Glaze" Gibbs no longer existed.

Re-entering society I had to create the person I am today. Keep in mind I had no prior job set or skills.

Fortunately, I developed working habits while incarcerated. Thanks Knot. Now it was about to pay off. Keep in mind I was 33 years old, just being release from serving time and my resume only included my accomplishments; Arm Robbery, Assault, Multiple Murders, Attempted Murders, and Several Drug Charges. Now my true test was filling out applications for employment opportunities with no working background which is a bit difficult to do.

I must admit I was scared. I was back out in the streets without a gun and a bullet proof vest. Instead of dealing with situation as my former self, I had to maybe call the police to help. It sure seemed strange.

As part of the witness protection program, I was picked up by two U. S. Marshall and was taken to LaGuardia Airport in Queens, New York. Literally I was like on Cloud 9 - FREEDOM -again - after all of those years. I was dropped off at the airport; the US Marshall gave me a ticket to Lexington, Kentucky with several hundred dollars for my pocket. Mind you I didn't have a piece of ID and this was four years prior to 911. I was in awe walking thru LaGuardia airport not in handcuffs or escorted by correctional officers or a US Marshall. I was free, heading thru the terminal looking at all the beautiful women of different nationalities. I felt like a big kid in a candy store looking at them and watching a few of them looking me up and down.

As I boarded the plane heading to Lexington it was like I was pinching myself to make sure I was not dreaming; I was truely free. I can recall Thursday November 10, 1988 when the FBI's and US Marshall arrested me in McDonald's in South Carolina they slapped three sets of handcuffs on me, and one of the FBI agents stated that I will never see the street as a free man again and here I am eight years, eight months and seventeen days later airborne in the sky to Lexington, Kentucky. God is good! My mind was racing thinking about my future.

The plane landed in Kentucky, as I went to baggage claim and was greeted by a U.S. Marshall who drove me to a hotel where I stayed for the next two weeks. Here it is I was stuck in no man's land. Back then cell phones were not as affordable. It was all about the Pre-Paid phone cards. The Marshall gave me approximately five hundred dollars to purchase some clothes: underwear and whatever I needed. But my mind was too busy thinking of my family and my new life.

Doing Retail - Good Working Habits

By developing those work habits in prison allowed me to return to society and obtain gainful employment. The first company I applied to was Johnston & Murphy Men's Shoes who had been in business since 1850. Every American president to President Obama received a free pair Johnston & Murphy shoes. President Bill Clinton's received a pair of blue suede shoes.

Would you believe I was a customer of a pair of Johnston & Murphy shoes which I ordered to wear home when I was released? Now I am free to roam in this new city, happy and grateful to have my freedom. I was downtown feeling out the city and doing a little shopping when I met two men, Doug and Terry with whom I would build a bond. They knew I was new in town and looking for employment. The opportunity became available and Doug plugged me into his regional manager for an interview. With very little to fill out on my applications I was still hired at J&M; my first job with my new life and it felt great. Beyond lucky, I couldn't stop saying it.

Being a salesman, selling shoes for Johnston & Murphy was easy for this Brooklyn street kid who had been selling stolen goods all my life.

So, in October of 1997, I started my first job in retail. I learn a lot like how to tie a tie. There are many ways to tie a tie, for every occasion, many of which you probably never knew existed. Each tie knot has been judged on four different factors: aesthetics, symmetry, difficulty, and knot size. I also learned how to run a store and stock room, indeed fun and different. Would you believe I used to take three buses each way just to get back and forth to work? I can recall getting about $6.00 per hour and 5% commission. That was a lot less than $40,000 per day and I was content. I recall my manager at the time was a crack head, Clay. He used to go in the bathroom for hours at a time and when he came out he would be wearing sun glasses. He also used to take cash out of the cash register -- a major no, no. That location eventually closed, and I was transferred to the downtown location which was a lot different. *I stayed with the company for approximately 10 years.*

In 1997 when I came home and started working at Johnston& Murphy by May of 1998, I was able to apply for a job with FDX and Bingo I got the job with very little work experiences. I worked fulltime at Johnston & Murphy, and when I got off from work my wife at the time was a home body, meaning she didn't like to do much. She was an early bird and I a night owl which was one of the reasons for taking a second part time job from 10:30PM to 3AM or until the job was done.

When with FDX I was able to work my way up from a part time package handler to a full-time human resource interviewer and recruiter, and eventually rising to a full time Operations Supervisor -- good old FDX.

Great Expectations

It's ironic the odds were definitely against me: a killer, and a career criminal. The US Marshall gave me a total of 45 days before I would commit a crime and return to jail. The US probation officer who was assigned to supervise my next 10 years of supervised release, well she gave me a whole ninety days before I would return to the slammer. I was determined to prove those that didn't believe in me, wrong. I wanted to be part of the American Dream; I wanted to be a homeowner. I wanted to be a law-abiding citizen, a great husband, an excellent father and a pillar of strength in the community. One can dream. *Would you believe in less than two years of my release my family and I were homeowners?*

My drive continued, I wanted to be more successful in corporate America. My plan was in motion at time when I left Johnston & Murphy. At night I had plenty of time to change out of my suit and tie and drive right into FDX parking lot and head through the guard shack heading into the facility. As I normally walked in, upper management would be heading out. My greetings were always the same. How are you doing on this m*arvelous* Monday, *terrific* Tuesday, *wonderful* Wednesday, *tremendous* Thursday and or *fabulous Friday*? First, they were all trying to figure out who the hell I was? What department did I work in? And where in the world was I getting all this positive energy late in the evening? Well, trust me when I say, my plan was indeed in motion and in full effect.

As I sit back and think about it, within one month of June of 1998 I was recruited by numerous managers to become a supervisor. I was flattered, and I can recall telling my suitors at the time, that I barely know my way in and out of the facility and what could I possibly teach my employees at this time when I didn't know all that I should. I told them to give me some time to get more familiar with the operation and I can go from there. As time went on I was fortunate to become a fulltime article 22 employee. Those positions came available after the August 1997 strike, when over 185,000 union employees went on strike. During the first half of my shift I would sort packages, which was very physical, and the second half of my shift I would do clerical work. Eventually due to the relationship I built with Kathy Koss, the Rocky Mountain Divisional

Manager I was introduced to Myron A. Gray. Myron at that time was the CEO of the Rocky Mountain District for Colorado, Wyoming and Montana. Myron was written up in Bloomberg Business Week when he served as President of U.S. Operations at United Parcel Service of America, Inc.

Helping Management Understand People

It's like Myron and I struck an instant bond. He became like a mentor to me and slowly, but surely, we became friends. During our daily conversations he always gave me a lot to think about. One day he asked me, "Why don't I sign up to become a supervisor?" My exact answer, "Myron the way FDX has it set up, I would have to start off part time and work my way up to become a full-time supervisor." Myron disagreed and countered by saying, "If you become a part time supervisor and apply yourself and stand out from your peers the opportunity for advancement is there."

I then came clean with Myron by telling him that when I first filled out an application with FDX I did not have a working background to fall back on, so I falsified my application to cover the gap of a man at 34 years old with no real employment history. Myron's exact words was, "A technicality, I can fire you, but let he or she who have not sinned cast the first stone." He told me going forward just put the truth down. He also told me a story that changed his life when he was a teenager living in Tennessee. He and a few guys were hanging out in the hood, when this guy came up to one of his friends and asked him, "Do you have my money?"
Myron's friend responded by saying, no I do not have your fucking money, and the guy responded by blowing his friend's head off with a sawed off shot gun. Myron stated he was drenched in his friend blood and was shaking in his shoes. That incident that made him realize that the hood wasn't the life for him and that helped mold

his future to become one of the most powerful CEO's in the United States at FDX.

Fighting Back - Glaze Almost Returns

As an hourly employee, occasionally the management team and I would go at it big time. Ninety percent of the management team was very rude and disrespectful. They would yell, scream, shout, and use profanity towards hourly employees and most often to supervisors that reported directly to them. One time me and a senior employee by the name of Benny Williamson was talking as we were placing mis-sorted packages back on a conveyor belt when supervisor Dan Schmidt approached us and start yelling and screaming, being disrespectful. All I know was that Benny was gone while Dan and I went at it head on. I told him, "Get the fuck out of my face before I break your jaw." He kept mouthing off and I took my right hand and shoved my hand in his face with a hard thrust causing him to move the fuck out of my space. Dan screamed, "That's your job!" I replied by saying, if that's my job, then that will be your ass." Long story short, he summoned Manager Greg Karners and the Divisional Manager Rick somebody. They talked to Benny Williamson and he stated that Dan and I were arguing and that I never touched him. After that incident I was really mad at myself. *How in the hell did I place myself in that predicament to allow "Glaze" to come out? It had been a while, but I honestly thought "Glaze" was a past memory until I got so upset that I placed my hand on another man. "Glaze" was taught to never place your hands on any man unless it's the final move. I had to regroup and get my emotions back in check before it become costly.*

I was eventually promoted into management as a Full Time Human Resource Specialist, interviewing and recruiting. I literally wanted to give jobs to those that were looking for a good part time job, with excellent benefit and with the opportunity for full time positions. I believed in giving people second chances. I recruited several individuals with prior felony convictions and each time they came in, they were shot down. One day the Human Resource District Manager, Stefan Wilson, came to me and personally instructed me not to bring in another person with a past criminal record. My argument, anyone can change. I went onto say if you really knew me from my past you would not have hired me. Stefan responded back by saying that I was different that I beat the odds and was not like them. I always say to myself, people, black, white, Asian, etc. can and do change if given a chance. Stefan Wilson is now recognized as a Multicultural Leader of the Year. Stefan Wilson -- formerly President of Gulf South, FDX - now President, Great Lakes, FDX. *Believe me; I'm not taking any credit.*

One of my most enjoyable positions was a salesperson in woman's shoes at Neiman Marcus *in Denver, Colorado.*

Beyond Lucky

Why was I spared, never mind a light sentence, I should be dead? That's not a suggestion. Why did God spare my life? I believe the reason I'm still alive is to get on the road and pass on my stories of the violence, pain, and death, to the kids and adults in the inner cities, tenements, and projects. I believe I can make a difference to prevent or put an end to the inner city teens using, or dealing drugs; if not for their selves, but for the misery they may cause their black communities. I want to teach the youth in drug and violent areas critical thinking, so they will be reminded to ask themselves, "Will my decisions cause me, and those I care about pain?"

To understand why I was so lucky, you have to understand it was more than just getting such a short sentence. Let's not forget that the final sentence of eight years was only part of the fourteen years and six months I spent in total. So, I was not as lucky or not as bad as it could have been. But I was truly beyond lucky when I was afforded the opportunity to enter the witness protection program.

I believe based on some criteria, that people coming out of prison should be given one "good" chance to put their past behind them, like myself, to be given a completely new identity. It is my intention to promote this concept and maybe the problem can be assessed. Wouldn't that be the biggest opportunity to make a change?

Again, stack up my escapes from being killed and you will have to agree I was beyond lucky. Not bragging, just saying. I was in the witness protection program, which gave me a new identity, (new name, new social security number and a clean background) which is something most criminals getting out of jail don't receive. Their record follows them. The benefit, I truly had a second chance at life. With a new identity I can fill out an application, and my background is as clean as yours; *that is if you never robbed or killed anyone.* But I'm willing to tell you my new name, providing this book sells and I can make a living inspiring, and speaking to kids and adults around the country to make a difference. Because, without the success of this book, the name, Brian "Glaze" Gibbs" isn't going to get me the job opportunities I have had.

Another reason, why I think I was given another chance at a normal life with a loving relationship with the mother of my son, and my son is because I had a good "Point of Reference." My point of reference, in my case, was my upbringing. I was thought to have a conscience, which I had for a while, but obviously misplaced it. Although, it was imbedded in my subconscious, it was slowly scratching the surface of my mind, rebuilding and finally restored during my last years in prison. I've been preaching to my son on the lessons I've learned. I'm sure like most kids, they hear the words of right and wrong: "Do onto others as you would have done unto you," fortunately for some the brain stores those words. Sometimes individual's morals are forgotten, until they mess up and then hopefully those words are there to guide them back. Unfortunately, there are many kids that weren't even taught the morals to build a conscience, so if never stored it could never be used as a point of reference, which can guide them and help make their lives better.

Effectiveness of the Witness Protection Program

Again, on July 28, 1997, I was free man after serving eight years, eight months and seventeen days in prison. Prior to my release my name was brought up before a special meeting of the senate committee in front of Joseph Biden and other Senators around June 18,1996, on effectiveness of the Witness Protection Program.

During that hearing, they also singled me out, stating how the US Government had given me given a deal after being responsible for fifty murders and was allowed to keep *thirty-five million dollars* from my trade as a drug lord. *You'd think there was a trade school for it, like auto mechanics.*

It was stated in exchange for my testimony against my own underlings; I only received a 10-year sentence and then was later reduced by Rule 35. Which states; Lehder and Mermelstein, the biggest cocaine suppliers, were those who spoke to the Senate Committee - They were not the only drug cartel figures who were playing the government. Despite the country's professed war on drugs, the leaders of the drug cartels are being allowed to testify against their underlings in order to gain their own freedom.

The facts were slightly distorted; I was in the Witness Protection Program. But I never testified against anyone that worked for me. By the time I got out of prison, most of my assets, homes were under other people's names and when my mother died, I lost all access to any cash. As I told a friend, "When I went into prison, I couldn't take my money, my wife, or my guns. All I took was my reputation. Unlike the corporate world, there was no 401K programs for drug dealers."

As for the $35,000,000 the Feds allowed me to keep; when my mother died on February 9, 1992, I assumed a close family member was in possession of my money. It was not until several months after my mother's death that I kept calling to have things taken care of. My family members stated that my mother didn't mind doing things for me, and where did I think she was getting the funds to have all of my requests granted? I responded by asking who is now in charge of my money. Their response was what money? Those words that I received were not what I wanted to hear. It was always speculated that they knew where my money was, but no one was telling. I still find it a little hard to believe, only my late mother knew, and she wasn't around to tell, so the guilty culprit got away "Scott free". Foolishly, I never thought of my mother dying. I wasn't released until five years after my mother's death. *And in reality, if I would have been released from prison sooner it's a strong possibility that anyone that I suspected was responsible for the theft of my money would have been tortured and murdered, and that's the sad part about that - lucky for them, lucky for me.*

After I was released, I was a model citizen and for that I only did two years and six months before they eliminated the remainder of the supervised release. I must laugh, women can usually remember and tell you how many days, months and years they dated someone, or how long they've been married, but not most men. But ask a convict how long he's been in prison, and he tell you how many years, months, days, hours and minutes. We usually let the seconds go.

Murdered Victims Family and the Guilt

I never killed an innocent person. I never did drive by shootings. Drive by shootings is more Gang Bang west coast style. I felt I was an expert shooter, reason being I made sure I was as close as I could get on an intended victim, so I could not miss. Back than it was no such thing as an innocent person, because truly no one was innocent, it was guilt by association, because the victim did something to warrant the death penalty or the victim was part of the act prior or after the act occurred. We were all in the game and we all knew the rules and consequences, or we should have known. *Death is probably the biggest deterrent for not getting in the business. I have regained my conscience, and I paid for my crimes with a discount.*

Most important, for whatever good it does, I don't know what closure they will receive however, I am truly sorry to the families for their losses. Although, I can assure you, most of them were not surprised or would have killed me first. I'm still sorry. The following are some of the names that they have asked me about and want to nail me with and or feel I'm responsible for.

Murdered Victims: Sybil Mims, Myeshia Horsham, Maurice Bellamy, Artel Benson, Keith Reedy, Clifton Rice, Trini Ahming, Supreme Bey Allah, Christopher Brothers, Jonathan a.k.a. Pen, Ka-son and his girlfriend Tawana, Toya Turner, Calvin Mc Cloud, Chip from Bushwick, two or three people in a bike cycle shop in Bedford Stuyvesant in 1988.

After you've seen enough bloody, dead faces with eyes and lips missing and with what is left of their faces and bullet ridden bodies looking back at you, you must learn to look forward. You also learn to see your life a little clearer. If you can understand what soldiers deal with after battling in war? I believe I may have some symptoms of PTSD. Don't laugh, please, and you don't have to feel sorry for me either, although I doubt you do, or should.

Joe Ponzi on Brian Gibbs with Joseph Verola

I, Joe Verola, met Joe Ponzi on October 16, 2014 at 12:00 at Ruddy and Dean's restaurant on Staten Island. His initial comment was, "Let me clarify, I never arrested Brian, I testified against him. I was not a cop with the NYPD, but an investigator for the district attorney office."

Joe Ponzi worked for the District Attorney's Office for 37 years and rose to the ranks from investigator to a chief investigator before retiring in October of 2014.

Mr. Ponzi went on to say, "My relationship with Brian "Glaze" Gibbs began when I had to gather information on him for the brutal murder of Sybil Mims.

"Brian is one of the few guys (criminals) that I met that truly turned his life around. It's been twenty to twenty-five years since he brokered his deal, and has been on the straight and narrow.

"I think he gives me too much credit for helping change his life; he was the subject of a Federal investigation. All the pressure was put on by the Feds. It was my job to gather the information that would be presented at his trial, which I did, but it was because of the long arm of Uncle Sam that he crumbled, and he basically took the plea.

"As time went on the Feds faded into the background and he and I continued to develop our relationship. That's why after all these years later he presents me as the face of all the law enforcement people. I don't want you to get the wrong impression, that I was the one that took him down. Brian has a tendency to present me as the face of all law enforcement and morphs us all into one.

"Brian gives the impression that Charlie Rose and Leslie R Caldwell saved his life? They did, but did so with the desire to get information?

"That's true, no doubt about it. It was a two-way street. But again, I wished I had a dollar for everyone that flipped; came in and decided to work for the government. However, as soon as they're out and get a whiff of freedom there back doing what they did before. But a guy like Brian, even when he was in the witness protection program, we were not supposed to be contacting each other. However, I could call him, and he would point me in the right direction; he had access to the streets still, not in a criminal way, but in an associate's way. And guys like that are jewels. So, when he would have a personal problem if I could help him I would."

Joe Verola to Joe Ponzi: What I said to Brian was, for people to read your story and like you, it can't be about what you say about your rehabilitation and your remorse. It's the fact that you have people like yourself (Joe Ponzi) and Leslie R Caldwell that keeps in touch with him, that shows that he is special. When do people like Leslie call Brian on their birthday and have lunch with him? Or someone like yourself that would invite him to your retirement party among others in law enforcement - the guy must special and unique.

Joe Ponzi: "Right; I can't speak for Leslie, or did I have conversations about Brian, but as for my conversations with Brian, what I saw was a recognition that he's not apologetic about the things he did, which is weird, you know. It's not liked a callousness, but he'll talk about them rather matter of fact. But once that part of his life ended, it most definitely ended. He never, ever, ever went back. For most of them it's the allure of that lifestyle. The money, the trappings of the trade: the cars, the jewelry, the girls. It's easy. When you get out of jail, many guys can't get back on their feet, get any stability, or get a legitimate job. It's hard; you got this black mark to carry around. I'm not justifying or rationalizing why they go back. But you can almost understand why they go back to what they know. He never did.

"What's interesting to me, he sometimes held two to three jobs; he worked for FDX, and for Johnston & Murphy. He was busting his ass, and he was used to having thousands of dollars just lying on the table. When I testified at his trial for the murder of Sybil, I didn't know Brian and I had only one objective, to see him convicted. When he beat the rap I was pissed, strange how things turn out. I sometimes speak to Brian a couple times a week and I did invite him to my retirement party."

Leslie R. Caldwell, My Savior

Thirteen years after my release I was able to meet up with Leslie R. Caldwell on August 31, 2010 for lunch to celebrate her 53rd birthday and to thank her for saving my life.

Specializing in complex litigation, Caldwell Leslie & Proctor, PC ("Caldwell Leslie") provides strategic, creative and cost-effective representation in cases that matter most. Our record of success at trial, on appeal and in alternative dispute resolution proceedings has attracted a loyal roster of clients, including Fortune 500 corporations, closely held businesses, major studios and networks, cities and counties, state and local agencies, foreign companies, professionals and community groups. Even prominent law firms rely on Caldwell Leslie for excellent representation in high-stakes litigation.

If we have what someone would call a mortal ANGEL, then Leslie R. Caldwell would be the angel that God sent to save me.

It is funny how two different individuals come from two separate geographic areas and walks of life can have such a profound impact on someone else's life. It's interesting when I first met Leslie R. Caldwell how we connected from the beginning. I know she had a job to do, but in an around and about way I sensed from the start she had my best interest at heart. It is very hard to believe and trust someone on the opposite side of the law, but I could truly say that I trusted her. To be frank, I didn't have much of a choice. I was a 25-year-old African American born in an urban environment of Brooklyn, N.Y., the concrete jungle. And I was a violent career criminal with four felony convictions, facing numerous federal charges, and was the prime suspect in dam near every unsolved homicide in the Metropolitan area of N.Y.C.

Leslie was this pure 31-year-old white young lady from Steubenville, Ohio entering year two as Assistant United States Attorney in the Eastern District of Brooklyn, NY. I was a hardcore N.Y. Knicks fan, due to their rough and tough street ball mentality lead by the likes of Charles Oakley, Anthony Mason and John Starks. Leslie was a big Pittsburg Penguins fan, especially of Mario Lemieux. She loved the fact that he was one of the best players in the league at the time and his ability to refrain from violent behavior when the opposition was being physically violent with him. He retaliated by his excellence in his play which normally lead to an assist, a score or both; she really respected his professionalism. We would go back and forth about why he wasn't fighting back. I wanted him to fight back and got tired of watching him get pounded on ESPN. She admired his restraint and how he beat the opposition with his play. I guess if I was born in Steubenville, Ohio opposed to being born in a back seat of a NYPD police car, I too probably would have been a bit more passive.

Based upon my cooperation with the Federal Government Leslie R. Caldwell helped me to gain my freedom, despite that Brooklyn and Queens' law enforcement wanted me badly, and the fact that I received a deal in the first place with both counties screaming foul play. They believed and felt that I got away with murder. The State felt and were pressured to convince Ms. Caldwell and the Federal Government that I was a sociopath. Leslie didn't judge me by what she heard or read. I believe she judged me over the course of time, based upon our face to face encounters, and realized deep down inside, despite my reputation and all of the negative comments and statements that she heard, I believe she decided to give me the benefit of the doubt by judging me strictly by her interaction with me.

I can recall using the race card with Leslie regarding white defendants verses black defendants receiving better deals. I would be the first to say that Leslie is the most honest and fairest person I know, and her action were illustrated when she put together the 5K1.1 letter to the Honorable Edward Korman on my behalf, despite I never went in front of a Grand Jury or testified at any trial,

Since my release I have kept in touch with both Leslie Caldwell who recently left her partnership with a large white-collar law firm to be appointed to Assistant Attorney General under Attorney General Eric Holder, and with Joseph Ponzi who have recently retired from Kings County District Attorney Office. Leslie Caldwell and Joseph Ponzi and their team saved my life and believed in me enough to go to bat for me and help me to obtain another shot at life. If both of you should ever read this, for my family and myself, "Thank You Very Much."

Some Final Remarks

"Brian, or "Glaze," are not selfish individuals -- I say "are," because they are two separate personalities, in a way. Since birth, both were taught that it is always better to give than receive. The one thing both personalities hated more than anything is to have someone take their kindness for weakness.

"I sit back and reflect on life and remember when I wanted to be a major league baseball player. To this day, I feel that my dream could've become reality, if I'd only pursued it, instead of taking the other route. As far as school was concerned, I was always slightly above average student.

"It seems so strange how these two individuals came into each other's life. As I put down my thoughts, I try to pinpoint exactly when these two individuals clashed together. How? Why? If I wanted to take the easy way out, then I could blame it on the cruelty of the streets of New York City, or the drugs, or even try to find some mental disorder as an excuse. But I'm not looking for an easy way out, and I certainly am not looking for excuses.

As I sum up things, I believe I simply wanted to be accepted by the older crowd. I began abusing my body by indulging in chemical substances, as well as various kinds of alcohol. I always tried living up to others' expectations. Now I realize that nothing I did brought me any closer to the crowd, but just managed to make me feel awful for long periods of time after each hangover. But I kept going, and what I accomplished was to continually push myself farther and farther away from my true self.

Like so many young boys, I wanted to be grown up before my time. Instead of letting nature takes its course, I threw everything out of the window. Well I think I said it all. My mother was a wonderful person and a good parent. It seems strange how so many kids who go astray that have loving parents. It's a sad thing to analyze, but one day I hope someone comes up with a solution.

A lot of publicity surrounded everything I was involved in and no doubt the average citizen who might have read some of it would like to see a lunatic like Glaze off the streets.

However, Brian was born a survivor. He survived the odds against him and overcame the obstacles he encountered, and yes, he is blessed to still be alive and beyond lucky.

Remember the saying: "Don't talk the talk, if you can't walk the walk." I honestly believed all along that I could've done both. In the end I was proven wrong. When I grasped reality, I understood that when it came time for me to actually "talk the walk" I couldn't do it. It just wasn't in me anymore.

Out of everyone I spoke with, my brother, James (Kool-Aid), didn't agree with me cooperating with the feds. He told me that I knew what I was up against from the very beginning. He told me that out of everyone he just couldn't see me cooperating with the government. But I told him that the Feds weren't playing and that if I didn't cooperate, I could end up spending the rest of my life in jail. He said that he didn't want me spending the rest of my life in jail, either. Then he said that he wouldn't sanction anything, but that whatever I decided to do would be on me. Then he added that nothing would change the fact that we're brothers or the love he has for me. That really touched me, and I clearly understood what he was saying.

A snitch! Maybe cooperating with the government is something that I thought was against my principles. But the other things I did which eventually led me to cooperating with the feds were wrong. In making choices we sometimes must decide between the lesser of two evils. I swallowed a very bitter pill by turning against my former colleagues in the drug game, but I'm sure I chose the lesser evil. I'm a survivor and my family mean more to me than anything in the world, and I will be with my family and not spending the rest of my life in prison.

In Conclusion

As I mentioned, I never saw of the $35,000,000 the Feds allowed me to keep, shame on me. I've been out over 16 years and have been working 9 to 5 jobs. It doesn't get to me; in fact, I also worked as a security guard on the graveyard shift, five nights a week. I call it a legit hustle. I love being a salesman because I am good at it. When I am dealing with customers, I feel like I am on stage performing, as if I am seeking to win the academy award for best actor. Sales has its up and downs. When it is slow I am only making eight hundred dollars every two weeks, but when business is booming, I am making two to four thousand dollars every two weeks. With my security guard job, all I must do is show up and I receive a set salary every two weeks. Two jobs is a legit hustle for me, if I only had that mind set when I was a kid.

Now tell me that I, Brian "Glaze" Gibbs wasn't worthy of a second chance at life. Leslie R. Caldwell, Joseph A. Ponzi, the late Charlie Rose, Richard Martinez and David Higgins all who originally were my nemesis, were able to see a new man.

Let me finish by saying, nobody wants to be an asshole, everyone would like to be the best they could, if they knew how. Have you ever said to yourself, "That was an asinine thing to do?" I obviously learned my lesson.

Thanks for listening, Brian "Glaze" Gibbs.

Joseph Verola has written several screenplays including: two romance comedies (You're a Dog, Jack & A Beggar's Ball), two film Noir (Out of Control & Twisted Emotions), one personal true story (Don't Cry Pop) & one based on a memoir written with David Fisher (Louie's Widow). Synopsis available at UstarPublishing.com and clicking on the Author/Publisher pull down menu.

Joe also self-published several books, via ustarpublishing.com: Romance/Fantasy Novels (You're A Dog, Jack & ThePigeons.net); the memoir of a Drug Lord/Murder (Beyond Lucky – The Brian "Glaze" Gibbs Story) and the memoir (Snapped, The Gloria DeLaurentis Story – First Degree Murder or Manslaughter); two fictional memoirs (None That I Know Of & The Caregiver); one self-help book (How to Become a Movie Star in Ten Steps); one historic book (The American Idol Book). Synopsis available at UstarPublishing.com and clicking on the Author/Publisher pull down menu.

And three motivational CDs (Free High Cannabis, Free High 100% Proof and Free High Natural).

Understanding the desire and the need for self-publishing he created Ustar Publishing and aids others in that quest. Among those are A Camelot of the Biomedical Sciences - The Story of the Roche Institute of Molecular Biology by Herbert Weissbach and David Fisher, Chemo Saved My Life - Yoga Saves My Living by Faith Bevan, and Going the Distance "Try a Tri!" A Guide to Your First Triathlon by Clark Parry & Cindy Durkee.

Prior to perusing a career as a writer Joe's prior experience was the marketing of computer hardware and software to Fortune 500 companies, and with the advent of the PC genesis, he started Hi-Tech Cinema. The company provided hardware and software to Movie, TV, and Advertising industries. Software included, script writing program, budgeting, video editing and story boarding.

His passion for the entertainment industry also led to acting classes and hitting the stage. He showcased his work at comedy clubs which included, Catch A Rising Star and The Improv at a time that Pat Benatar, Larry David and Jerry Steinfeld were just starting their careers, working out in the same clubs.

Let Joe assist you in creating your legacy! Got Book? Visit
www.ustarpublishing.com

Best Wishes;
Joe V

CPSIA information can be obtained
at www.ICGtesting.com
Printed in the USA
BVHW040839261221
624839BV00026B/1049

9 781519 792242